Revenge on Mulberry Street

By Joe Bruno

Knickerbocker Publishing Company

© 2018

"Revenge is a dish that tastes best when it is served cold," Don Corleone, from the book "The Godfather."

Chapter One

Johnny Russo - 1984

A stiff wind played havoc with Johnny Russo's wavy black hair as he jogged around Columbus Park, opposite the New York City jail ominously called The Tombs. A muscular 210 pounds chiseled on a six-foot-two-inch frame, Johnny resembled an Italian Hercules consumed by his daily labors. Five miles of road work every day is no day at the beach, but if you want to become heavyweight champion of the world sacrifices have to be made.

The scorching noon sun caused pools of sweat to run down Johnny's Christian Dior sweat-suit and straight down into his Puma joggers. Johnny usually started his roadwork at dawn, but last night Benny Bastone, the dispatcher at Prestige Limo, had conned Johnny into taking a late-night ride.

What a hassle that broad turned out to be. Johnny couldn't wait to get his hands around Benny's scrawny neck.

"Johnny, you've got to see this hot broad!" Benny had told Johnny over the two-way radio, mounted under the dashboard of his black stretch Cadillac limo. "Mario drove her two nights ago, and he's been raving ever since. Mario's got a face like a gorilla. But with your good looks, Johnny, you're a cinch to get laid."

Benny knew well what Johnny's Achille's heel was: good-looking broads with long sexy legs and cleavages down to their belly buttons. But, Johnny was madly in love with the drop-dead-beautiful Linda McKay, and there was no way he would risk losing Linda by fooling around with another woman.

Johnny finished his seventh lap around Columbus Park. Eight laps equaled five miles; his daily objective. Johnny missed the soothing feel of his solid gold boxing glove, mounted on an 18-carat gold rope chain, which usually swayed gently around his neck. He had lost both the glove and chain the previous night. Johnny hoped it had merely been dislodged and had fallen onto the floor of his limo. He made a mental note to search for it later.

Johnny sped up his pace. One more lap to go and the last one was pure torture. The booze he had consumed the previous night was taking its toll, and Johnny swore it would never happen again. From now on Johnny would concentrate on two things only: Linda, and his boxing career, in exactly that order.

Johnny's sole mission in life was to make tons of money in boxing, marry Linda and move out of his Little Italy neighborhood, where sinful temptations stood around every corner. He decided to propose to Linda that very night. He couldn't wait to see her lovely face light up like the Christmas tree at Rockefeller Center.

Johnny stumbled through the last few paces of his five-mile jaunt. Then, he made a beeline for the Sons of Italy Social Club located at 91 Mulberry Street, just below Canal Street. The club was located on the ground floor of a red tenement, directly below Johnny's second-floor apartment. Once inside, Johnny collapsed on a weather-beaten armchair, and he picked up an early edition of the *New York Post*.

The club was deserted, except for Chickens, a bookie who ran the club for Johnny's uncle, Carlo Russo. Johnny didn't gamble often, and when he did it was a measly five-time bet: $27.50 to win $25. The local bookies bought Cadillacs with the ten percent vig tagged onto every bet. But the Yankees were in town, and they were on a ten-game winning streak, so Johnny decided to double his usual bet on the home team.

"Hey, Nappy, what's the line on the Yankees?" Johnny said.

"Hey, Dunski, what does it say in the papers?" Chickens said.

"It says the Yankees are favored 9-11."

"Then, what's the fuckin' question?"

Chickens poured himself a glass of water from the sordid sink behind the bar that had more rust on it than an abandoned tugboat. He popped two black pills into his mouth and chugged them down with the warm swill.

Chickens stood straight up, and his head barely cleared the top of the bar.

"Fucking doctors!" Chickens said. "You go visit them in their office, and they rob your fuckin' eyes out. Dr. DiPasquale changed me twenty bucks just to write out a damn prescription. You know what it says on the bottle? 'To be refilled 0 times.' When I run out of these heart pills, I have to go back to that thievin' bastard, so he can write me another damn prescription. That's another 20 bucks down the drain."

Johnny looked up from the newspaper and smiled.

"My heart bleeds for you," Johnny said. "Now, give me the Yankees 10 times."

"Yankees ten times," Chickens said. He put his hand out, palms up. "55 clams. Cash on the barrelhead."

"I'm in my freaking sweatpants," Johnny said. "I'll bring the money down when I leave for the gym."

Nappy Chickens. "Then, I'll write the bet down in my mind when you deliver the cash,"

Johnny let out a deep sigh.

"You're relentless," he said.

Johnny picked up the newspaper and turned it around to the front page.

The headline read: **MAFIA INFORMER TO TAKE THE STAND TODAY!**

Under the headline, a picture of two men, handcuffed to two plain-clothes police officers, extended to the bottom of the page. Both men covered their faces with their free arm and elbow.

Johnny turned to page three. The accompanying story read:

Mafia stool pigeon Gregory Piazza will take the stand today in the trial of Paul Mirada and Tony Palumbo; two reputed Mafia henchmen. It is anticipated that Piazza will tell the jury how Miranda and Palumbo extorted thousands of dollars from him as protection money for his uptown nightclub. Piazza is expected to weave a gory tale of murder and the sale of drugs, most notably cocaine.

The district attorney will also unveil a surprise witness, revealed today to the defense attorneys under the law of discovery, who will corroborate Piazza's allegations. The presence of the mysterious witness will deliver a crushing blow to Miranda's and Palumbo's defenses. According to District Attorney William O'Neil, if convicted, the loss of these two vicious enforcers will greatly diminish the influence of organized crime in New York City."

Johnny threw down the paper in disgust.

"What bullshit!" Johnny said to Chickens. "Did you read this crap on page three?"

"Nah, I never read the back of the paper," Chickens said.

"When the cops make a pinch, there's always a rat involved," Johnny said. "And the stupid public thinks that the police are like Sherlock Holmes, walking around with a magnifying glass inspecting the sidewalk for clues. When, in fact, most cops couldn't find their asses with both hands. Some rat spills his guts, and the cops look like geniuses."

"Who gives a fuck?" Chickens said. "As long as it ain't me getting pinched."

Johnny pushed himself off the armchair, exited the club, and tramped up the steps to his apartment. A cold shower cleared the cobwebs from the night before, and as he shaved, Johnny noticed three long red scratch marks on his neck.

Friggin' Hamilton broad.

Johnny decided he'd tell Linda he got the scratches from sparring.

Johnny donned his black chauffer's jacket, folded his tie, placed it in his inside jacket pocket, and he exited the apartment.

The black limo sat by a hydrant near the corner of Mulberry and Hester, in front of Casa de Carlo, the most exclusive restaurant in Little Italy. Johnny's uncle Carlo Russo owned that place, too. It seemed to Johnny that Uncle Carlo owned everything and everybody in Little Italy.

Unfortunately, a parking ticket adorned the limo's windshield wiper.

Screw Benny, Johnny thought.

If it weren't for Benny's con-job the night before, Johnny would have been back early enough to park the limo in the company garage before it closed.

Johnny ripped the ticket into little pieces and flung them in the gutter. He then checked inside the back of the limo looking for his gold chain and the gold boxing glove.

No luck.

Then, he searched the floor in the front of the limo.

Still no luck.

Johnny slid his hand into the crevice behind the driver's seat.

Still nothing.

Shit. A thousand bucks down the fucking drain.

Prestige Limo stood the corner of Houston Street and Sixth Avenue. Outside the garage, five shiny black stretch limos were lined up, double parked, and two black men waxed them like their lives depended upon it. Since Prestige Limo was a mobbed-up business, murder was possible and sometimes inevitable.

Johnny parked his limo behind the last double-parked limo, and he strode into the garage.

Behind a gray stretch limo, a glass window divided the entire width of the garage in half. To the right of the window, a door led to the inner office. Benny did all his business behind the glass window. No drivers were allowed in Benny's office except for Johnny. Benny banished all the other drivers to a cubby-hole inside the garage, which had room for four drivers stuffed in like sardines.

No heat.

No bathroom.

No respect.

Johnny walked past the driver's room and banged on the interior door. A new secretary opened the door. Johnny didn't know her name.

"Where's Benny?" Johnny said as he pushed inside.

The girl noted Johnny's black suit, and he shoved a hand into his chest.

"I'm sorry, but Benny told me no drivers are allowed inside his office," she said.

"I'm an exception," Johnny said. "I'm also his doctor, and he's going to need a doctor after I break his scrawny neck."

Johnny pushed past the startled secretary just as Benny emerged from his private bathroom. When Benny spotted Johnny, his face stiffened.

"Come into the back room," Benny said.

Benny Bastone was an angelic-looking 25-year-old with fine chiseled feature not unlike Felix Unger of television's *Odd Couple*. Benny was born to money and the prospects of an eternally happy life; that is unless one of his drivers ended it for him at an early age. Still, Johnny was Benny's best friend, and maybe his only friend. The other drivers hated Benny with a passion, but they wouldn't dare raise a finger because Johnny was Benny's protector.

Benny led Johnny into his father Mike Bastone's office. A copy of the latest edition of the *New York Post* was lying on his desk. Benny handed Johnny the newspaper.

"I guess you haven't seen this yet," Benny said.

In place of the front-page photo, Johnny had seen earlier, stood one of a dead body covered by a blood-stained sheet. A snapshot of the murder victim sat in a corner inset.

The headline read: **KEY MAFIA WITNESS SLAIN. WAS DUE TO TESTIFY TODAY.**

The color drained out of Johnny's face when he recognized the person in the snapshot.

It was Diane Hamilton.

The story on page three now read:

The body of Diane Hamilton, a reputed drug dealer, was found by an early-morning jogger in an alley near Cherry Street under the Manhattan side of the Manhattan Bridge. She had been shot three times in the back of the head in an apparent mob rubout. Police confirmed reports that there was a considerable amount of money in Miss Hamilton's purse, and robbery was ruled out as a motive.

Miss Hamilton was slated to testify as a surprise witness in the trial of alleged mob enforcers Tony Palumbo and Paul Miranda. Informant Gregory Piazza was schedulable to take the stand today and identify Miss Hamilton as his corroborating witness in this sensational extortion and murder case. Police believe someone silenced Miss Hamilton in order to prevent her from testifying.

Sweat formed on Johnny's brow as he continued reading.

Police have one piece of concrete evidence concerning the identity of the possible killer or killers. A gold boxing glove connected to a gold rope chain was held tightly in the dead woman's hand. The chain is being examined at police laboratories for fingerprints. Detectives are questioning city jewelers and the inhabitants of the city's boxing gyms as to whom the owner might be. Police Commissioner Barry Walden predicted an arrest within the next 24 hours.

Johnny looked at Benny through frightened eyes.

"Benny, you've got to believe me. I didn't have anything to do with this," Johnny said.

Benny shook his head.

"It's not what I believe," he said. "It's what the cops believe. You have an uncanny knack for getting into big trouble, my friend."

Johnny crumpled the newspaper and flung it onto the floor.

"You got that right," Johnny said. "Trouble is my middle name."

Chapter Two

Mary Italiano 1950

Mary Italiano, the youngest of 11 children, was born in 1925 in a tiny two-bedroom apartment at 104 A Bayard Street in New York City's Little Italy. In the early part of the 20th Century, her parents had emigrated to the United States from the province of Salerno, in the Campagna region of Italy, 25 miles from Naples.

Her father, John Italiano, hard-pressed to support his 11 offspring, sold vegetables from a stand in an open-air market on Mulberry Street between Hester and Grand Streets. His wife Carmella took in laundry to make ends meet. As each of the children married and raised their own families, Giuseppe Italiano's financial burden gradually decreased.

104 A Bayard Street is a four-story red brick tenement located between Mulberry and Baxter Streets across the street from Columbus Park. Each floor contains two apartments; one facing the Bayard Street, and the other facing the backyard. By 1930, all eight apartments in 104 A Bayard Street were occupied by John and Carmela Italiano and their married children. Mary, along with her unmarried brother, Joseph, lived with her parents in the front apartment on the second floor.

Directly across the street from 104 A Bayard Street stood Columbus Park's landmark Park House, an open-air dance hall built in 1897 under the administration of William L. Strong, Mayor of New York City.

"I remember my parents going across the street to the Park House every Friday night to dance," Mary told her sister-in-law Rita, who was married to her brother, Johnny. "It was the only night they ever spent alone together. My father sold vegetables, seven days a week, from seven in the morning to ten at night. But on Friday nights he came home at six. All nine daughters had to leave the kitchen so that my father could take his weekly bath in the tub, which was part of the kitchen sink. When he finished bathing, he called all his children into the kitchen and gave them each a quarter. It was the only time I ever saw my father smile."

In the backyard of 104 A Bayard Street stood 104 B Bayard Street, one of the rare back-buildings in New York City. Until the mid-1930s, the toilets for both buildings sat in the backyard of 104 A Bayard Street, or if you wish, the front yard of 1904 B Bayard Street.

"When I was a little girl, I remember my mother taking me downstairs to go to the bathroom," Mary told Rita. "There were only six bathroom stalls for the 16 apartments, so sometimes you had to wait a long time to go to the bathroom. But when I was about six years old a miracle happened: bathrooms, connected by pipes to the kitchen sink, were built in all the apartments. People celebrated for days, but will 11 children in my family, there was still a long wait to go to the bathroom."

Mary's life almost ended at the age of fifteen. While she babysat for his sister Anna's three children, Piero, then six, managed to open the living room window and wander onto the fire escape.

Little Theresa, then five, ran into the kitchen and screamed, "Come quick, Aunt Mary. Pietro's on the fire escape, and he can't get back inside."

Mary hurried into the living room and eased her way onto the fire escape. She grabbed Pietro as he was about to fall and flung him inside the apartment. But she lost her balance and fell over the railing towards the pavement below.

The bright red canopy of the Red Horse Saloon broke Mary's fall. But the canopy collapsed under her weight, and she landed on the head of Jimmy Clark, just as Clark was leaving the Red Horse Saloon after his customary three nightly beers. Miraculously, Mary escaped with only a few bruises. However, Jimmy Clark's neck was broken, and he never walked again.

Whenever Mary saw Samantha Clark pushing her husband's wheelchair, she was overcome by an enormous wave of guilt. Samantha Clark never said an angry word to Mary, but her cold blue eyes said everything.

The Clarks had only one son, Billy. The neighborhood pranksters called Bill the "pigeon," not because he was an easy mark, which he was, but because he was born with a deformed spinal column that forced him to walk with his head permanently pointed towards the pavement.

The neighborhood jokesters yelled "coo, coo, coo" when Billy Clark waddled down the block. This induced Samantha Clark to carry a huge wooden umbrella, rain or shine, when she accompanied her son on their jaunts. She had honed the point of the umbrella to a sharp point, and if any of the local rabble insulted Billy in his mother's presence, Samantha would shove the point of her umbrella into crevices of their bodies where the sun never shined.

Tall and shapely, Mary Italiano was, without a doubt, the prettiest of the nine Italiano daughters, most of whom were built like linebackers. Mary had raven black hair and penetrating brown eyes. Despite her wondrous appearance, Mary never seriously dated until her early twenties. This was partly because Mary was her eight sisters' "designated babysitter," and partly because her older brothers, Johnny and Joe, were talented professional prizefighters who could do serious damage with their fists. The two bruisers made it clear to the local male rabble that Mary was off limits, or else. That is unless marriage was in the cards, and then the two brothers would adjudicate those proposals on a case-by-case basis.

One bright sunny day in May of 1950, while Mary strolled down Baxter Street, she saw two roughnecks antagonizing poor Billy Clark. Blessed with the same fighting spirit as her brothers,

Mary snatched the tops off two garbage cans and chased the two bullies down the block.

After Mary had handled the situation, Billy sat on the stoop of his Baxter Street tenement, put his hands over his face, and cried.

"It's all right Billy," Mary said. She put her arm around his frail shoulders. "Those two have nothing to do except cause trouble. You finished high school, and now you have a fine job at the bank. With your intelligence, you'll do just fine. Those two have trouble even spelling their own names."

Mary and Billy became a regular item in the neighborhood. They were a strange but beautiful sight walking down the pavement arm in arm. Mary so tall, dignified and so beautiful, and Billy with his noble head eternally pointed towards the ground, a proud smile on his face. Thoughtless people shook their heads when Mary and Billy passed. But Billy's former tormentors kept their distance, and, mindful of the Italiano brothers proficiency with their fists, they minded their manners, too.

Johnny Italiano, now an undefeated heavyweight boxer with great promise, had laid down the law to all concerned: "Make fun of my sister or Billy Clark, and I'll use your heads as a punching bag."

The smart and the not-so-smart all heeded Johnny's warning.

Christmas of 1950 was a sad time for the Italiano family. John Italiano had contracted pneumonia two days after Thanksgiving, and he passed away a week later. His wife Carmella took his passing badly. She screamed at the walls and pulled her hair every night before she finally fell asleep. Her children were uncertain whether to commit their mother to a nursing home so that she could get the proper treatment and not be a danger to herself or to others. But, with Mary being her mother's constant companion, they had universally decided against it.

On Christmas Eve, Mary and Billy attended Midnight Mass together at Transfiguration Church on Mott Street. After Mass, they decided to take a stroll in Columbus Park. Snow felt lightly, but it was not cold, and Columbus Park, with its snow-cover trees, resembled a Norman Rockwell painting.

Billy brushed the snow off a park bench with his handkerchief, and he invited Mary to sit down next to him. The snowflakes melted into the ground as Billy put his arm around Mary's shoulder.

"Mary, I love you very much," Billy said. "I know I'm a cripple, but I also know that looks don't mean everything to you."

"You're a fine-looking man, Billy Clark," Mary said. "Don't talk about yourself that way."

"Thank you, Mary," Billy said, "But I want to make my intentions clear. I have a good job at the bank, and I'm up for a promotion. I know I can provide for you properly, and I'm sure I'd make a fine husband. Mary, will you marry me?"

"Billy, I do care for you very much," Mary said. She wiped a moist spot from Billy's cheek. It could have been a snowflake, but Mary knew it was a tear. "But with the condition my mother is in, I can't make any plans right now. Please forgive me, but now's not the proper time."

Bill stood up, and said, "I understand, Mary. I can understand you not wanting to marry someone like me."

"That's not true, Billy," Mary said. "It's my mother. *I swear it is*. Just give me time. Things will be different when my mother gets better."

Billy offered her his hand, and she took it.

"It's getting late. I'll take you home," Billy said.

Mary stood, and as the bell from Transfiguration chimed, announcing the birth of the Messiah, she tilted Billy's chin upwards and kissed him on the lips. At that instant, she knew that she loved Billy Clark.

"Billy, take me home," Mary said. "I don't remember the last time I felt so happy."

A siren blared, as a police car chased a stolen black Buick down Baxter Street and past the city prison called The Tombs. The driver of the stolen Buick was Bobby Bello who had recently been released from prison after a five-year bit for grand larceny. A stolen car rap would send Bello back to prison for at least another five years, and Bello was determined not to get caught.

The Buick's tires squealed as Bello made a gangster left turn onto Bayard Street.

As Mary and Billy strolled arm and arm on Bayard towards Mary's apartment building, Billy spotted the danger. A split second after he pushed Mary in the back propelling her into the front door of the Red Horse Saloon, the Buick hit Billy squarely, propelling him 30 feet up into the air.

They buried Billy three days later at Calvary Cemetery in Queens. While a pulley lowered Billy's coffin, Mary pushed Jimmy Clark's wheelchair toward the dark hole in the ground. Samantha Clark followed them, propped up under each arm by Johnny and Joe Italiano. As snow fell lightly as it had done three days earlier, Mary threw a red rose onto Billy's coffin.

She bent forward and whispered into Jimmy Clark's ear, "As long as I live, I'll never meet a better man than your son."

Four days later, while Mary attended to her mother Carmella on the second floor, the Italiano family congregated in Anna's fourth-floor apartment to welcome in the New Year. Mary cradled her mother's head in her arms and gently rocked her to sleep. Just before the bells, Mary trudged upstairs to join her siblings.

Ten minutes after the bells chimed in Transfiguration Church signaling the start of a new year, Carmella Italiano climbed the stairs to the roof. She made the sign of the cross, then jumped off the roof, landing in the backyard between the two buildings.

After her mother's horrible death, Mary Italiano never again ventured into the backyard of 104 A Bayard Street.

Chapter Three

After the holiday tragedies in the winter of 1950, Mary Italiano rarely left the safe confines of 104 A Bayard Street, except to work as a checkout girl, five days a week, from 9 am to 5 pm, at the Lexington Diner on 23rd Street and Lexington Avenue. The only time she ventured out at night was to see her brother Johnny fight at various boxing arenas throughout the five boroughs.

Joe Italiano had retired from boxing after he suffered a detached retina in his right eye, courtesy of a well-aimed and ill-intentioned left thumb delivered by Rocky Kelly at Madison Square Garden. Clancy's mischievous thumb, which was delivered in round two, caused Joe to see two, and sometimes three, Kellys. Despite his handicap, Joe's well-timed left hook, originating from someone where near the ring apron, deposited Clancy into Slumberland in round five.

Joe's eye operation at the Eye and Ear Hospital on 14th Street was deemed a success. But the attending physician told Joe that another thumb could result in complete blindness in that eye. Not wanting to be relegated to selling pencils on street corners, Joe retired from boxing, and instead, became his brother Johnny's manager and trainer.

Mary and her sister-in-law Rita, Johnny's wife, sat ringside at St. Nick's Arena to see Johnny win his twenty-first consecutive fight against King Lewis. An overhand right hand turned the King into a knave at 1:10 of the fifth round.

The punch was so devastating; the referee didn't even bother to count.

During the fight, Mary noticed that between rounds, instead of Joe, a complete stranger was in the ring attending to Johnny as he sat on his stool. Joe stood outside the ring, bent over, whispering instructions into his brother's ear. Still, Mary sensed something was not quite right.

After the fight, Mary and Rita entered Johnny's dressing to congratulate their brother. The newcomer, who Mary later found out to be Dominick Russo, was busy cutting the tape off Johnny's hands with round-tipped surgical scissors. While newspaper reporters fired their questions at Johnny, Joe stood off to the side, seemingly uninvolved in the festivities

"Were you surprised King didn't get up?" one dim-witted reporter asked Johnny.

"Why would I be surprised?" Johnny said, smiling. "A horse wouldn't get up after being hit with that right hand."

While he was being interviewed, Mary thought her brother, with his white shiny piano-key set of teeth, looked more like a Hollywood movie star than he did a prizefighter.

After the interview ended, Johnny called to his wife, "Hey honey-bunny, how about a kiss?" Then, he motioned to Mary. "You too, sis."

Mary gave Johnny a quick buss on the check, and then she motioned for Joe to meet her outside the dressing room door.

Joe complied. And when they were in the hallway, Mary said, "Look, Joe, I don't know much about boxing, but something's wrong. Who's that new guy in Johnny's corner? Why is he doing everything you used to do?"

Joe didn't like being questioned by his younger sister.

He said, "Hey sis, why don't you stick to what you know best, and I'll stick to what I know best," Joe said.

He was not smiling.

"But you and Johnny are barely speaking, even at home," Mary said. "I noticed something has been wrong for weeks. Cue me in. Maybe I can help."

Joe shook his head and said, "Sorry, sis. But this is something I gotta handle myself."

He gave Mary a soft hug and a quick peck on the cheek. Then, he said, "I know you mean well, but don't worry. I have everything under control. Everything will turn out just peachy. Trust me."

Then, he flashed her his biggest smile.

Still, Mary was unconvinced. She knew when her two brothers were lying. They just weren't very good at it.

Rewind to a few weeks earlier.

His name was Carlo Russo, a rising young hood on Mulberry Street. Carlo had recently been given his button, designating him a "made-man" in a secret society, which had originated in Carlo's town of birth, Palermo, Sicily, in the Thirteenth Century. The American press called this group "The Mafia," but no Mafioso ever used that term. When conversing among made- members, they used the phrase "Cosa Nostra," which, loosely translated meant "Our Thing."

At first, only Sicilians were allowed admission into this esteemed society. But gradually, the rules were loosened. Soon, men whose families came from all part of Italy were invited to join.

Dating back to its time of origin, men who were proposed for membership had to "make their bones" by actually killing someone, or at least be involved in the conspiracy of murder, even it if only meant luring the victim to his death, or cleaning up the blood, or disposing of the body afterward.

But in recent times, the rules had been eased to include men, who were not killers, but, in fact, "good earners," which meant that they put big bucks into their bosses' pockets.

In the Mafia, the money and the prestige flowed up, while the hard work and risk dribbled down.

Once a man becomes "made," or "a wiseguy," he was compelled to follow orders explicitly and without question. If ordered to kill, he must do so in a timely manner, or be killed himself. And if ordered by his boss to a meeting or a "sit-down," he must show up promptly, or be killed, even if he suspected the reason for the meeting was to initiate his own demise.

Carlo Russo was not a good earner. He was a stone-cold killer who actually enjoyed his job. Carlo killed his prey with the same gusto as a Major League Baseball player hitting a grand slam homerun.

Carlo's favorite manner of execution was the icepick, which he would gleefully insert into of his victim's ear, while his free hand covered the dupe's mouth to muffle the screams.

To Carlo, guns were just too damn noisy. But sometimes they were necessary.

Whereas murder was his profession, boxing was Carlo's obsession. It was the ultimate high for a wiseguy to become the manager of the Heavyweight Champion of the World. It gave him the ultimate respect within the organization and also in the legitimate world.

If the Mafia is about anything; it's about respect.

As an added perk, Carlo knew that if he controlled the Heavyweight Champion of the World, he would have a bearhug on the entire sport of boxing. Then, the big bucks would flow into Carlo's coffers like pressured water from a fireman's hose.

That's where Johnny Italiano came into the picture. Carlo knew that Johnny had the natural ability to beat most of the top heavyweights in the world. And the ones Carlo felt Johnny could not beat, he would make sure that Johnny avoided them like leprosy. Carlo knew that a win over the ageing heavyweight champion Bill Brannigan could be bought at a reasonable price. And if Carlo could not convince Brannigan to be reasonable, then Johnny would fight for the vacant title after Brannigan untimely demise.

The only flaw in Carlo's plan was that he was not, as of yet, Johnny Italiano's manager. But with a little friendly persuasion, and more than a little pressure, Carlo was sure he could convince Joe Italiano to sell him Johnny's contract.

Carlo did not want something for nothing. After all, Carlo was a man of respect. He was willing to pay fair market value for

Johnny's contract. And that fair market value would be determined by Carlo Russo and Carlo Russo alone.

That was another perk of being a wiseguy.

Carlo had sat at ringside when Johnny had won his 20th straight fight, a second-round knockout of Killer Keyes. After the fight, Carlo visited Johnny's dressing room with his top aide and enforcer, Butch Salerno.

Carlo, the personification of gangster fashion, was decked out in a $300 black Hickey Freeman shark-skin suit, silk white dress shirt, with a red and white striped tie, and black patent-leather shoes. Barely five-foot-seven-inches tall, but with the strength of a coiled snake, Carlo had a rodent-like face, with a large pointed nose and his upper lip curled down in a permanent snarl.

It was a simple fact that Carlo Russo would win no beauty contests; which made him all the more determined to gain the proper respect, no matter who, or how many people, he had to kill to do so.

When Carlo entered Johnny's dressing room, Johnny was positioned face-down on the dressing room massage table, while his brother Joe expertly kneaded his brother's bulging back muscles.

"Great fight, kid," Carlo said to Johnny. "You looked fantastic tonight."

Johnny, giving Carlo the Invisible Man treatment, spun around and jumped off the table. Then, he stormed into the bathroom and slammed the door behind him.

Carlo said to Joe, "What's with this kid? He acts like I got bad breath."

Joe wiped his hands on the sides of his pants and extended his right hand to Carlo.

"He's got a bad stomach, that's all," Joe said. "It was nice of you to come to congratulate him. I know he appreciates that, and I do, too."

Joe glanced over Carlo's left shoulder, and he spotted Butch Salerno, like a mastiff, standing guard at the dressing room door. At six-feet-four-inches and as wide as Sicily, Butch's frame blocked the entire entrance.

"I gotta tell you, Joe," Carlo said. "You're doing a great job training your brother. I can tell he's in tremendous shape thanks to you. Most heavyweights today eat themselves out of contention, but not Johnny. He's solid as a rock."

"Well, my brother just loves to train," Joe said. "It's in his blood. He runs seven days a week, rain or shine. The kid's like an animal."

Carlo decided to get right to the point.

"Listen, Joe. Come over to my joint tomorrow night," Carlo said. "I have a proposition I'd like you to consider."

Joe stiffened at the tone of Carlo's voice. Joe knew Carlo was not a man to take no for an answer, especially on his own turf. And those who did say no to him usually wound up wrapped in a rug and thrown into the East River.

"Gee, Carlo, I'm sorry, but I already have plans for tomorrow night," Joe said.

Carlo's eyes turned dark, and he spat out, "Well, break them. Be at my place tomorrow night, eight pm sharp. And no bullshit excuses."

That said, Carlo did an about-face, and after Butch opened the door for him, he stormed out of the dressing room.

Butch started to follow his boss. But suddenly, he spun around and said to Joe, "Remember, eight pm sharp."

While Butch was reinforcing Carlo's edict, Johnny came out of the bathroom

"What was that all about?" he said to his brother.

'Ah, don't worry about it," Joe said. "I got everything under control.

"Why do you treat that asshole Carlo with such respect?" Johnny said. "He's a big load of dog shit."

Joe smiled, and said, "Hey, it costs nothing to be nice. You'll learn that when you grow up and get some manners."

The following night at eight pm sharp, Joe entered the Silver Coin, Carlo Russo's bar and principal place of business, located on Hester Street between Mulberry and Baxter Streets. Joe immediately spotted Carlo, who was sitting at his customary table in the back facing the front door.

Wiseguys never sat with their back to the front door, just in case.

With Carlo was Butch and Carlo's younger brother, Dominick.

Carlo motioned to Joe with a wave of his right forefinger.

"Hey, Joey boy. Sit down and join us for a drink," Carlo said.

As Joe headed towards Carlo's table, Butch shuffled over to the front entrance and locked the door.

It suddenly hit Joe that he was now in Carlo's domain, playing with Carlo's ball, in a game rigged in Carlo's favor.

All things being equal, Joe would rather have been sitting in a sneak pit with his hands tied.

Joe plopped down in the chair Carlo had designated for him, directly across the table from Carlo. Butch and Dominick took seats on either side of Joe, sandwiching him like a red piece of meat between two fat slabs of Italian bread. Joe took note that, besides the bartender, the scar-faced Frankie Fish, they were the only people in the joint.

Things could have been worse, but at this moment, Joe couldn't think any. But at least he was still alive – if just for the time being.

It was three against one, and any thoughts Joe might have had about fighting his way out had faded away like smoke from a cigarette. Joe knew he could take out any of the three hoods individually with his fists. But the odds of him being victorious against all three at one time was nil, especially since Joe knew all three mobsters traditionally carried deadly weapons.

Carlo took a sip of anisette and washed it down with a gulp of espresso, or "black coffee" as the Italians called it.

"Hey, Frankie!" Carlo yelled across the room to the bartender. "Give Joey here what he wants."

What Joe really wanted was a ticket out of this joint, but when Frankie came over to their table, he ordered a Dewars and club soda instead.

After the bartender returned with Joe's drink, Carlo said, "Listen, Joe, I'll get right to the point. I like your brother's style, and I absolutely love the way you're training him. But what your brother needs is a manager like me who has all the right connections to guide him to the top: the Heavyweight Championship of the World."

Joe sat there dumbfounded, and when he didn't react to Carlo's statement, Butch patted Joe on the back and said in a voice that sounded like gravel, "Drink your drink. You'll feel better."

While Butch patted Joe's back, Joe remembered what an old mob boss had said a generation ago: "The best way to deal with your enemy is to keep patting them on the back until a bullet hole appears between your fingers."

Joe took a sip of his drink, but he still said nothing. There was nothing he could say until he heard Carlo's proposition, and even then, there was not much he could say if he wanted to not leave the joint toes up

When it was obvious Joe was tongue-tied, Carlo resumed his soliloquy.

"Now Joe, I don't want you to get the wrong idea. I don't want you to feel I'm making an unreasonable offer. I want this to be a win-win situation for the both of us. I'm willing to give you ten grand for your brother's contract, and I want that contract extended for a ten-year period. On top of that, I'll give you ten percent of all his future purses. And, as his trainer, I'll also hit you with a cool hundred bucks a week. That's a very generous deal I'm giving you, Joe."

Carlo stood and leaned across the table until Joe could smell the booze on his breath.

"And remember this," Carlo said. "I'm not a man who takes no for an answer. So be smart, and do the right thing here."

Joe removed a handkerchief from his pants pocket and wiped the sweat from his brow. Butch patted his back a second time, and said, "Drink up before your ice melts."

Finally, Joe forced the words out of his mouth.

"Look, Carlo. What you're saying sounds good to me," Joe said. "But you don't know my brother Johnny. He's a funny kid; a real hot-head. If I make this deal without his consent, there's no telling what he might do. He might even retire from boxing rather than have you as his manager."

Carlo's rat-like face twisted into a wicked smile.

"I knew you'd come out with a smart answer like that," Carlo said.

He slowly removed a 38 caliber Smith and Weston revolver from his shoulder holster and placed it on the table.

"I want you to take a good look at this piece," Carlo said. "It's my opinion that a man can accomplish much more with a kind word and a gun, rather than with a kind word alone. You get my drift?"

Butch resumed patting Joe's back. Joe glanced towards Butch, and then towards Dominick. Maybe Joe imagined it, but it seemed to him that Dominick looked slightly embarrassed at what he was witnessing. Joe filed that thought away for future evaluation.

Carlo snatched the gun off the table and slipped it back into his shoulder holster.

"Now, go to your brother," Carlo said. "It's up to you how you present my offer to him. You've always been a smooth talker. I don't care how you do it, but convince your brother I'm making you an offer you can't refuse. And remember my gun. The next time you see it will be the last time you see anything. Capisce?"

Joe downed the rest of his drink in one long gulp. Then, he stood, and said, "Okay, Carlo. I'll speak to my brother right away."

Joe turned and headed for the front door. Butch made like his shadow, patting Joe's back all the way to the front door. Once there, Butch unlocked the door, and Carlo said, "Joe, I'll give you 24 hours. I want an answer by tomorrow night at 8 pm, sharp."

"No problem, Carlo. I'll see you then," Joe said.

As Joe was exiting the establishment, Butch's right hand spun Joe around, and he said, "Remember. Tomorrow night. 8 pm. Sharp."

Joe shot Butch a sickly smile. Then, he exited the Silver Coin and stepped onto Hester Street.

As he trudged down the block, Joe knew what he had to do. Carlo Russo had given him no choice.

Chapter 4

After leaving the Silver Coin, Joe made a beeline for Tony's Drugstore, located on the southwest corner of Mulberry and Canal Streets. He sped past the soda fountain and slipped into the phone booth located in the back. He dialed Johnny's home number, and Johnny's wife Rita answered the phone.

"Hey, sweetie pie," Joe said. "Is your husband home?"

"Sure, he's home. Where else would he be at this time of night?" Rita said. "And what's with this sweetie pie stuff? Are you in trouble again?"

Good old Rita. Joe knew she was sharp as a tack with a mouth to match. There was no fooling her.

Rather than keep playing this game, Joe decided to do an end-run around her.

"Just put my brother on the phone," Joe said.

Before she could reply, Johnny snatched the phone from Rita's hand.

"What's up, big brother?" Johnny said. "We live in the same building, and you have to call me on the phone. Are you too lazy to walk up two flights of freaking stairs?"

"Listen, Johnny, I'm jammed up," Joe said. "I can't talk on the phone. Meet me in Columbus Park. I'll be sitting on the park benches near the Motor Vehicle Building on Worth, Street on the Baxter Street side of the park."

Johnny glanced at his wife who seemed attached to his left elbow. She was not smiling.

Instead, she bit down hard on the forefinger of her right hand. That was a warning gesture all Italians were all too familiar with.

"Okay, I'll be there in half an hour," Johnny said. Then he banged down the receiver.

"What the hell was that all about?" Rita said to Johnny. "Is he betting those three-legged ponies again? Or, did he lose a bundle in a card game?"

"I'll find out when I talk to him," Johnny said.

"I'm telling you one thing," Rita said. "We're not lending him any more money that he never pays back. I'm saving money in my cookie jar for my new winter coat. He ain't touching a dime of that money."

Johnny had given up arguing with Rita years ago. The little spitfire was only 100 pound soaking wet and bulging with brains; unlike Johnny, who had the reputation of being a might slow upstairs. Rita, who was half-Irish on her mother's side, was always locking horns with his brother Joe, who Johnny knew was the toughest guy in the neighborhood.

So, Johnny did what he thought the wisest thing to do – he lied.

"There's no way we're giving Joe any more money," he said. "He's on his own this time."

Rita stuck her right forefinger under her husband's chin.

"What kind of fool do you take me for?" Rita said. "Joe could sweet talk honey from a beehive. But he ain't getting my winter coat!"

"Look, babe, my brother has his weaknesses, but we both know he's a good man," Johnny said. "He gave up his career to manage me. He was so good; he could have fought even with his bad eye. He quit boxing to manage me, and he's doing a bang-up job, ain't he? I'm undefeated, ain't I? So, let's cut him a little slack. I owe him big-time, and so do you."

"Yeah, I owe him a big kick in the ass," Rita said. She turned her back on her husband. "There goes my winter coat."

"Maybe it won't be so bad," Johnny said. "I'll find out in a few minutes."

"Okay, do what you have to do," Rita said. "Tell Joe I love him, too. But if he ever does this again, I'll wring his freakin' neck."

It was late October, and autumn was still in its youth. Scattered red and yellow leaves dotted the tarred surface of Columbus Park, and a brisk wind blew north on Baxter Street until it dissipated around the corner of Worth.

Joe sat in deep thought opposite the children's wading pool, which had long been the alternative to Coney Island for the neighborhood youths.

Joe was in a jackpot, and he knew it. You just don't mess with a man like Carlo Russo and lived to tell about it. Joe was always more level-headed than Johnny, who would not think twice about making the suicidal move by putting his hands on a made-guy like Carlo. It was up to Joe to break the news to Johnny without putting both their lives in jeopardy.

Joe spotted his brother coming across the softball field and headed in his direction.

Showtime was about to start.

Joe arrived at Joe's bench wearing a blue windbreaker over a white turtleneck shirt. A blue New York Yankee had sat slightly tilted on his head. He sat down next to Joe.

"Hey, what's with the Yankee hat?" Joe said. "You know I'm a diehard Giant fan."

"Screw the Giants," Johnny said. "We just kicked your ass in six games in the World Series."

"Yeah, but DiMaggio is on the way out," Joe said. "Word is out that he's retiring. His legs are shot. Plus, that kid Mantle screwed up his knee in game two of the World Series, and who knows if he's any good anyway?"

"He's better than that showboat Willie Mays, who's always running out from under his baseball cap," Johnny said. "Besides, Yankee Stadium is a ten times better place to watch a game instead of that decrepit the Polo Grounds the Giants play in. It's like comparing the Taj Mahal to a shack in the woods."

"Well, that's good, because Yankee Stadium is where we're headed for," Joe said. "If we can get Bill Brannigan into the ring, we'll fill up Yankee Stadium. With all the Italians and Irish in New York City, Madison Square Garden won't be big enough."

"Enough of this baseball bullshit. What the heck am I doing here anyway?" Johnny said. "We just got our new television set, and I could be home snuggling in front of the TV with my wife."

Joe put his arm around Johnny's shoulder and hugged him tightly.

"Kid, I'm in big trouble," Joe said. "And I need your help to keep my head above water."

"How much cash did you blow this time?" Johnny said.

"A lot more than we both have - *combined*," Joe said. "I lost a bundle at the track, and I tried to make it back by doubling up my bets on the Giants to win the World Series. And we both know how that went."

"Who did you bet with?" Johnny said. "And how much are you in the hole?"

"Ten grand worth, and I owe it to Carlo Russo," Joe said. "But Carlo offered me a way out. I took it, or you'd be seeing me in a pine box at Bachigalupo's Funeral Parlor."

Suddenly, it hit Johnny. Joe had sold him out to cover his betting losses.

"Don't tell me you sold out your flesh and blood to that bastard," Johnny said.

"Listen, Carlo covered my ten grand, plus he gave me another ten grand for your contract," Joe said. "That extra ten grand is yours. You and Rita could do a lot with that money. I'll be okay because Carlo is giving me a hundred bucks a week to be your trainer."

Johnny shook his head in dismay.

"I can't believe you did this to me," he said. "You married me to a mobster. Whatever I do now, people will say Carlo fixed everything for me. You know his reputation in boxing. He buys off everybody, even the New York State Boxing Commission. The referees. The judges. Everybody!"

"What else could I do?" Joe said. "We can't fight a guy like Carlo. He's got his button, and he's surrounded by muscle like Butch Salerno. My only other option was to go on the lam. But if I did that, he'd go after you; go after our family."

"Since when did you become a punk?" Johnny said. "You always taught me not to be afraid of anyone. Now, it's my big older brother who's turned yellow."

Joe jumped up and pulled Johnny to his feet. They stood eye to eye, their noses an inch apart.

"I'm no coward, and you know it," Joe said. "Sure, we could have fought them. Me and you against all the wiseguys on Mulberry Street; not to mention their pals all over the five boroughs of New York City. We wouldn't have stood a chance. We'd both be six feet under if they ever found our bodies."

"I'd rather be dead than sell my soul to the Devil," Johnny said.

"Listen to me," Joe said. "What do we need this aggravation for? Let me sign over your contract to Carlo. But I promise you that I'll make all the decisions. Carlo just wants to be a figurehead. It makes him look like a big shot with his mob buddies."

"What, you haven't signed over my contract yet?" Johnny said. "Then fuck Carlo. Let him go shit in his hat."

"I can't do that," Joe said. "I'm thinking about the safety of our entire family."

Johnny pushed his brother away.

"Then, you're a friggin' coward like I said," Johnny said.

Joe smacked Johnny hard across the face. Johnny started to fire an overhand right, but he stopped the punch in mid-air.

Suddenly, the two brothers fell into an embrace, and they both spilt tears on the other's shoulder.

It was Joe who spoke first.

"Listen, kid. Let's do it my way, at least for the time being," he said. "Let's give Carlo his piece of paper, and when the time is right, we'll tell him to wipe his ass with it."

Johnny pushed Joe away.

"All right. Do what you gotta do," he said. "But I'll never forgive you for this. For our family's sake, I'll put on a good face. But you'll know how I really feel. My big brother turned out to be a pussy. Who would have fuckin' believed it?"

Johnny spun around and headed across the softball field towards 104 Bayard Street.

The crisp autumn air cut through Joe like a knife. He sat back down on the bench like he was in a deep trance. It seemed like days to him, but it was only minutes later when Joe trudged out of Columbus Park and headed up a steep hill called Park Street to Transfiguration Church located on the corner of Mott Street.

Joe pushed open the massive oak front door and crept inside the church. He was alone, except for three old Italian women with black shawls covering their heads, who stood by the altar up front, lighting candles and mumbling prayers in Italian.

Joe dipped his hand in the holy water and made the sign of the cross. He knelt in the back pew and said a silent prayer.

"Dear God, forgive me," Joe said. "But if it's the last thing I ever do, let me be the one who drops Carlo Russo into the fires of hell."

Chapter Five

It was nine am Thanksgiving morning, and Johnny, after finishing his early morning roadwork, returned to his apartment at 104 Bayard Street with a large white box in his hand with lettering that read: "LaBella Ferrara's Pastry Shop."

He was greeted by his wife Rita, who snapped at him, saying, "What are you freakin' nuts? That's a two-pound box of pastries. If I have to sleep on the couch because we can't have sex while you're training for a fight, you better not even think about eating those pastries."

"Today's Thanksgiving. Forget my diet," Johnny said. He patted his rock-hard stomach. "I'm going to eat like a horse today. I hope you and Mary made enough food. Turkey. Stuffing. Sweet potatoes. And all the trimmings."

Rita smiled, and said, "Okay, if you're going to eat like a horse today, we're going to screw like rabbits this morning."

"It's a deal," Johnny said. "Now, where's my coffee, to go along with these wonderful pastries?"

Rita smiled, and then winked at her husband, "I'll prepare your coffee, but we're going into the bedroom first."

A little after noon, Johnny and Rita bounded down two flights of stairs from their fourth-floor apartment to Joe and Mary's apartment on the second floor. Of course, the two women were preparing the traditional turkey dinner that Americans had expected to consume on Thanksgiving Day. But the turkey dinner would be the final course of an all-day feast and would be the only concession to American customs.

Starting the previous night, Mary had cooked a scrumptious meat lasagna, while Rita had arranged a tray of Italian antipasto cold cuts, consisting of prosciutto, sopressata, and capicola, as well as Italians cheeses including provolone, asiago, and pecorino. The tray was then decorated with roasted peppers and black and green Italian olives, and rimmed with anchovies.

On the stove, a large cast-iron pot was boiling a dozen artichokes, while the traditional red Italian meat-sauce (or gravy as it is called in New York City) was simmering in a huge stainless-steel pot containing meatballs and Italian sausages. Two pounds of spaghetti was lying on the kitchen table waiting to be cooked after the artichokes were done, and two pounds of homemade cavatelli stood in line to be prepared after the spaghetti.

For starters, Mary placed a tray of cooked chestnuts on the kitchen table next to the antipasto, and the two men began chowing down while the two women handled the cooking on the kitchen stove.

Joe stuffed a piece of cheese in his mouth and yelled to his sister Mary, "Don't forget to keep stirring that gravy. And turn down the heat to low, or you'll burn it."

Mary turned towards Joe with her hands on her hips.

"How about you cook, and I eat?" she said.

Joe belched and inserted another piece of cheese into his yap.

"No, I'm sure you're doing just fine," he said. "But as your older brother, I need to do a little supervision here."

Rita strolled over to the kitchen window and opened it halfway. After the cooking smoke escaped outside, the kitchen inhaled the crisp November air.

"Good, now we can at least breathe," Rita said. "These two mooks ain't gonna lift a finger all day."

Mary poured two glasses of wine from the gallon jug sitting on a side table, and she handed one to Rita.

"Let's get into the holiday spirit," Mary said to Rita.

The women took sips of their wine and then resumed cooking.

"Hey, what about us?" Johnny said. "You didn't pour me and Joe any wine."

"What are you crippled?" Rita said. "Help yourself, and don't break our balls while we're cooking for you two cafones."

It was around three pm when Johnny and Joe fled to the living room to rest up before the main course of turkey and all the Thanksgiving trimmings, which was scheduled for 4 pm. Both were sipping red wine, and on Joe's 17-inch RCA television set the traditional Thanksgiving football game between the Green Bay Packers and the Detroit Lions was in the middle of the third quarter. The Lions, an habitual powerhouse, was kicking the crap out of the lowly Packers by three touchdowns.

Johnny took a sip of wine, and then he said to Joe, "What's up with Carlo's brother, Dominick? He don't know shit from shinola about boxing, and he looks like my chief second between rounds."

"So what?" Joe said. "I'm still giving you all the instructions between rounds from behind you, outside the ring."

"That's no good," Johnny said. "In my next fight, I want you in the ring between rounds, not Dominick. It's easier for me to concentrate on what you're saying when you are in front of me, not behind me. This is my career we're talking about. Let's cut the bullshit. I don't want any screw-ups."

Joe positioned his glass of wine in front of his face and gazed into it like it was a crystal ball.

Finally, he said, "Nah, let's keep it how it is for a while. It makes Carlo look like a bigshot by having his brother in the ring between rounds. Besides, Dom ain't such a bad guy. He's nothing like Carlo. He actually has a good heart."

"It's bad enough Carlo is now my manager," Johnny said. "I don't want it to appear like I'm taking boxing instructions from his jerkoff brother between rounds."

"Look at it this way, kid," Joe said. "The main thing is to keep Carlo off our backs. With Dom hanging around and looking important, Carlo stays away. Get my drift?"

"Yeah, you got a point, Joe," Johnny said. "But I'm still not comfortable with the situation. But I will say one thing. I kinda like Dom myself. Last week he loaned me his car to drive Rita to her mother's house in Brooklyn. I didn't even ask him for the car. I just mentioned I was walking Rita to the subway, and he handed me the keys to his car."

"I told you Dom has a good heart."

"He even stuffed a five-dollar bill in my pocket for gas. He wouldn't take no for an answer."

Joe lowered his voice and leaned towards Johnny. He said in almost a whisper, "I think I know why Dom is being so nice to us. He's stuck on our sister Mary. He even approached me last week about setting up a date between the two of them. I didn't give him a definite answer. What do you think?"

"I think you're freaking nuts, that's what I think," Johnny yelled.

Just then, Rita stuck her head into the room, and said, "Are you two morons fighting again? It's a freakin' holiday. Can't you two keep peace in the family even for one day?"

"We're not fighting," Joe said. "We're just talking loud. We're Italian, for Pete's sake. What did you expect?"

"All right," Rita said. "But just keep it down to a low roar. You're giving me a headache."

After Rita left the room, Johnny leaned forward and whispered into Joe's ear.

"Are you friggin' nuts," he said. "We can't let our beautiful sister go out with that ape. Dom's so ugly when he was born the doctor spanked his mother."

"Come on, your exaggerating. Dom ain't ugly," Joe said. "He ain't Tyrone Power either, but he's a decent looking guy. Besides, Mary ain't doing herself any good by staying home all the time. She needs to get a life of her own."

"But Dom is almost a head shorter than Mary," Johnny said. "When they'd walk the street together, he'd look like her pet monkey. All she'll need is an organ grinders organ and a tin cup."

Joe tried to stifle a giggle.

"Think of it this way," Joe said. "Mary's 26 years old, and the only real boyfriend she ever had was Billy Clark. She's the best-looking of all our sisters, and she's the only one not married. She's always babysitting for one of our nieces or nephews, and she never goes out except to see you fight."

"But he's Carlo Russo's brother," Johnny said. "He has bad genes."

"No, Johnny. Dom is a gentleman," Joe said. "He even suggested that you and Rita chaperone him and Mary on their first date."

"Now, I know you're losing your mind," Johnny said. "That chaperone shit is something they used to do in the old country; not in America."

"But Mary has nothing to lose," Joe said. "She could dump Dom after one date. Like they say in basketball, no harm, no foul."

"Okay, let's leave it up to Mary," Johnny said. "If she's okay with going on a date with Dom, me and Rita will go along as chaperones. But I guarantee you, Rita will watch Dom like a hawk."

"That's what I'm counting on, little brother," Joe said. "Mary is the apple of my eye. If I thought this was bad for her, I would have told Dom to go fly a kite."

Johnny stood from his chair.

"It's almost 4 pm. Let's go inside and attack that turkey," Johnny said.

Joe glanced at his wristwatch.

"It's not even 3:30," he said. "The turkey's probably not even ready yet."

"Then, we'll pick on what *is* ready," Johnny said. "Like I said, I'm freakin' starvin'."

"But don't discuss anything about Dom until we finish eating," Joe said. "I don't want to kill anyone's appetite, especially mine."

At the kitchen table, Johnny Italiano washed down the last morsel of his Thanksgiving dinner with his sixth glass of wine.

"That's it for me," Johnny said. "if I eat one more bite, I might puke."

As Mary and Rita cleared the table, Joe sat back in the kitchen chair and held his stomach with both hands.

"That's it for me, too," he said. "You two girls really did a great job cooking for us today."

Joe stood up and walked over to where Mary was cleaning the dishes. He hugged her and said, "Hey, Mary, you haven't been getting out much lately, have you?"

"Not really," Mary said. "Why do you ask?"

"I don't know. You get up in the morning, go to work, and then come home and stare at the four walls. I think it's time for you to start thinking about a life of your own."

Mary stared at the ceiling in frustration.

"What do you want me to do," she said. "Hang out in bars looking for men? You know I'm not like that."

Sensing a commotion, Johnny stood from the table. He grabbed Rita's arm.

"Come on. Let's go into the living room and watch TV," Johnny said.

After Johnny and Rita exited the kitchen, Joe said, "Mary, there's a neighborhood guy who's dying to go out with you. He's an honorable guy, and he did the right thing by asking me to make the introductions. He's very concerned that things are done properly."

"What's his name?" Mary said.

"Dominick Russo."

Mary flashed angry eyes.

"You're kidding me," she said. "Carlo Russo is tearing you and Johnny apart, and now you want to fix me up with his brother? Am I part of that deal, too?"

"Sis, it's nothing like that. Dom's a really nice person. He's nothing like Carlo. He's no John Derek in looks, but I think you and him will make a great match."

"If he's Carlo's brother, how can he be a nice guy?

"Dom's nothing like his brother. He even asked that Johnny and Rita accompany you on your first date. Johnny said it's fine by him."

"What about Rita?"

Joe nodded towards the living room.

"I think that's what they're discussing right now," he said.

Suddenly, Rita booming voice came in loud and clear from the living room.

She screamed, "ARE YOU FREAKIN' CRAZY?"

Mary said to Joe, "I think we better go inside before Rita sticks a fork in her husband's eye."

Chapter Six

At seven am, the day after Thanksgiving, Joe Italiano banged his ringing alarm clock quiet. The heat from the lone gas heater in the living room barely crept into Joe's bedroom. So, Joe pulled the covers over his head and shivered.

Joe knew his brother Johnny now slept warmly with his wife Rita snuggling next to him, and he decided that, after he married Mary off to a suitable fellow, he'd find himself a nice, plump, Italian wife, preferably from the old country.

His ideal wife had dark hair and brown eyes, with a voluptuous body. She had to be a good cook and not someone whom you might run into at a Mensa meeting. What Joe didn't need was an intelligent and bossy ball-breaking wife.

Joe jumped out of bed, and he passed Mary's bedroom. The door was half open, and Joe noticed that Mary was still sleeping.

"Hey, Mary. Wake up," Joe said. "Don't you have to be at work at nine?"

His loud voice rebounded off the walls and thudded into Mary's ears. She pulled the covers over her head to stifle the commotion.

"Come on, sleepy-head," Joe said. "You heard me. It's time to get up. We ain't so rich that you don't have to work."

Mary stuck her head from out under the covers, and said, "Leave me alone. Today's my day off."

"Sorry, kid," Joe said. "Go back to sleep. I'm going out for a walk to get the newspapers."

"Come back in about two weeks," Mary said.

"Don't get rambunctious. I'm walking all the way down to the South Ferry where the air is fresh, the coffee is hot, and the seagulls are more friendly than certain relatives of mine."

Joe gently closed Mary's bedroom door.

In the kitchen, Joe, his frigid breath visible in the cold apartment, doused his face with cold water to clear the cobwebs caused by too many glasses of Thanksgiving wine. After he brushed his teeth and ran a Gillette razor across this face, he tipped-towed past Mary's bedroom and into his own. He scanned the inside of his closet, and he decided on the Navy pea coat, Navy issued sweater, and a dark blue pair of dungarees – all purchased at the used Army-Navy store downtown on Whitehall Street.

Fully dressed, and with the apartment temperature barely above freezing, he went into the kitchen and turned on all four jets on the gas range to provide more heat.

Joe turned on the kitchen radio, and he heard Frank Sinatra singing "Nancy With the Laughing Face."

Joe thought, maybe I'll give Nancy a call today. He hadn't spoken to his former girlfriend since they had broken up three months earlier.

Nancy Romano was the prettiest girl in Little Italy, but she possessed the temper of the wildest hurricane. She was the daughter of Pete Romano, the benevolent Mafia boss of Little Italy. Carlo Russo, for all his bluster, was merely an underling who took orders from Pete. If Pete Romano told Carlo to sit, Carlo wouldn't even look for a chair.

Pete Romano earned a nice living controlling the neighborhood gambling and loansharking. But Pete strictly prohibited the sale of narcotics. Anyone, who was foolish enough to disobey Pete's non-drug decree, would not be long for this world.

Near the end of the summer, Pete Romano had sent word to Joe to meet him at his Hester Street social club, the hub of Pete's operations, which had a strict "members only" policy. When Joe arrived, he spotted Pete sitting at a circular table where all the sit-downs took place. After Joe took a seat opposite him, Pete folded his hands over his ample gut, and he got right to the point.

"Joe, you've always been a good kid," Pete said. "I've known you since you were in diapers. But it's time that you explained to me your intentions with my daughter Nancy. Nancy will be twenty-five in January, and you must be close to thirty."

"Twenty-nine to be exact," Joe said. "I'll be thirty in December."

"So, what's the story, Joe?" Pete said. "Do you have any plans to marry my Nancy?"

As if on cue, Nancy Romano marched through the front door.

Tall and erect, Nancy looked like a high-priced fashion model. Her jet-black hair was parted on the right side, and it was curled up at both ends, barely touching her shoulders. Her raven eyes had a strange way of flashing when she was angry, that was both attractive and a little bit frightening; especially since she was Pete Romano's daughter.

Nancy wore a black and white polka-dot dress that ended just under her knee, exposing long, shapely legs. She sat next to her father and kissed him on the cheek. Then, she peered coldly into Joe's eyes.

Joe felt nailed to his seat.

Pete Romano turned to his daughter.

"Nancy, I just asked Joe a very important question," he said. "And I'm waiting for his answer."

Nancy leaned forward and continued staring into Joe's eyes like she had x-ray vision into his innermost thoughts. Joe felt her eyes burning through to the back of his skull.

"Joe, we've discussed this before, and you never gave me a straight answer," Nancy said. She tapped the fingers of her right hand on the table like she was playing the piano. "I want to know where we stand, and I want to know now!"

Joe chose her words carefully. Incurring the wrath of Pete Romano was bad enough, but the thought of an angry Nancy Romano sent chills down Joe's spine. Joe figured if he pulled this off and walked out of the club unscathed, he was a better actor than Lawrence Olivier.

He said, "Yes, Nancy, I love you, and nothing would please me more than you someday being my wife."

Joe took a deep breath, and continued, saying "But now is just not the right time. I still have my younger sister Mary at home, and I have my obligations to her. When I marry her off, thing's will be different. Also, I'm very involved in my brother Johnny's boxing career. So, maybe is a year or so I'll be in a better position to contemplate marriage."

Peter Romano started to speak, but Nancy silenced him with an angry wave of her hand.

"WHAT A CROCK OF CRAP!" she screamed. "How about that exotic dancer you've been seeing uptown!"

Joe squirmed in his seat as Nancy continued her tirade.

"Oh, you didn't think I knew about her, did you! The one with the long legs and a gap between them as wide as the Holland Tunnel! Explain her to me, Mr. Italiano!"

For Joe, this was not good news. He decided to take the path of least resistance. He lied.

"What dancer? I'm not seeing any dancer," he said while scratching his head "Oh, wait a minute. You don't mean Lauren McGee, do you? Her brother Bobby's a fighter. He wanted me to train him, but I told him I didn't have the time. His sister asked me to meet her for a drink. She tried to get to reconsider about Bobby, but I......"

What Nancy did next, Joe had seen John Wayne do in Westerns. She jumped to her feet, picked up her end of the table, and flipped it over onto Joe's lap. Bottles and glasses flew in all direction and shattered on the floor.

"YOU THINK I'M A MORON, DON'T YOU!" she screamed.

Both Pete Romano and Joe sat transfixed in their chairs; their mouths wide open, and a shocked look on their faces. Beer dripped onto Joe's lap, but he was too terrified to move.

Nancy screamed louder, "GET OUT OF MY LIFE, JOE ITALIANO! I DON'T EVER WANT TO SEE YOU AGAIN!"

That said, Nancy rushed out of Peter Romano's social club, slamming the door behind her.

Pete stood up and handed Joe a handkerchief. Joe tried to wipe the beer off his pants, but it still dripped down onto his socks, saturating them.

Pete picked up the table and placed it right-side-up.

"Well, I guess that's that," Pete said. "When Nancy gets her balls in an uproar, even I can't control her. I wish you would have thought of a better excuse than that bullshit story about that dancer."

"Sorry, Pete but that dancer was a one-night stand," Joe said. "I don't know how Nancy found out."

"Look, Joe. You and Nancy ain't married yet, and men have to be men," Pete said. "I know how it is. Now, if you had been married, or even engaged, you'd be in deep shit now."

"I know Pete. I know," Joe said.

"Look, kid. She cares for you," Pete said. "Leave her alone for a while. Give her a chance to cool down. Then, make your pitch, but make it a good one. You hear what I'm saying?"

Joe told Pete that he indeed understood what he needed to do.

Now, it was the day after Thanksgiving, three months after the incident in Pete Romano's club, but Joe still didn't have the courage to dial Nancy's phone number.

"Nancy with the laughing face..."

Sinatra finished the song that Joe was listening to on the kitchen radio.

Then, Joe heard the 7:30 am news.

Hank Kelly, the manager of heavyweight champion Bill Brannigan, was found shot to death in his midtown apartment.

Joe turned up the volume on the radio.

Kelly was found sitting at his kitchen table, face down, with two bullet holes in his forehead. According to the police report, there was no sign of forced entry. The police believe that Kelly knew his killer, or killers, and was engaged in a meeting when he was murdered. The police found three used glasses and a bottle of Irish Whiskey on the table. The police lab dusted for fingerprints, but the glasses had been wiped clean.

Joe poured himself a cup of hot coffee, black, no sugar. His mind raced, listing possible suspects. The radio report continued:

Police say that at this time there are no clues as to who the murderer or murderers may be. But they are investigating Kelly's ties to the boxing world and underworld figures for clues as to a possible motive."

Joe snapped off the radio.

Joe figured Kelly's murder smelled of Carlo Russo. Joe knew for a fact that Carlo had talked with boxing promoters about a possible title fight for Johnny against Bill Brannigan.

But why kill Kelly? Kelly would have jumped at the chance to match the champion with an untested, unknown commodity like Johnny. Brannigan was a wily veteran who knew every trick in the book; legal and otherwise. He would be a prohibitive favorite over Johnny, who had a load of natural talent but was not ready, physically or mentally, to fight a fighter of Brannigan's caliber.

Hank Kelly had always insisted, that for any title fight concerning Brannigan, they would get a significant percentage of the gate, in addition to a guaranteed minimum. With the Irish coming in droves to root for Brannigan, and the Italians doing the same for Johnny, they could fill any park, including Yellowstone Park, and Kelly stood to make a bundle when the fight took place.

Johnny donned his pea coat, pulled navy-blue stocking hat over his ears, and exited the apartment.

Twenty minutes later, Joe arrived at a 24-hour coffee shop/diner at the base of the South Ferry. This small eatery was one of the few 24-hour restaurants in downtown Manhattan, and everyone in Little Italy showed up there sooner, or later, especially after an all-night bender. After picking up a copy of the *Daily News* and the *Daily Mirror*, Joe ordered a hot cup of coffee to stay, and six jelly donuts and six apple turnovers to go.

While Joe sipped his coffee and waited for the counterman to fill his order, he spotted a familiar figure exiting the South Ferry with his back to Joe so that he couldn't see his face. The man wore a black fedora pulled down over his mug, and a grey overcoat buttoned to the top with the collar rolled up over his ears. It was cold at the South Ferry, but not that cold. It was obvious to Joe this man didn't want to be recognized.

The mysterious man made a right turn onto South Street, where he hailed a cab. Joe caught a quick glance at the man's face as he stepped into the cab.

He looked like Dominick Russo.

But why would Dominick Russo be exiting the Staten Island Ferry at eight am in the morning the day after Thanksgiving? Joe wrestled with that question all the way back to 104 Bayard Street.

Chapter Seven

After Joe arrived with the donuts and the morning newspaper, Mary placed a freshly brewed pot of coffee on the kitchen table. Then, he greeted her big brother with a kiss on the cheek.

"Sorry I jumped all over you this morning," Mary said. "I had a terrible nightmare last night, and I woke up all bent out of shape. Funny thing, I can't even remember what the nightmare was about, only that I was scared."

"That's alright, Kiddo," Joe said. "We all have our bad moments." Joe took a sip of his coffee. "Give Rita a call. Tell her and Johnny to come down and sample these delicious donuts I bought by the South Ferry. That's Johnny's favorite place."

"Good idea," Mary said.

She walked into the living room, picked up the phone and dialed Rita's number.

While Mary was talking to Rita on the phone in the living room, Joe flipped through the pages of the *New York Daily Mirror*. There was no mention of Hank Kelly's murder in the news section of the paper. So, Joe flipped the paper over to the sports section in the back. He scanned through a couple of pages and stopped when he saw Dan Parker's boxing column.

While he was reading, Mary came back into the kitchen.

"Hey, Mary. Look what Dan Parker wrote about Johnny," Joe said. "He said Johnny is the best prospect in the heavyweight division. I'm going to clip this and put it in Johnny's scrapbook."

"That's nice," Mary said. "You're going to need a bigger scrapbook pretty soon. By the way, Rita said thanks, but she's staying in bed for a while. I'll save her a few donuts for later on."

"What about Johnny?" Joe said. "Is he still home or did he go out jogging. He better put in an extra mile or two after what he ate yesterday."

Mary smiled. "No, Johnny's still home. That's why Rita is still staying in bed."

"That figures," Joe said. "What the hell? Let them have fun until Monday morning. Then we'll go back to work. I can't let the kid get out of shape. You never know when we might get a big fight."

Joe took a large bite of a jelly donut, and the jelly squirted down onto his chin. After giving his mug a quick wipe, he said to Mary, "What do you have planned for your big day off?"

"I have a three-day weekend to be exact," Mary said. "Me and Rita are going to the movies. There a new Joan Crawford movie playing at the Venice Theater. Everybody is raving about it. We both adore Joan Crawford. She really knows how to handle men."

"Joan Crawford depresses me," Joe said. "Why don't you go see a nice Betty Hutton movie instead. They're always fun. Men like women who are sweet, soft, and cuddly. Not a vampire like Joan Crawford."

"Yeah, guys like you want women you can step all over," Mary said. "By the way, what's the story with you and Nancy Romano? I haven't seen her around lately."

"Ah, we broke up a while back," Joe said. "I had a sit-down with her old man last summer. She wanted to get engaged right away. I told Pete I wanted to wait awhile, and she exposed like a Cherry Bomb. I haven't seen her since."

"See, that's your problem," Mary said. "You always want to be the boss. But with Nancy, you can't be the boss. She has a mind of her own, and you can't take it. You don't want to admit it, but she the perfect girl for you. Men like you need a woman who can keep them in line."

"Better I should marry a cop," Joe said. "If I get even a little bit out of line with Nancy, I have to deal with her father and his gorillas. My life expectancy would be zero, zip, zilch."

"Why don't you just give her a call?" Mary said. "It can't hurt, and you've been close since you were kids."

"I'll think about it," Joe said. "But first, I'm going to have myself another one of these delicious jelly donuts."

At precisely high noon, Joe entered the Silver Coin. He sat at the bar and ordered an espresso. Both Carlo Russo and his brother Dom were conspicuous by their absence; as was Butch Salerno. That was odd, but Joe figured he knew why.

"Is Carlo or his brother Dom around?" Joe asked Frankie Fish the bartender.

Frankie was counting out the new day's cash register bank, and he didn't even look up when he said, "Haven't seen either one yet."

Joe knew asking too many questions in a joint like this was not the wisest thing to do, so he just sipped his espresso and pondered his future.

Since he had retired from boxing, Joe had shaped-up three nights a week at the mob-controlled Fulton Fish Market on South Street, loading and unloading crates of fish. The pay was good; fifty bucks per 12-hour shift. But sturdy young men like Joe swiftly grew old and decrepit schlepping fish on South Street.

During the steaming summers, the workers barely survived the heat; mainly because they slipped in and out of the refrigerated fish lockers. But when the temperature dipped below freezing, it was pure torture. The frigid and damp air blasted through the worker's bones like hot flames through a dry forest. The combination of the unbearable weather conditions and the heavy lifting stamped deep lines on the worker's foreheads and injected arthritis into their bones.

Joe's burning ambition was to save his hard-earned money and move to a warmer climate far from the harshness of the Fulton

Fish Market, not to mention the treacherousness of the New York City Mafia.

Joe ordered another espresso and waited. The heavy caffeine from the Italian coffee pumped up Joe's awareness, and he was wide-eyed alert when Carlo Russo trudged through the front door at 12:30 pm.

Carlo sauntered past Joe like Joe was a cockroach on the floor. And after he sat at his customary table, he grumbled to Frankie Fish, who was waiting for his assignment with baited breath, "Espresso with Anisette on the side, and make it quick."

Joe stood up and paced to Carlo's table. He sat in the chair opposite Carlo, and said, "Don't you say hello anymore?"

As soon as Joe saw the rage in Carlo's eyes, he knew he had made a big mistake.

"Who the fuck are you that I have to say hello?" Carlo said. "You're nothing but a piece of shit to me anyway."

Joe wanted to crack the ugly bastard right in the face, but he knew that since Carlo was a made-man such action would be suicidal.

"Look, Carlo, I didn't come here to argue you," Joe said. "I wanted to talk to your brother Dominick about my sister Mary. What time do you expect him?"

Carlo lifted the glass of Sambuca to his lips and downed it in a single gulp.

"Dom's home sleeping," Carlo said. "We were out playing cards all night. I haven't the slightest fuckin' idea when he'll be around. Now, go pedal your shit someplace else. Nobody invited you to sit in the first place."

Joe knew Carlo was lying. He was sure it was Dom he had seen at the South Ferry.

"Okay, sorry for the intrusion," Joe said. "Just tell Dom that Mary agreed to a date with him tomorrow night at eight pm. He can pick her up at our apartment at 104 Bayard."

"Are you trying to make a fool out of me?" Carlo said. "I'm no messenger boy. Tell him yourself."

Joe's blood was beginning to boil, and before he lost his temper, and probably his life, he said, "Suit yourself. I'll be back later."

Joe walked back to the bar and picked up his change, leaving Frankie a dollar tip.

"Frankie, when Dom comes in, tell him I was here looking for him," Joe said. "Tell him I'll be back around five pm."

Frankie scooped up the buck and said, "Ok, will do."

A split second after Joe exited the Silver Coin, Carlo hurled his glass against the front door, and slivers of glass sprayed in all directions.

Frankie Fish dove behind the bar, expecting to hear bullets. He didn't get back up until Carlo had stormed outside, slamming the door behind him."

After exiting the Silver Coin, Joe hiked to Canal Street where he hailed a cab. He told the driver to take him to Stillman's Gym located at 48th Street and Eighth Avenue, just down the street from Madison Square Garden. While the cabby weaved his way through Midtown traffic, Joe sorted out the puzzle of Hank Kelly's murder. And no matter which way Joe arranged the pieces, it still came up the handiwork of Carlo Russo.

The question was why.

Thirty minutes later, Joe entered Stillman's Gym, and the sweet stench of sweating bodies hit him like a swift kick in the face. No matter his many times Joe slipped into any one of the scores of New York City boxing gyms, dotted throughout the five boroughs, this odor still repulsed him. Some things you never get used to.

Pee Wee, a dwarfish, bald-headed man in his early 70s, ran Stillman's Gym. Before Joe got five feet inside, Pee Wee stopped him with a hand to his chest.

"Hey, fork over the month's dues for your brother's locker," Pee Wee said.

"See Carlo Russo," Joe said. "He's my brother's manager, and he's responsible for the financial side of things."

"No, you see him," Pee Wee said. "He never comes here anyway."

"Okay, Pee Wee. But what did you do with the money?" Joe said.

"What money?" Pee Wee said. "I never got the money. That's why I'm asking you for it."

"No, not that money," Joe said. "I'm talking about the money your mother gave you for charm school."

"Fuck you in spades," Pee Wee said. "Now fork over the cash."

Joe smiled, and then he palmed Pee Wee's bald head like it was a basketball. Pee Wee wiggled and squirmed, but Joe still held firm.

"Hey, let go of my head!" Pee Wee yelled.

"I'll let go if you tell me if Bill Brannigan has shown up yet," Joe said.

"Yeah, he upstairs," Pee Wee said. He pulled a penknife from his pocket, and said, "Now let go, or I'll stab you in the balls."

Joe let go of Pee Wee's head. Then, glaring at the knife, he said, smiling "Who are you scaring with that? It's the size of a toothpick."

Pee Wee was quick with the penknife, but Joe was quicker. Two quick sidesteps and Joe was out of the little man's reach.

Laughing so hard his sides hurt, Joe sprinted towards the steps leading to the second floor. He bounded up the steps two at the time.

For five bucks a month, the fighters training at Stillman's had the privilege of storing their boxing equipment in broken down lockers and showering in an unsanitary cubby hole equipped with one rusted shower head. But befitting his status as the Heavyweight Champion of the World, Bill Brannigan received the red carpet treatment. He had his own private room and his own private shower, that was only slightly more sanitary that one used by the rabble.

Joe stopped at a faded green door. The named "Brannigan" was chicken-scrawled on it in black paint. Joe turned the doorknob, but the door was locked from the inside. Joe knocked hard, three times. But, but no one answered

"Come on, Bill. I know you're in there," Joe said. "I only need a couple of minutes."

A feeble voice said from inside, "I ain't talking to no reporters."

"Hey, Bill. It's Joe Italiano. Johnny's brother."

In seconds, the door opened and Bill Brannigan, all six-feet-four-inches and 230 pounds of him, blocked the entrance.

"What's on your mind, Joe?" Brannigan said. His voice had an edge to it.

"Bill, I just want to tell you I'm sorry about Hank Kelly," Joe said. "I also wanted you to know I had nothing to do with it, and I was shocked when I read it in the papers this morning."

Brannigan turned and lumbered inside. He did not close the door, and Joe followed him in. Brannigan sat hunched on a wooden bench, and Joe sat next to him.

"Yeah, you're sorry, alight," Brannigan said. "Hank was just another cockroach, and you guys stepped on him."

"No, Bill, you have it all wrong," Joe said. "Carlo is my brother's manager on paper, but I call all the shots. At least that's the agreement we have. But as soon as I read about Hank, I knew Carlo was involved. I just didn't know why. Was Carlo trying to broker a fight between you and Johnny? If he did so, it was without my knowledge or consent."

Brannigan stood and shuffled over to his locker. He removed a pint of Irish whiskey from the top shelf and took a long gulp. Then, he sat back down next to Joe and offered Joe the pint bottle. Joe grabbed it and took a small sip. It burned all the way down. He handed the bottle back to Brannigan, who finished it off.

"Yeah, Joe, I guess you're on the level," Brannigan said. "You've always had the reputation of being a stand-up guy. I couldn't believe it when I heard you and your brother were mixed up with that scumbag Carlo Russo."

"Yeah, Bill. I couldn't believe it either. It wasn't my doing, but that's another story. Tell me what you know, and I swear it won't leave this room."

"Funny, I was just sitting here wondering what I'll tell the cops when they show up. I was going to lam-it, and let my lawyer issue a statement or something. And I still might do it if I have the time, but it's probably too late. They'll probably be here any minute. So, before the cops get here and I clam up, here's what really happened."

A week ago, Carlo Russo had cornered Brannigan just as he was leaving the Stillman's Gym. Butch Salerno was with Carlo, and after Butch strong-armed Brannigan into an empty tenement hallway, he stuck a 38 caliber pistol into Brannigan's ribs.

"You and your manager Kelly are going to come to my joint on Mulberry Street," Carlo had said. "Tonight at midnight. Don't be late, and don't make me come looking for you."

"Our first mistake was going down into Carlo's territory," Brannigan told Joe. "As soon as we entered his joint, they drew pistols and forced us into the back room, where Carlo, that ugly fuckin' midget, slapped Hank in the face. Once. Twice. Three times. Then, he told Hank that me and Johnny were going to fight for the title within three months, or else. That was no problem with me. Your brother's good, but he's green. It should be an easy fight for me. I'd beat him on experience alone."

Joe figured, with the way Brannigan was hitting the Irish whiskey, experience may not be enough.

He let Brannigan continue.

"But the kicker was that I had to go into the tank. They had a gun to my head. What was I to say or do? So, I agreed with the proposition. Carlo told me he'd give me fifty grand to throw the fight. Twenty-five grand after I signed the contract, and twenty-five grand after I splashed. After we left the joint, Hank told me not to worry. He said he knew how to handle those guinea bastards. That's the last I heard about it until last night."

Brannigan stood and went to his locker. He removed another pint of Irish whiskey, took a swig, and offered the bottle to Joe. Joe refused it with a wave of his hand.

"So, what happened last night?" Joe said.

Brannigan spoke as he paced the room.

"It was after midnight, and I was sleeping," Brannigan said. "The phone rang, and I heard Hank's voice. It sounded like he was crying. The bastards then made me hear Hank beg for his life. He was saying over and over, 'Don't kill me. I have four kids and a sick wife.' And that's the truth. I knew it, but Carlo didn't care. Then, I heard the shots. Two quick ones. And, a second or two later, another shot. Then the phone went dead.

"I prayed that it was all a sick joke; that they were just trying to scare me. But this morning, I heard the news on the radio. That's all I can tell you. I was waiting for Carlo to get in touch with me. When you knocked on my door, I figured you were here as Carlo's boy."

"So, what are you going to do?" Joe said.

"What am I going to do? I tell you what I'm going to do. I'm going to fuck everybody. I'm retiring and giving up the crown. I ain't taking no dive, and I'm going out as champ."

"Think this through, Brannigan," Joe said. "You think Carlo's going to let you retire? Just like that? You have a wife and kids?"

"Yes, me and Millie have three kids, and one is on the way."

"So, that's it," Joe said. "He'll grab your wife, or one of your kids, and hold them for ransom until you do the right thing. You don't know Carlo like I do. He'll do anything to get what he wants, and a human life means nothing to him."

Brannigan sat on the bench, put his head between his hand, and began sobbing. His massive back muscles bobbed up and down.

"But what can we do?" Brannigan said between sobs.

Joe stood up and approached a speed bag hanging from the ceiling in the back of Brannigan's dressing room. He started tapping the bag slowly, first with his left hand; then with his right hand. Then, with both hands, increasing the intensity and the cadence.

Ratta tat tat... Ratta tat tat... Ratta tat tat............

Joe stopped attacking the speed bag, and he turned towards Brannigan

"No way, Brannigan. No freakin' way!" Joe said.

Then, he turned and hit the bag with increased speed and vengeance.

"We'll make our stand now," Joe said, while still punching the bag. "If we don't stop Carlo, he'll be up our asses the rest of our lives."

"But how?" Brannigan said. "How do we fight back at Carlo with all the muscle he has surrounding him?"

Joe fired one last right hand at the speed bag that knocked it completely off its moorings, propelling it against the back wall with a *TWARP*!

Joe turned back to Brannigan.

"Don't worry, Bill," Joe said. "I have an ace in the hole that even Carlo can't trump. And now I'm going to use it. In spades."

Chapter Eight

Joe exited Stillman's Gym, and he made a beeline for Gilhooley's Bar, a smelly dive on Eighth Avenue just down the block from Stillman's. Gilhooley's was a joint where hordes of greedy fight managers contrived their next fistic move. The crowd in Gilhooly's resembled rush hour at Port Authority, but instead of bus tickets, flesh was sold at pennies a pound.

The décor at Gilhooley's was early Depression, and the cockroaches outnumbered the customer at a rate of ten to one. The hundred-foot rotten oak bar ran from the front entrance back to the urine-stained men's room, inside of which a sign read: **We aim to please. Your aim will help.**

Gilhooley's owners saw no need, nor did they have any desire, to construct a companion ladies room. No real lady would ever enter Gilhooley's anyway.

Fight managers who frequented Gilhooley's were notorious for treating their fighters like slabs of beef; impersonally pushing them around from fight to fight, with the endgame being the swift upward explosion of the fight manager's bottom line. Bigtime fight managers wore hundred-dollar suits and sparkling pinkie rings. Most fighters were lucky if they had a decent pair of shoes.

Gilhooley's bartender was a pleasant chap named Lefty Porter, who had been an excellent welterweight before the Second World War. An exploding mine in France had left Lefty with a 12-inch stump for a right arm, but despite the handicap, Lefty could fill a drinker's beer mug as well as any of this two-fisted contemporaries.

Joe ordered a draft Schaefer, and Lefty expertly drew the beer from the tap with his right stump, while his left hand held the mug in place.

After Lefty placed the mug in front of Joe, Joe said, "Has Ray Brown been around lately?"

"Not so much," Lefty said. "He ain't been feeling well these days. He spends most of his time at home. The word is that he's disgusted with the fight racket, and I can't say I blame him."

"Could you contact him for me?" Joe said. "It's really important."

"You're not making a comeback, are you kid?"

"Not me, Lefty. I like the idea of being able to see with both eyes. It's my brother Johnny. He's ready for the big time, and I've taught him all I know. I needed someone like Ray Brown to apply the finishing touches."

"I don't know, kid. The last time I spoke with Ray, the old man was really down on the sport. He said he lost all interest in the game when you quit on him. "

"I didn't quit Ray," Joe said. "The doctors did that for me."

"You know what I mean," Lefty said. "Ray's tired of everybody lying through their teeth. Ray just couldn't deal with them bastards anymore. He's like a square peg trying to fit into a round hole."

Joe downed his beer. He ordered another and Lefty obliged him. Joe took a sip and headed for the single pay phone located at the back of the bar. Pat Petrone, a washed-up pug five years older than Joe, screamed into the phone as Joe respectfully waited in line eight feet behind him. Still, Joe couldn't help but hear Petrone's rampage.

"Please see what you can do for me," Petrone whined into the phone. "I'm in good shape, and I really could use the cash. I'll give you six good rounds, or whatever you need. Then, I'll take an exit. Your boy will look good, and everybody will be happy."

The phone clicked dead on the other end.

"Son of a bitch!" Petrone yelled.

Petrone turned and spotted Joe. He put his head down and hurried past Joe without even saying a word.

Poor bastard, Joe thought. They just don't know when to quit; especially when they're broke, which is most of them.

Joe dropped a dime into the phone and dialed Nancy Romano's phone number.

After three rings, Nancy's answered, "Hello, the Romano residence, who's speaking?"

Joe took a deep breath, and then he said, "Hello, Nancy. It's Joe."

Nancy hesitated for a split second, and then she snapped, "Oh, so it's the great Joe Italiano. What do you want? My father's not home."

"I don't want to speak to your old man," Joe said. "I wanted to speak with you. Could you meet me, say, in an hour?"

"Joe, I thought I made it clear I didn't want to be bothered with you anymore."

Joe felt his heart sink into the pit of his stomach.

"Look, Nancy. This will only take a few minutes," Joe said. "The last few months have been miserable for me without you. Please."

"Okay," Nancy said. "I'll give you exactly ten minutes of my time. Where do you want to meet?"

"How about Dave's Corner?" Joe said.

"All the way down on the corner of Canal and Broadway? That's some hike from Mulberry Street."

"Yes, but we've had some of our best times there; having a burger and a Cherry Lime Ricky. You remember, don't you?"

"Okay, I'll be at Dave's Corner in an hour. But I can only give you a few minutes. I have a date."

"Give me ten minutes, and I guarantee you you'll break that date," Joe said.

"Don't hold your breath," she said.

Then, the phone line went *click*.

Dave's Corner is one of the few luncheonettes in Manhattan that never closes. Because it's one of New York's taxi driver's favorite hangouts, the place is just as crowded at four in the morning as it is at four in the afternoon. Sometimes busier.

Besides the usual inside seating, there is outside counter service on the Broadway side, where a white-capped counterman dispensed such delicacies as egg creams, malted milks, hamburgers, hot dogs, French fries, and an occasional knish: a square potato pancake that is usually cut in half widthwise and slapped with a schmear of mustard.

Joe arrived at Dave's Corner 15 minutes early, and he sat at the first booth by the cash register, facing the front door. It was the only empty booth in the establishment. Almost all the other tables were taken by men Joe knew as cab drivers, engaged in conversations on topics ranging from baseball to boxing, to their favorite pastime - horse racing. Joe had gotten tips on three-legged ponies by the very men sitting at these tables. Partly for that reason, Joe made believe they were strangers.

From the side window, Joe could see the Canal Street entrance. He ordered a Cherry Lime Rickey and waited.

In minutes, a black Cadillac double-parked in front of Dave's Corner. A tall, elegantly dressed man wearing a grey pinstriped suit exited from the driver's side. He sauntered around the front of the car to the passenger side like he was modeling his suit, or, maybe, his walk. He opened the door, and Nancy exited the Caddy. She looked like a fashion model ready to traipse down the runway.

Joe's heart almost stopped.

The man in the suit took her hand and led her to Dave's front door. He opened the door for her, but before she went inside, she threw her arms around the man's neck and kissed him on both cheeks. The man then strode back to his car, sat behind the wheel, and waited.

Joe shook his head. If that man was Nancy's date, Joe had a rough road ahead of him.

As Nancy approached Joe's booth, Joe stood at attention. He tried to kiss her on the lips, but she turned her face and offered her cheek. Joe reluctantly took the offer, and said, "Have a seat."

After she sat opposite him in the booth, Joe said, "Who's the man in the grey suit?"

"That's my boyfriend," Nancy said.

"Nice suit," Joe said. "Nice car, too."

"Look, I'm here like you requested," Nancy said. "Please get to the point."

"How about a Cherry Lime Rickey?" Joe said. "Just like old times."

"No, thank you," Nancy said. "That's ancient history anyway."

Joe decided this was no time for half-measures, so he reached across the table, held Nancy's hands in his and said, "Nancy, I truly love you, and I want you to marry me."

For an instant, Joe wasn't sure if he said what he just said, or maybe he was dreaming. But when he saw the stunned look on Nancy's beautiful face, he knew he was indeed awake.

"Alright, let's cut the crap," Nancy said. "What do you really want?"

"I just said it," Joe said. "Do me the pleasure of being my wife. My life is miserable without you. Please, just say yes."

Nancy shook her head with a curious smile.

"Joe, I know you like the back of my hand," she said. "There must be a catch. What is it? Are you in some kind of trouble."

"I'm always in trouble, you know that," Joe said. "But right now my only problem is that I don't have you. Say yes, and I'll speak to your father tonight; ask him for permission to marry you."

Nancy reached across the table, cupped Joe's face in her hands and kissed him gently on the lips.

"Joe Italiano, you certainly pick the most romantic places to propose to a young lady," she said. "No ring. No champagne. No candlelight. No romantic music. And here we are in Dave's Corner surrounded by cab drivers scratching their butts and picking their noses."

Joe smiled. "You forgot the belching and cursing."

"Yes, that too," Nancy said. "So, how can I refuse? Of course, I'll marry you. It's about time I made you an honest man. The only question is what took you so long? And why now? I know you too well. There's something else you're not telling me."

"Wait, did you just say yes?" Joe said. "What about the man outside waiting in his car?"

"Yes, I said yes," Nancy said. "And don't worry. I'll take care of him."

That said, Nancy rose from the table and went outside. Joe watched as she leaned into the driver-side window and said something to the man. After the man rolled up the window, he started the car, turned left on Broadway and headed south.

Nancy went back inside Dave's Corner and sat in the booth next to Joe.

"Who was that guy and what did you say to him?" Joe said. "I never saw him before."

"Just an associate of my father's," Nancy said. "I was trying to make you jealous. I just told him to go see my father and tell him you wanted to talk to him tonight."

"Did you tell him why?

"Of course not. That's your job to talk to my father. I'm not going to make it any easier for you."

"Wow, that was quick," Joe said, smiling. "You don't leave anything to chance, do you?"

"Of course, it was quick," Nancy said. "Once I have a fish like you on the line, I'm going to reel you in, pronto, before you wiggle away. Now, tell me what you have been neglecting to tell me. Don't forget, I read the newspapers, too. It's Carlo, right? You and Johnny are in trouble, right?"

Joe told Nancy everything; from the time Carlo forced him to sell him Johnny's contract, up until Joe's meeting with Brannigan earlier in the day.

"Joe, you should have come to my father right away when Carlo threatened you about Johnny's contract," Nancy said. "Carlo works for my father. My father has Carlo firmly under his thumb. If you had done that right away, none of this other mess would have ever happened."

"Looking back, you're probably right," Joe said. "But I thought I could handle Carlo. But after what happened to Hank Kelly, I see that I can't handle everything. I just want to make sure nothing happens to Johnny or the rest of my family. As for me, I can handle myself. Carlo's not the only tough guy in Little Italy."

Chapter Nine

Joe and Nancy walked blithely hand and hand north on Mulberry Street. They turned right on Hester Street and stopped in front of Nancy's apartment building, two doors down from her father's social club.

Joe kissed Nancy on the cheek and said, "I'll see you at eight at your father's club. I'll bet he'll be surprised by what I have to say, that's for sure."

Nancy smiled and said, "Not as surprised as I was this afternoon."

She kissed Joe full on the lips, then headed into her apartment building.

Joe's feet barely touched the pavement as he glided down Mulberry Street to the Silver Coin. Once inside, Joe spotted Carlo and Dom sitting in the back at their customary table. Knowing his place, Joe sat at the bar next to two neighborhood men and ordered a draft beer.

After Frankie Fish placed the beer in front of him, Joe said, "Did you give Dom my message?"

"Sure did," Frankie said. "He seemed really excited that you wanted to talk to him."

Joe downed his first beer, and he ordered a second.

He told the bartender, "Frankie, do me a favor. Me and Carlo ain't getting along too well these days. Tell Dom I want to speak with him when he finished talking with his brother."

"Sure thing, Joe," Frankie said.

Five minutes later, Dom bellied up to the bar and sat next to Joe. He offered his hand and said, "What's up, Joe."

Joe shook Dom's hand. He noticed Dom's eyeballs were streaked in red, and he was wearing the same overcoat he had worn that morning at the Staten Island Ferry.

"Dom, I spoke to my sister Mary, and she agreed to go on a date with you," Joe said.

"That's great," Dom said. "When would it be convenient?"

"How about tomorrow night at eight?" Joe said. "It will be six of us. You and Mary. Johnny and Rita. And me and Nancy."

"I thought you and Nancy were on the outs?" Dom said.

"We were," Joe said. "But now we're back together, for good."

Dom seemed slightly taken back. Then he said, "How about if we eat at Forlini's at 5 Baxter Street? It's a small joint, but the food is great."

"That sounds good," Joe said. He decided to throw a curveball, when he said, "Did you hear what happened to Hank Kelly last night? Someone put a couple of bullet holes in his forehead."

"No. This is the first I'm hearing about it," Dom said.

"I wonder why somebody would want to murder Kelly," Joe said. "He always seemed like a nice guy to me."

Dom stiffened, and said, "Well, I head he don't like us Italians too much. Always throwing around disgusting words like guineas and greaseballs. Maybe the potato-picker got what he deserved."

Dom stood up from the bar, and said, "Well, me and my bother have some unfinished business to take care of. You'll have to excuse me."

The two men shook hands, and Dom said, smiling, "I'll meet you people over at Forlini's tomorrow night at eight sharp. "

That said, Dom headed back to Carlo's table.

Carlo was not happy when Dom returned to his table.

"What was that big conversation all about?" Carlo said.

Dom lowered his eyes in apparent shame, but it was really fear. For as long as he could remember, Dom could never look directly into Carlo's eyes. When he did, he saw the Devil.

"I asked Joe if he could set me up on a date with his sister, Mary," Dom said. "We're on for tomorrow night at Forlini's."

"Mary's a good looking broad," Carlo said. "But if you ask me, the whole family stinks. Especially that scumbag you just spoke to."

"Joe told me something else," Dom said. "But I don't want you to get sore."

"What the fuck? You playing games with me?" Carlo said. "Spill. I want to know what he said."

"Joe said he's back with Nancy Romano," Dom said. "They're coming out with me and Mary tomorrow night. Johnny and his wife Rita, too."

Dom waited for the explosion. He wasn't disappointed.

Carlo stood and banged his fist on the table.

"That fuckin' cunt! I've been asking her out for weeks, and she kept putting me off," Carlo said. "Now I know why. Not that I give a fuck about her to start with. But she's Pete Romano's daughter, and that would have put me in real tight with Pete."

"Look, don't get all sore," Dom said. "Maybe Joe was just blowing smoke. I'll find out tomorrow night."

"Yeah, you do that."

Dom hesitated before he said, "Joe also asked me about Hank Kelly. You don't think he knows anything, do you?"

"Now don't get all spastic on me," Carlo said. "Joe's a smart guy. Too smart. It's been all over the papers. He's probably put two and two together already."

Carlo leaned across the table and stuck his forefinger into Dom's chest.

"Now don't say nothing stupid to him tomorrow night," Carlo said. "You'll do anything for a piece of pussy, you ugly bastard."

"I'm not ugly," Dom said weakly, his head down, like a beaten man.

"Well, you ain't Clark Gable either," Carlo said.

Dom decided to change the conversation.

"That was a good idea of yours; having me ditch the pistol off the Staten Island Ferry," Dom said.

"Yeah, there's probably enough rods in the water between Manhattan and Staten Island to start another World War," Carlo said.

Carlo's face got mean again.

"By the way, are you sure nobody spotted you pitching the pistol overboard?" Carlo said. "Besides being ugly, you ain't exactly Albert Einstein either."

Dom's face turned a bright red, and his voice cracked when he said, "I'm fuckin' positive no one saw me. I threw the gun into the water from the bottom deck of the ferry. And it was in a paper bag anyway. Besides, you're not so smart yourself. It was my idea to take the stairs when we left Kelly's apartment. If it were up to you, we could have been spotted in the elevator. So get off your high horse!"

"Okay, so you're a fuckin' genius," Carlo said

"Just don't sell me short, I've got brains, too," Dom said.

Carlo smiled when he said, "If brains were gunpowder, you wouldn't have enough to blow your nose."

Carlo was relentless in his insults, so Dom decided to change the subject again.

"Well, what's our next move?" he said.

"Simple," Carlo said. "All we have to do is lay low for a while. Let Brannigan stew in his own juices. Then, we'll pay him a little visit. He'll fold like a cheap suitcase. Those Irish cocksuckers got big mouths, but when you get them alone, they have no balls."

To Carlo, the act of killing was almost like getting laid. Even though Dom was present when it happened, Carlo described his killing Hank Kelly to Dom with savage glee. While Carlo gave his brother a detailed account of Kelly's murder, Dom's stomach began to churn. He couldn't get any sleep all day long. Every time he shut his eyes, trying to nod off, all he could see where Kelly's dead fish eyes staring at him.

"The only thing I regret is not cutting the Irish fuck into little pieces and feeding them to the rats in Chinatown," Carlo said. "Imagine, that rat bastard telling his cop uncle in the Fifth Precinct what we were planning. What did he expect me to do about that? Nothing?"

Late Thanksgiving night, Carlo had told Dom, "You know what? I think we should pay a little visit to Hank Kelly at his apartment."

As soon as Kelly had opened his front door, Carlo stuck a gun in his face and ordered him to sit at the kitchen table. After Carlo cracked Kelly across the face a few times, Kelly quickly admitted that he had told his cousin, Captain Jim Clancy of the Fifth Precinct, all about Carlo's plan for Brannigan to relinquish the heavyweight title under duress.

Finally hearing the truth from Kelly's own mouth, Carlo went berserk. He ordered Kelly to phone Brannigan, and while Kelly spoke to his fighter, Dom had held the muzzle of his gun against Kelly's forehead. But when Carlo ordered Dom to shoot, he just froze. Carlo could kill someone, then devour a roast beef sandwich dripping with blood five minutes later.

Dom was cut from a different cloth.

When it was apparent Dom was not going to shoot Kelly, Carlo screamed, "Give me that fuckin' gun!"

Carlo snatched the gun from Dom's shaking hand, and he fired two bullets into Kelly's forehead, propelling his head backwards and killing him instantly. Then, he fired another one into the ceiling, just for fun.

But Carlo was not finished.

After hanging up the phone, Carlo grabbed Kelly's bloody hair and smashed his head, face-first, onto the glass table top, pulverizing the glass into little pieces.

Since that horrible moment, all Dom could see was Hank Kelly's mangled face dripping blood onto the fractured glass.

Carlo summoned Frankie Fish from behind the bar with a wave of his scrawny forefinger.

"Two more Jack Daniels, straight up," Carlo said.

After Frankie returned with the drinks, Carlo said to Dom, "You coming with me to the trotters in Yonkers tonight? I have a tip on a horse that can't lose. I want to get there before the odds drop."

"No, I'm going home to get some sleep," Dom said. "I'm still bushed from last night."

"Okay, but I want you to remember one thing," Carlo said. "Tomorrow night I don't want you making a fool of yourself with this Italiano dame. You'll be out in public, and everyone knows I'm your brother. Everything you do reflects on me."

"Don't worry, I'll be cool," Dom said. "It's only our first date anyway."

"And another thing," Carlo said. "Be careful with that asshole Joe Italiano. He's got more moves than a belly dancer."

"Joe ain't such a bad guy," Dom said.

As soon as the words left his mouth, Dom knew he had made a mistake.

"*Joe ain't a bad guy!*" Carlo screamed. "That's because you want to get into his sister's pants! Remember, you're a Russo, and all us Russos got pride. Don't you dare do anything to embarrass the family name."

Dom started to rise from his chair, but Carlo reached across the table and grabbed his arm in a vice-like grip. He screamed loud enough for the bartender to hear, prompting Frankie Fish to decide this might be a good time to go into the men's room, which he did; just in case things got ugly. The two neighborhood men at the bar sat silently, trying to ignore the commotion in the back.

"Reme*mber, watch out for those Italiano brothers!*" Carlo yelled.

Dom stood up and shrugged off Carlo's grip on his arm.

"Don't worry about me. I can take care of myself," Dom said. Then he added, "Besides, I get along fine with the Italiano brothers. You don't because you have a personality conflict. I don't have that problem."

Carlo became so angry at his brother's statement; he struggled to speak. When he couldn't get the words out of his mouth, he backhanded Dom, hard, across the lips, causing blood to trickle down Dom's chin.

Dom started to react in kind, but then he changed his mind.

"*Don't you ever speak to me in the tone of voice again!*" Carlo bellowed. "*I'm your older brother! Don't you ever take a stranger's part over me again!*"

Dom wiped the blood off his chin with a handkerchief. Then, he glanced at the bar, where the two men sat turned around facing them with their mouths open.

"Carlo, you're my older brother, and I respect you," Dom finally said. "But don't you ever put your hands on me in front of people again."

Carlo reached for the gun in the holster under his left armpit, but after spotting the two men sitting at the bar, and Frankie Fish peeking from inside the bathroom, he changed his mind.

Carlo yelled at Dom, "*Now get the fuck out of here! You make me fucking sick! You have no fuckin' respect!*"

Dom stared at Carlo, hard, for a second. Then, he did an about-face and headed for the exit. But before he got there, Carlo picked up a glass from his table and hurled it at Dom. The glass missed Dom's head by inches and smashed against the wall. Glass flew in all directions.

Dom turned and glared at Carlo. Then, he left the Silver Coin without saying another word.

Carlo looked like a man possessed by the Devil.

He yelled in the direction of the two customers at the bar and Frankie Fish, "*No fucking respect, that's what I get!*"

Then, he pointed his finger at his bartender, and said, "And you. You're getting too friendly with that Joe Italiano. Don't forget who's the boss around here."

As Frankie Fish cringed in fear, Carlo approached the bar.

He yelled at the bartender, "And if I ever find the register short again, I'll cut off all your fingers."

Carlo turned and exited the Silver Coin, slamming the door behind him.

A minute later, the two customers also exited. And as soon as they were outside, Frankie Fish returned the ten-dollar bill he had taken from the register an hour earlier.

Chapter Ten

Joe Italiano entered Pete Romano's Social Club on Hester Street at precisely eight pm. After he stepped inside, he spotted Nancy sitting next to her father at Pete's usual table, her hands sedately folded on her lap. At this time of night, the joint was usually buzzing with activity, but Joe noted that they were the only three people present.

Joe wondered where were the men guzzling beer and playing knock rummy; the neighborhood's favorite card game. And where were the men watching sports on the small black-and-white 17-inch RCA Victor television set mounted high on the wall behind the bar? And most importantly, where were the bookies quickly tallying the day's betting results?

Why was the joint empty?

But before Joe could contemplate that question, Pete motioned for Joe to sit opposite him. When he did, Nancy smiled broadly. And it was Pete who broke the heavy silence.

"Hey, Joe, how about a little wine?" Pete said. "Nancy says you have something to say to me, and I've always said that a little wine loosens up the tongue."

"Now that you mention it, I could use a little glass of wine," Joe said.

Pete poured Joe a hefty portion of red wine into a 12-ounce glass from a gallon jug he had placed on the floor next to his chair. Joe eradicated three-quarters of the wine in one long gulp.

Joe glanced at Pete, who now wore a benevolent smile on his chubby face. Nancy winked at Joe, but Joe was so petrified, he barely noticed. With a lump in his throat, Joe knocked off the rest of his glass of wine

"You see Pete, me and Nancy had a little talk today," Joe said. He glanced at Nancy, then at his empty glass. "Can I have a little more wine?"

"Sure, you can have all the wine you want," Pete said. He handed Joe the entire gallon bottle. "Help yourself."

Joe resisted the urge to lift the jug to his lips and guzzle the wine like a *cafone*. Instead, he shakily poured himself a glass, spilling some of it on his lap.

Joe forced the words out, saying, "Look Pete. We, er… We decided that we… er… er… We thought it would be a good time for us to. Er… that is, er… If you would only give us er… uh… uh…"

Nancy couldn't contain it any longer. She burst out laughing and said, "Go ahead, Daddy. Tell this moron you know already. This poor bastard is scared shitless."

"No, I'm not," Joe said. "I'm just a little nervous. What the heck! Pete, I like your permission to marry my, no, I mean marry *your* daughter."

Pete's grin erupted into a smile the size of Sicily.

"Jesu Christi, he finally spit it out!" Pete said. "I thought the man was going to have a heart attack right here in my club. Then, what would I tell the cops?"

"Go ahead, Daddy, *tell him*!" Nancy said. "Before he *does* drop dead on the floor."

Pete stood reached across the table and offered his hand to Joe.

"Of course, you have my permission to marry my daughter. My only question is 'What took you so long.'"

As if on cue, the club's back door opened, and half of Little Italy scrambled through the door, yelling, ***"Surprise!"***

Johnny, Rita, and Mary led the stampede, and Johnny grabbed Joe in a playful bear hug, almost fracturing Joe's ribs.

"It's about time you broke down and did the right thing," Johnny said.

Rita and Mary took turned hugging and kissing Joe and doing the same to Nancy.

Suddenly, about a dozen hired waiters scurried through the back door carrying folding tables and large trays of hot food. They set up shop, transforming the grubby social club into a fancy catering hall.

After hordes of people surrounded Joe and Nancy offering their congratulations, Joe squeezed Nancy's hand, and said, "Wow, that was some surprise trick you played on me. I didn't have a clue this was going to happen."

"Sorry, Joe, but it was my father's idea," Nancy said. "I couldn't help telling him when I got home. And you know him. He always wants to make a big splash. He had all his men running all over the neighborhood rounding up all the people and rounding up all the food. It was crazy what he accomplished in just a few hours. Look at all these people!"

"He *is* Pete Romano," Joe said. "People jump when he tells them to."

"Even you," Nancy said.

"Especially me," Joe said. "I jump even higher."

From the corner of his eye, Joe spotted Carlo Russo entering the club, alone.

Carlo approached Joe and offered his hand. When Joe took Carlo's hand, it felt like a damp cold fish.

Carlo was truly pissed he had to give up going to the Yonkers Racetrack to attended a party for a man he absolutely loathed. But Pete Romano was the boss of Little Italy, and Carlo was merely one of his men who took his orders, whether he liked them or not.

"Congratulations," Carlo told Joe in a hissing monotone.

Carlo quickly bussed Nancy on the cheek, and then he fled to the bar to get himself come much-needed booze.

Nancy had noticed the visible animosity between the two men, but she decided to say nothing.

The party lasted well into the night. Every few minutes, Pete called for a toast to "my beautiful daughter and my future son-in-law."

And every time Pete called for a toast, everybody drank, which led to the revelers getting loaded, all except Joe. All party long, Joe kept his eyes glued to Carlo, who was drinking heavily at the bar and obviously not having a very good time. Carlo's face displayed a perpetual sneer, which became more sinister the more he drank.

The sight of his Carlo's malicious face kept Joe sober all night.

At around three in the morning, the party began to disintegrate. Johnny and Rita were the last to depart, leaving Nancy, Joe, and Peter Romano the only ones left in the joint.

Pete rubbed his belly as he said, "Well, I guess it's about time for me to call it a night too." He turned to Nancy, and said, "If your mother were still alive, she'd be grabbing me by the ear by now."

Pete handed Joe a set of keys. "Here, Joe. You lock up for me. Okay?"

"Sure thing, Pete," Joe said.

Peter exited the social club through the front door with a gleam in his eye and a stagger in his step.

"We better go home and get some sleep," Joe said. "With all the excitement I forgot to tell you we're going out tomorrow night as chaperones on Mary's first date with Dom Russo at Forlini's. Rita and Johnny are coming along, too. Dom did the right thing and asked me for my permission to date my sister. And it was his idea for all of us to come as chaperones."

Nancy faced dropped when she heard the news.

"You're letting your sister date Carlo's brother?" she said. "Besides, she's a head taller than him!"

"So what? Dom's a good guy," Joe said. "He's nothing like his brother Carlo."

"Yeah, maybe you're right," Nancy said. "Dom seems like a decent guy. But I cringe at the thought of having Carlo in the family."

Nancy gently took Joe's hand and said, "Joe, there's something I have to tell you. Carlo's been hounding me for a date for months, but I kept putting him off. He couldn't even look me in the eye tonight."

"That explains his actions tonight," Joe said. "Carlo doesn't like me to start with, but tonight he was doubly pissed off at me, and now I know why."

Joe and Nancy exited the social club. Joe locked the club door and walked Nancy back to her apartment on Hester Street.

They arrived at her tenement building, and Joe kissed Nancy, first on both cheeks, and then full on the lips.

"That should keep you until tomorrow," Joe said.

"Just barely," Nancy said, and then she turned and entered the building.

On his walk back to 104 Bayard, Joe decided he would soon have to take on Carlo Russo head to head. Even though Carlo was a killer, he didn't frighten Joe.

Joe said to himself, "Fuck Carlo. He doesn't understand that I'm Sicilian, too."

Chapter Eleven

Dom Russo rolled out of bed at eight am on Saturday morning totally exhilarated. Tonight was the night he had dreamed about for so long. He was finally going on a date with the lovely Mary Italiano.

How could a man be so lucky?

The previous night, wanting to look and feel his best for his date with Mary, Dom had slipped into bed at eight pm. There was no usual trip to the track. And no Friday night drinking marathon, the objective of which was to find a gorgeous young girl to take home, but which always ended with Dom going home alone with copies of the *New York Daily News* and *New York Daily Mirror* stuffed under his arm.

Dom had just turned thirty, but he had never had a steady girlfriend. His short, stocky body, combined with a weak-chinned face, had always made Dom less than a popular attraction amongst the local female population.

Dom didn't have much luck with the uptown or Brooklyn girls either.

After tending to his morning necessities, Dom slipped into dark-blue shark-skin trousers, and a grey-and-blue Italian knit shirt. He opened a suit bag and removed a three-quarter-length soft black leather coat, which he donned over the Italian knit. All three had been purchased the evening before at Al Kaplan's on Canal Street.

Dom examined his appearance in a full-length mirror mounted on the back of his bedroom door. Satisfied, he exited his apartment and walked down the four flights of stairs to the Mott Street pavement below.

As he traipsed down the block, Dom sniffed the marvelous rich aroma of the baked bread emanating from Parisi's Bakery, which had been a neighborhood staple since 1903. On an average day. Dom would knock down at least two loaves of Parisi's 25-cent Italian bread, which led to him carrying almost 200 pounds on his five-foot four-inch physique. Dom knew that the scrumptious combination of Italian pastries, pasta, bread, red and white sauces, and garlic-coated delicacies shortened the lifespan of the Italian/American male. But what's the good of being Italian if you can't eat?

Dom made a right on Hester, and he stopped at Gino's Barbershop, owned and operated by an Italian Immigrant who had come to this country three decades earlier with just the clothes on his back and a five-dollar bill in his pocket. Gino employed no other barbers, and sometimes men had to wait more than an hour to sit in Gino's coveted barber chair.

Dom entered the establishment, and he heard the tingling of the doorbell signaling to Gino that a new customer had arrived.

"Good morning, Gino," Dom said. He took off his leather coat and hung it on the wooded coat tree. "I see I'm next."

The shop was empty except for a youngish uniformed police officer on whom Gino was displaying his tonsorial talents.

"Good morning, Dominick," Gino said in his broken English accent. "Captain Clancy just called, and he'll be here in a few minutes. So Clancy is next, and then you are after him. Have a seat. I'll get you some coffee. Black or brown?"

Unlike in most of the rest of the world, in Little Italy black coffee meant espresso, and brown coffee meant the traditional American coffee usually served with milk and sugar.

Dom ordered the black coffee with a little Anisette on the side, and before he could take a sip, Captain Jim Clancy, the commander of the Fifth Precinct on 19 Elizabeth Street, strode through the front door. Clancy's precinct supposedly protected the Lower East Side, which included Little Italy. But in truth, Fifth Precinct cops had very little to do with respect to controlling crime, since the only crime in the Fifth Precinct was organized crime; Italian and Chinese.

Clancy was a giant of a cop, standing six-feet, six inches tall, the maximum height allowed for a New York City police officer. His hair resembled newly-fallen snow, which enhanced Clancy's image as a respected figure of authority.

Clancy hovered over the diminutive Gino. He patted the barber's bald head and said, "Good morning, my little greaseball friend."

Gino stiffened. He ran his forefinger across his pencil-thin moustache, as he said, "Good morning Ill Duce. I see you're always on time for your free haircut."

Clancy removed his navy-blue regulation three-quarter length cloth winter coat resplendent with gold buttons, and he hung it on the coat tree next to Dom's leather coat. Clancy sat in the chair next to Dom and waited. He didn't even slightly acknowledge Dom was in the establishment.

A few minutes later, Gino spread talcum powder onto the young cop's neck. Then, he used a wooden bristled brush to sweep it off with a flourish.

The young cop stood, reached into this pocket, and handed Gino a crisp dollar bill.

"Thank you, young man," Gino said. "I hope you captain is just as generous."

Clancy shot the young cop a dirty look, and then he plopped down in Gino's barber chair.

Gino spread a white pin-striped barber sheet over the good Captain's torso and secured it in the back with a safety pin.

As Gino performed his magic, Clancy peered into the mirror in front of him, and he noticed Dom's face was buried in the *New York Daily News*.

"Hey, Russo," Clancy said. "I heard Pete Romano's daughter got engaged last night to Joe Italiano."

Dom said, without looking up, "I know they're dating, but I don't know nothing about no engagement."

"Yeah, I guess you're so low on the mob totem pole, they don't tell you anything," Clancy said. "By the way, tell your brother Carlo I'm sending over a new man on Monday to collect. His name is Rubenstein. And tell Carlo to make sure the amount is right. I don't want to come to your place myself all pissed off. You know what that means."

Whenever Police Headquarters assigned a new sergeant to the Fifth Precinct, Clancy made him in charge of the weekly graft collections. The new sergeant made his rounds every Monday during the eight am to four pm shift. He arrived at each location carrying a large blue leather satchel, and when he left, the satchel was always substantially heavier. When his rounds were completed, he would deliver the satchel to Lieutenant Morelli at an uptown bar, the location of which changed every week, just in case. Then, the sergeant would immediately vacate the premises.

Lieutenant Morelli took the satchel into the bathroom and into one of the stalls, where he would drop his drawers so as not to be disturbed. After counting the cash, Morelli took out 15% for himself and 10% for the new sergeant. He put the rest of the money back into the satchel, with a slip of paper saying how much money was in the satchel, and then he made a beeline for the Port Authority Bus Terminal where he placed the satchel into a locker, the key to which he would give to Captain Clancy the following morning. Captain Clancy would pick up the satchel as soon as possible, and take it home with him where he would have some privacy.

After taking half the remaining money for himself, Clancy would divide the rest of the money by the number of cops on the take in the Fifth Precinct, which was just about everyone. The resulting amount was the amount of money the new sergeant would dispense Tuesday to the crooked cops, which consisted of most of the Fifth Precinct.

This was the way it had been done in the Fifth Precinct for decades, and everything went smoothly.

No muss. No fuss. No risks involved.

And that suited Captain Clancy just fine.

How else could he have afforded his massive home in Bay Ridge, Brooklyn, containing four bedrooms, four baths, a two-car garage, a fully remodeled basement complete with a bar and pool table, and a heated swimming pool? Of course, Clancy was shrewd enough to put the deed under his wife's mother's name, just in case someone got nosey.

Gino put the finishing touches on Clancy's free haircut: parting his hair, powdering and de-powdering his neck, and patting his back, signally Clancy's haircut was done.

Clancy rose to his full height and examined himself in the mirror. Then, he said to Gino, "Gino, my man, here's your big tip. Bet the five horse in the fifth race at Aqueduct, across the board. That's the biggest tip you'll ever get from me, wop-face."

Gino forced a half-a smile, and said, "You're such a big sport, Captain. You toss around nickels like fucking manhole covers."

"Fuck off, Dago," Clancy said, as she donned his overcoat.

As Clancy opened the door to leave, Gino yelled at him, "Hey, Captain, you know I had a wet dream last night. I dreamed I slit your throat with my straight razor while I was shaving you. It was the best load I shot in years."

Without answering, Captain Clancy exited Gino's Barbershop and slammed the door behind him.

Dom Russo took Clancy's place in Gino's barber chair.

As Gino was fastening the barber sheet around Dom's neck, Dom said, "I don't know how you take that arrogant donkey's bullshit."

Gino said, "What choice do I have? What choice do we all have? We all paid up before Clancy got here, and we'll all be paying after Clancy is gone. That's just the way it is, was, and always will be."

"Yeah, I guess you're right," Dom said. "But I know one thing for sure, there's going to be a long line to piss on Clancy's grave when he's six feet under."

While Gino cut Dom's hair, Dom closed his eyes and smiled. He thought of nothing but the beautiful Mary Italiano, who he would formally meet for the first time in just a few short hours.

At this very moment, Dom was as happy as he had been in his entire life. And he was intent on not doing anything that could possibly spoil his bliss.

Unfortunately, circumstances beyond his control would occur that would throw his life, and the lives of those he loved, into the chasm of despair.

Chapter Twelve

Captain Clancy paraded double-time from Gino's Barbershop to the Fifth Precinct just a few short blocks away.

The Fifth Precinct, located at 19 Elizabeth Street, was the oldest police precinct in the city. Built in 1881 for less than $40,000, the now-decrepit building, both outside and inside, stands between a row of aging tenements, whose storefronts house mostly Chinese restaurants, whose daily garbage attract hordes of hungry rats. The cat-sized rats make their grand appearance at the early morning closing time, when the restaurant owners pile their trash in front of their establishments, tolling a silent dinner bell for the tens of thousands of the four-legged creatures on the prowl. By the time the Sanitation trucks pick up the rotting garbage a few hours later, more than half of it has already been eaten by the rats.

Clancy marched through the front door, and his spit-shined boots thumped loudly on the wooden floor. He shot a summary salute to the desk sergeant sitting on the right at a decrepit desk located three steps off the floor. The desk sergeant, at least fifty pounds overweight, was chomping down on a huge meatball sandwich he purchased from Tony's Italian Deli just down the block.

The desk sergeant quickly put down the sandwich and said. "Good morning, Captain."

Clancy shook his head in disgust, and said, "Sergeant, every time I see you, you're stuffing your face with a big Italian hero. Haven't you ever heard the word - salad?"

The sergeant wiped the red meat sauce off his lips with a napkin, and then he said, without much conviction, "Yes, sir!"

"Get me the Silver Coin on the phone," Clancy said. "I want to speak to Carlo Russo. Transfer the call to my office."

Clancy marched down a long pea-green corridor, with the paint chipping on both sides, past the detention cells and into his private office. He locked the office door and availed himself of the private bathroom reserved for the ranks of Captain and above.

Once inside, he unzipped his fly, and using his faithful right hand, he induced a huge erection. Seconds before ejaculation, he stuffed his penis back into his pants.

Clancy had learned this neat trick years back when he attended the New York Military Academy in the rural town of Cornwall, 60 miles north of New York City. Of course, this maneuver was not in the official military manual but was taught on the sly by the amply-named Commandant of Cadets, Dick Hertz.

The lesson was depicted thusly: "*If you want to become as mean as a slithering snake before combat, effect, then abort, the completion of the act of masturbation.*"

His blood boiling to the pressure point, Clancy went back into his office and picked up the phone. Frankie Fish, the bartender at the Silver Coin, was on the line.

"What the fuck are you on the line for?" Clancy said. "I want to speak to your boss."

Frankie Fish said, "Carlo told me to hold the phone while he went to the john. He'll be right back."

Clancy wondered maybe if Carlo had attended the New York Military Academy, too.

After two minutes had expired, Carlo's voice appeared on the other line.

"Captain Clancy, what a pleasant surprise," Carlo said. "How nice of you to call. What can I do to help you?"

"Cut the bullshit?" Clancy said. "You have some nerve keeping me waiting on the phone."

"Well, you know. Nature calls."

"After you hear what I have to say, I guarantee you nature is going to call you again."

"Just get to the point, Captain. My time is valuable."

"Alright, you Dago fuck, I'll get to the point. You killed Hank Kelly, and I can prove it."

"Is this some kind of joke, Captain?"

"No joke, Carlo. In case you didn't know it, Hank was my eldest sister's son. He was the apple of Lucille's eye. Damn, he was a fucking altar boy until he graduated high school. And just last week Hank told me about a problem he was having with you."

"Listen, Captain, just in case you're taping this conversation, murder is not my line of work. I take a few bets here and there, and that's it. I make a few bucks, and you make a few bucks. In fact, you make a damn good living just on my back alone."

"Yeah, and I'm going to make a lot more."

"Well, meet me at my place so we can speak in private," Carlo said.

"Your place? My ass!" Clancy said. "Do you think I'm some sort of moron. I know what goes on in your place. Meet me in an hour at Patrick's Pub on 32nd Street and Broadway. It's right opposite Gimbals. And make sure you're alone."

That said, Captain Clancy slammed down the phone.

Forty-five minutes later, Butch Salerno's black Buick eased into an illegal parking spot by the hydrant in front of the Broadway entrance of Patrick's Pub.

"I'll see you back in the neighborhood," Carlo said.

Carlo Russo emerged from the passenger's side, and he entered the bar, as Butch directed the Buick south on Broadway.

During the week, Patrick's Pub was pick-up paradise, where on any given night, fifty to a hundred women and men congregated with the hope of finding a sleeping partner for the night. However, on the weekends, when most of the local businesses in the neighborhood were closed, the place was practically deserted.

A solitary sanitation department worker sat at the bar and guzzled down a mug of beer, as the bartender tried to solve the daily *New York Times* crossword puzzle. Two waiters sat at the first table by the door, and when Carlo entered, they quickly threw in their gin rummy hands and stood at attention.

"May I help you, sir?" a tall, blond beach-boy-type waiter said to Carlo.

"Table for two," Carlo said. "The last table in the back will be fine. I'm meeting someone here."

Carlo always made it a point to arrive early for any meeting, just in case of an ambush, which was not entirely out of the realm of possibility considering he was meeting a police captain with an attitude, who had the law on his side, even when he was breaking the law.

Carlo sat at the round table, facing the door. He ordered a gin and tonic and waited, without great patience.

Ten minutes later, Captain Clancy burst through the front door, resplendent in his full dress uniform, metals sparking. He eyed the sanitation worker at the bar, and then he marched back to where Carlo was sitting. He hovered over Carlo like a vulture ready to dive-bomb a rotting carcass.

"Give me your seat," Clancy said. "I'm not sitting with my back to the front door."

Carlo stood up. He gave Clancy his seat, and *he* sat with his back to the door.

Carlo said, "Captain, I think you've been watching too many cops and robbers movies."

Clancy stood up and said, "Stand up again. I have to frisk you."

Carlo stood up, raised his hands over his head, and said, "Now I know you've been watching too many cops and robbers movies. Do you think I'm stupid enough to carry a rod when I'm meeting a fuckin' New York City police captain?"

Clancy gave Carlo his best professional frisk, even fingering between Carlo's legs.

"Okay, you're clean," Clancy said.

Both men sat back down.

"You sure you ain't queer, touching me between the legs like that?" Carlo said.

Clancy grunted, and when the waiter arrived, he ordered a scotch and soda.

They sat in uneasy silence until the drink arrived. When the waiter left, Clancy took control of the situation.

"Okay, Carlo, this is the deal," Clancy said. "I know you killed Hank Kelly, and I have a witness locked up tight. You thought you were smart taking the stairs at Hank's place, but you were spotted and positively identified from mug shots.

"You're full of shit," Carlo said.

"Am I? Are you willing to take that chance?"

"You're still full of shit. Cops like you always lie through their teeth."

"Look, I can go to the District Attorney's office with my story," Clancy said. "But why should I when I can make you pay through the nose?"

"So, that's your angle," Carlo said. "It figures. I never met a cop who didn't have his filthy hands out."

"You shouldn't complain," Clancy said. "I'm going to save your Guinea ass. But only if you come across."

"What's the numbers?"

Clancy smiled and said, "So, I got your attention. This is the deal. I want ten grand up front. That's for my sister Lucille so that she can bury Hank properly."

"Bury him properly?" Carlo said. "Why don't you just stick a torch up his ass and roast some fucking marshmallows?"

"I'll ignore that tasteless remark; you're nothing but a Goddamn animal anyway," Clancy said. "Besides the ten grand, I want $200 a week for as long as we both are breathing. By my estimate, you make about ten times that, so it won't break your back."

Carlo leaned back and folded his arms. "Do have anything else in mind?" he said.

"No, that's it," Clancy said. "Ten grand up front and two hundred clams a week. That's a small price to pay for not spending the rest of your life in jail. Think it over, and get back to me. You have twenty-four hours."

Carlo drained the rest of his gin and tonic, and then he looked straight into Clancy's eyes.

"I've already thought it over, Captain," Carlo said. "Shove your offer, and your supposed witness, up your ass. I ain't biting."

Carlo spotted thick red veins bulging in Clancy's neck.

Clancy started to speak, but all he could manage were short gurgling sounds like he was drowning in his own saliva. Clancy grabbed for his drink, and he downed the scotch and soda in one huge gulp.

"You know, you're a stupid fucking wop!" Clancy said. "Here I am throwing you a lifeline, and you're acting like an idiot. Play it smart, and take the deal. Do the right thing here."

"I am doing the right thing," Carlo said. "I'm telling you plain and simple – *GO FUCK YOURSELF!*"

Carlo reached across the table and poked his forefinger into Clancy's chest. Clancy stiffened like someone had just inserted an iron pole up his butt.

"Listen to me, copper," Carlo said. "I figure you made up the story about the witness. You cops like to bullshit and figure guys like me will lap it up. But I ain't buying. In any event, you're right about one thing; you're not asking for that much money. I can easily afford it. But I'm not going to give you the satisfaction of shaking me down."

Before Clancy could reply, Carlo reached across the table and grabbed Clancy's wrist.

"Listen to this, Captain," Carlo said. He leaned forward and said in almost a whisper, "Sure, I blew out Kelly's brains, and I'll do the same to you if you give me any more trouble. Fuck you. And fuck your badge."

Carlo released Clancy's wrist, and Clancy's mouth started to twitch rapidly like he was going into convulsions.

Clancy stuttered, " Youuuuuu... mother... fuckerrrrrrrrrr! *I'LL KILL YOU MYSELF!*"

Clancy started to reach for his police issued revolver under his armpit, but Carlo just smiled and Clancy froze.

"You won't do a fuckin' thing, captain," Carlo said. "Not with those four witnesses in the joint. You're not going to do a fucking thing except put your tail between your legs and get the fuck out of this bar. *NOW WALK!* I'll pay the tab. That's the least I can do considering what I did to Hank, that prick nephew of yours."

Clancy lurched to a standing position, he eyes wide open and his mouth agape. Carlo thought the big cop was going to have a heart attack right in front of him.

Instead, Clancy staggered to and out the front door of Patrick's Pub.

Carlo dropped a twenty-dollar bill on the table, and he too exited Patrick's Pub. He got outside just in time to see Captain Clancy flag down a passing police patrol car. Carlo opted for a cab.

"The corner of Baxter and Canal," Carlo told the cabby.

Ten minutes later, Carlo paid the cab driver in front of Most Precious Blood Church on Baxter Street, just north of Canal. He entered the church, dipped his right finger into the holy water, made the sign of the cross, and genuflected. Then, he counted out ten twenty-dollar bills from a huge wad of cash he had in his pocket and deposited them into the poor box. He faced the altar, genuflected a second time, and then he exited the church.

Carlo didn't exactly know why he donated $200 a week to the Catholic Church. He just knew when he did it made him feel a whole lot better than when he first had entered the church.

And if there was indeed a God, which Carlo sincerely doubted, maybe the man upstairs would give Carlo a special dispensation when it came time for Carlo's Judgement Day.

Just maybe.

Captain Clancy ordered the policeman who was driving the squad car to drop him off at the corner of 14th Street and Second Avenue.

"I'll take the subway from here," Clancy said.

As soon as the patrol car disappeared, Clancy hot-footed it to a dilapidated tenement on 12th Street, just east of Second Avenue. After glancing both ways, Clancy slipped into the building. He climbed the stairs and stopped at apartment 3 C. He took off his police hat and rang the bell. A tall, slender young man, barely in his twenties, with straw-colored hair, opened the door. He motioned for Clancy to take a seat on the couch.

"Can I get you a drink?" the young man said.

"Double Johnny Walker Black on the rocks," Clancy said.

The young man went into the kitchen. He returned with the drink, and Clancy downed it in one huge gulp. He handed the glass back to the young man.

"Another," Clancy said.

After the young man filled Clancy's glass a second time, Clancy imbibed it just a little slower than he did the first one.

"I want the full hour session today," Clancy said.

The commander of the Fifth Precinct handed the young man the empty glass. Then, he rose from the couch, entered the bedroom, and closed the door behind him.

After Clancy had carefully removed his uniform and hung it in the closet, someone knocked at the bedroom door.

"Come in," Clancy said.

The young man with the straw-colored hair entered the bedroom holding two double scotches. He wore a blond shoulder-length wig.

And nothing else.

Chapter Thirteen

At 7:45 pm, Dom Russo entered Forlini's Restaurant, and he took a seat at the bar facing the front door. He ordered a Dewars and soda and waited. Dom wore a muted blue-pinstriped suit, with a powder-blue shirt, and a red-and-white tie. Dom made it a point not to don flashy mobster-wear, which was his brother Carlo's favored mode of attire.

Forlini's, located at 3 Baxter Street near Park Row, was a neighborhood eatery known for its scrumptious Italian food. It was not a hangout for the neighborhood mobsters, who liked to frequent the establishments on Mulberry Street one block to the east. Instead, Forlini's was a haven for legitimate neighborhood people who were looking for a good, inexpensive meal, without having to worry about who-was-who, and who-was-looking-at-who cross-eyed with malicious intent.

Forlini's was also a meeting place for workers from the nearby criminal court buildings, and it would not be strange to see an occasional judge, police detective, or assistant District Attorney chatting about which neighborhood criminal they were trying to put into prison.

That was another reason the neighborhood wiseguys and would-be wiseguys preferred their Mulberry Street haunts.

At 8:15 pm, Joe Italiano entered Forlini's accompanied by Nancy Romano. Mary and Rita followed arm and arm, and Johnny Italiano brought up the rear. Mary wore a black shawl over a salt and pepper cotton dress, and when her eyes met Dom's, it was apparent that she was just as nervous as he was.

Dom stood up from his bar stool, like a marine waiting for dress inspection. Joe spotted him, and he walked over, his right hand extended.

"Hiya, Dom. I'm sorry we're late," Joe said. "But you know how women are. Sometimes, you have to light a fire under their rear ends to get them moving."

Dom smiled and said, "That's alright. I didn't even realize you were late. It's so good to see you all."

Joe took Mary's arm and introduced her to her date. Their eyes met, and Dom just melted.

Mary offered her hand. Dom took it, raised it to his lips and gave it a short kiss of respect.

Neither could summon the courage to speak right away, and it was Mary who broke the silence when she said, "Hello, Dom. I'm pleased to meet you."

Dom felt sweat dripping down his back. He turned to Joe, and said, "Would you like to have a drink at the bar first, or would you prefer to sit at the table?'

"We'll have a drink at the bar first," Joe said.

The three women sat on bar stools, while the men stood behind them. The conversations were gender-specific; the men talked about which baseball team was the best in town, the boxing racket, and horseracing in general, especially the art of horse race-fixing. The woman spoke about the latest fashions, current movies and movie stars, music trends, and what actor was the best looking of the bunch.

Standing behind Mary, Dom couldn't take his eyes off her, and more sweat poured down his back. Loosening his tie made Dom more comfortable, but only just a little.

After one drink, Johnny said, "Hey, my stomach is growling. Let's hit the dining room."

Minutes later, they sat at a round table in the middle of the dining room. As Dom gazed around the room, he could hear the neighborhood people's buzzing conversations. He was certain that the topic of conversation was his odd appearance at a table with the Italiano family, whom everyone in the neighborhood knew to be legitimate and hard-working people; or civilians, as the mobsters called them. Everyone knew Dom was Carlo's brother, and Dom hated this guilt by association, even though, considering what just happened to Hank Kelly, it was totally justified.

For appetizers, all six people wolfed down Forlini's special Fettuccine Alfredo, which consisted of long thick macaroni, bathed in a garlicy white cheese sauce. For dinner, the men chomped on steak pizzaiola: shell steaks drenched in a tomato sauce made with onions, garlic, mushrooms, Italian spices like basil and oregano, and Italian plum tomatoes. Nancy and Rita sampled the shrimp scampi: large shrimps resplendent in a clear white sauce consisting of garlic, shallots, olive oil, lemon and butter, and placed on a bed of linguine. Mary ate a simple golden brown boneless chicken.

During dinner, Dom's eyes were riveted on Mary's beautiful face. He was overcome by her mystical power that was entrancing him. He was certain that if he looked away, even for a second, he would surely turn to stone.

Dom sensed that Mary was wholly unlike Nancy and Rita. The other two women held their heads haughtily up high, with their faces tilted slightly upward, as if they were balancing an invisible object on the point of their chins. Mary, on the other hand, appeared humble and somewhat embarrassed, which was precisely the way Dom felt.

After a dessert of cannoli's and cappuccino, the waiter placed the check in the middle of the table. And just as Joe was reaching for it, Dom dove in and gobbled up the check.

"Thanks, Joe. But this is my treat," Dom said. "It's been my pleasure to be in the company of you and your wonderful family."

The excellent wine and food had lifted everyone's spirits, and the six happy people pranced north on Baxter Street as if they were gliding on a silver cloud.

While they were strolling, the girls in front and the men in the back, Mary thought to herself how Dom was so unlike his brother Carlo, who Mary considered a pig in every sense of the word. No, Dom was reserved, and even if he was a little shy, he was actually fun to be with. Although Dom would never be called handsome, he had a quiet, dignified manner that made his appearance appealing.

When they reached 104 Bayard Street, fifty feet east of Baxter Street, Mary said to Dom, "Will you join us upstairs for a nightcap."

Dom agreed, and while Nancy and Rita stood in the kitchen making coffee, they insisted that Mary stay in the living room and kibitz with the three men.

Joe poured three snifters of Remy Martin. Mary abstained, saying to Dom, "I really don't like the taste of liquor. I'll have a little wine at times, but hard liquor is not my cup of tea."

Dom stared at Mary, and his face felt hot, as he said, "Mary, is it all right if we see each other again."

Mary felt warm and comfortable inside.

"That would be very nice, Dom," she said. "Very nice, indeed."

Chapter 14

It was late afternoon on Christmas Eve at Stillman's Gym, and the place was nearly deserted. As Johnny Italiano stood pounding away at the heavy bag with both hands, sweat poured down both sides of his face and down onto his chest. After the gym bell rang, signaling the end of a three-minute round, Joe Italiano wiped his brother's face with a blood-stained towel. Then, Dom Russo put a plastic water bottle up to Johnny's mouth. Johnny took a swig, rinsed his mouth, swallowed a bit, and then spit the remains into a rusty bucket.

Joe turned to Dom and said, "That's four rounds on the heavy bag and four on the speed bag, right Dom?"

Dom nodded in the affirmative.

Joe turned to Johnny and said, "Alright kid, give me four rounds of jumping rope and that's it for today. No sparring. If you sit down for dinner with a black eye on Christmas, Rita will stick me with the knife instead of the meatballs."

A shriveled old man with stooped shoulders shuffled into Stillman's Gym. He wore a rumpled navy-blue pea coat and a dirty tweed cap pulled down over one side of his face. The old man dragged himself over to where Joe was standing with his back turned and tapped him three times between his shoulder blades.

"I hear you've been looking for me," Ray Brown said. "Well, I'm here, so what's on your mind?"

Joe's face erupted into a big smile. "The heavyweight championship of the world is on my mind, Ray. But I need your help."

Joe grabbed Ray in a bear hug and kissed him on the cheek.

Ray Brown had trained world-class prize fighters since the turn of the 20th Century when fighting was illegal in most states, including New York. But because of circumstances beyond his control, like the lack of a backer with big bucks, Ray had never trained a world champion.

"And who may this potential world champion be?" Ray said.

"My brother, Johnny," Joe said.

Joe turned to Johnny and said, "Say hello to Ray Brown; the best boxing trainer on this planet."

Johnny shook Ray's hand, and Dom did the same.

"Let's go upstairs and talk," Joe said.

The four men climbed the steps to Johnny's dressing room, and as Johnny took a shower, Joe and Dom sat on a wooden bench. Ray sunk into a dilapidated armchair with the springs exposed on the bottom that Joe had salvaged from in front of the building next door just before the sanitation truck had arrived.

Ray spoke slowly like it was an effort to emit each word.

"You know, when you quit boxing, Joe, my heart dried up inside of me," Ray said. "You were the best middleweight in New York City, and maybe even in the country, or maybe even in the world. Fifty-two years I've been in this rotten game. *Fifty-two fuckin' years*. I've seen scores of half-assed trainers come and go. All they knew how to do was wipe down their fighters and yell, *TIME!* Yet, these bums got the chance to train fighters who became world champions. I never was that lucky."

"We know all that, Ray," Joe said. "Everybody in the fight game knew you were the best. But the wiseguys wanted to control you, and you wouldn't give them the satisfaction."

"Damn right, I wouldn't, Joe," Ray said. "Anybody I trained, and I trained some damn good fighters, were put on the shelf because I wouldn't play ball with the wise-guys. Once my fighters left me, bam, they got title shots."

Ray wiped a tear from the corner of his eye with the sleeve of his pea coat.

"You were my biggest chance, Joe," Ray said. "You wouldn't deal with those bums either. We could have gotten a title shot out west where the New York mobsters don't have a foothold. But you quit on me, just like that. And don't give me that bullshit about your eye. I was born in the day, but it wasn't yesterday."

"Ray, I did have one bad eye, but an operation might have cleared it up," Joe said. "I knew the pressure you were under from the mob. They even approached me personally and told me to dump you. I told them to go shit in their hat. I used the eye as an excuse to get out with nobody getting hurt."

"You never told me that before," Ray said. "You just discarded me like an old shoe. No conversation. No nothing."

Joe got up off the bench, walked over to Ray, and held the man's wrinkled hand.

"You're right, Ray," Joe said, "I'm ashamed that I never told you the whole truth. But I figured the less anyone knew, the better it would be for everyone."

Joe stood and pointed to his brother who was still in the shower.

"That's the past, and my brother is the future," Joe said. "He's all gift wrapped for you and waiting for you to open the package. I've taught my bother all I know, but it ain't enough. We need you to complete the picture."

Ray pointed at Dom and said, "No offense, but I heard Johnny is with his brother, Carlo. You don't get any more mobbed-up than that."

"Ask Dom yourself," Johnny said to Ray. "Carlo's just Johnny's manager of record, but I make all the decisions about Johnny's career, including who I want as the head trainer. And I pick you."

Dom spoke in almost a whisper.

"Joe's right," Dom said. "I'm just here as window dressing to make Carlo look good. Joe is the boss as far as I'm concerned. Carlo just wants the glory of owning a heavyweight champion. But he knows even less about the sport than I do, and I don't know a damn thing."

Johnny walked naked out of the shower dripping wet, and pools of water appeared around his feet. Dom handled him two towels. Johnny draped one towel around his waist and dried himself with the other.

"What's this big pow-wow all about?" Johnny said.

Ray stared at Joe and then at Johnny. Then, he shook his head and dragged himself to his feet. He staggered to the door, but before he opened it, he turned around and said, "Okay. January 2. Three pm sharp. I want to see all three of you bums downstairs. Then you, Johnny, you and I go to work. No bullshit. Hard, hard work."

Ray opened the door and said, "Heavyweight champion of the world. This I've gotta see for myself."

Ray left the room and gently closed the door behind him.

Ray Brown exited Stillman's Gym and took in the crisp evening air. He shuffled up Eighth Avenue and passed under the brightly lit marquee of Madison Square Garden.

The Mecca of Boxing.

Ray craned his ancient neck upwards toward the blinking lights. Then, he slammed his right fist into the palm of his left hand.

"Fuck those gangsters!" he said to himself. "I'm old, but I ain't dead yet."

A broad smile creased the old man's weather-beaten face.

Chapter Fifteen

Joe and Johnny Italiano, and Dom Russo sat in the living room of Joe's apartment and watched the New Years' Day Rose Bowl Game between the Michigan Wolverines and the California Golden Bears. Upstairs in Johnny apartment, Rita and Mary Italiano, along with Nancy Romano, watched the *Bells of St. Mary* with Bing Crosby portraying a priest and Ingrid Bergman playing his favorite nun.

The men had started watching the game upstairs, but Rita chased them from the apartment wielding a mean rolling pin.

"There's going to be no football games in my home on New Year's Day!" Rita had said. "It's bad enough I have to miss Lawrence Welk because of the stupid Friday Night Fights."

"But, sweetheart, I have a bet on the game," Johnny had said.

"BET ON THE GAME," Rita screamed. *"WHO TOLD YOU TO BET MY MONEY ON A STUPID FOOTBALL GAME?"*

To prevent bodily harm to themselves, the men decided to watch the game downstairs in Joe and Mary's apartment.

It was near the end of the third quarter and California, 9-0-1 on the season and the fourth-ranked team in the nation, was leading 6-0, against the 5-3-1 and unranked Wolverines. After initially liking California, Johnny had bet ten times ($55 to win $50) on the underdog Michigan, who for some reason were only 1-point underdogs. Johnny had figured someone in-the-know had to know something to keep the odds so close, so he changed his mind at the last minute and bet the dog. Forty-five minutes into the game, the dog was playing like a dog, not even sniffing the end zone, which was putting a damper of Johnny's New Year's Day.

Joe poured himself and Dom a Dewars on the rocks. But Joe put Johnny firmly on the wagon.

"Tomorrow we start training with Ray Brown," Joe had said. "I don't want you showing up all hung over."

Joe handed the glass of scotch to Dom and said, "By the way, I told Carlo about Ray Brown taking over Johnny's training."

"What did he say?" Dom said.

"He was pissed. He doesn't want me making any more boxing decisions without his prior approval."

"Well, that's Carlo. He always wants to be in total control."

"Fuck Carlo," Johnny said. "Do you have any nuts in the house? I'm dying for some cashews. And this game sucks. I can't even watch it."

"No nuts except chestnuts," Joe said.

"I'm sick of chestnuts," Johnny said. "We had them on Thanksgiving and on Christmas Day, too."

Johnny turned to Dom, and said, "Hey, Dom, can I borrow your car? There's a place open on 14th Street. They sell nuts and candy, and they never close. Not even on Christmas Day."

"The owners are Jewish," Joe said. "Why would they close on Christmas Day?"

"Well, they don't close on Harmonica either," Johnny said.

Joe shook his head, and then he said to Dom, "Please give him your keys. His stupidity is starting to grate on me."

"What stupidity?" Johnny said. "They don't close for Don Kippers, either."

Joe took a sip of scotch, and then he said to his brother, "One thing for sure: they'll never pick you as a contestant for *Twenty Questions*."

Dom reached into his pants pocket, took out his car keys, and handed them to Johnny.

"Thanks, Dom," Johnny said. He turned to Joe. "I ain't the smartest guy in the neighborhood, but I got that question right on *You Bet Your Life* when Groucho Marx asked some guy, 'Who's buried in Grant's Tomb.' Everybody knows it's Mrs. Grant."

"I think you better go," Joe said to his brother. "You're giving me agita."

Johnny started for the front door, and then he turned to Joe, "Hanukkah, Yom Kippur, and President Grant. See, I was just breaking your balls. Let me know how the game turns out. I think I'm giving myself bad luck by just watching it."

After Johnny exited the apartment, Dom said to Joe, "Look, Joe. I need some advice."

"What about?"

"It's about Mary."

"What about Mary?"

"Look, I'm really crazy about Mary, but I'm not sure how she feels about me," Dom said. "Has she mentioned to you anything about me?

"Only that you two are getting along great. Mary's not much of a talker."

"Yeah, that's my problem, too. Whenever I want to tell her something important, I get a little tongue-tied. See, the thing is this. I want to ask Mary to marry me, but I need to get your, you being her oldest brother, permission first."

"Of course, it's alright with me," Joe said.

"That's great to hear, Joe. But I don't know if I can bring myself to pop the question. I want to tell her I love her, but the words keep getting stuck in my throat."

"Dom, listen to me. This is how to handle it. Buy her an engagement ring first. Nothing too gaudy. No big rock. She's not big into showy things like that. Is that something you can handle?"

"Sure, Joe. No problem. I have a friend who's a jeweler on Canal Street."

"Then, just take her out to dinner. Forlini's would be nice since you had your first date there. After dinner, take out the ring, get on your knees, and ask her to marry you."

"But suppose she says no," Dom said.

"That's impossible!" Joe said. "I know my sister Mary better than anyone. She's dying for you to ask her to marry you. If she says, no, and that will never happen, I'll pay for the damn ring myself."

The Rose Bowl was history when Johnny sauntered through the front door of the apartment. He held a large paper bag filled with nuts and chocolates.

"Well, what was the final score?" Johnny said to Joe. "Did Michigan even score a point?"

"You're one lucky bastard," Joe said. "Some doofus named Dan Dufek scored two touchdowns in the fourth quarter, and Michigan won 14-6."

"See, I knew somebody knew something about this game," Johnny said. "On paper California should have been at least a 10-point favorite."

"Hey, Johnny, I have some good news for you," Joe said. "Dom and me just had a little chat, and we've decided it's time for him to propose to our sister, Mary."

"That's great!" Johnny said. "I'm all for it."

Then, out of nowhere, Johnny hit Joe with a short right cross to his shoulder. Not too hard, but hard enough to get Joe's attention.

Joe flinched, and said, "Hey, save that stuff for the gym. You might outweigh me by 30 pounds, but I can still whip your butt."

Johnny popped a chocolate-covered cherry into this mouth and said, "Bullshit. Even my wife can kick your butt."

"So what?" Joe said. "Rita can kick your butt, too. I've seen it happen. The difference between you and me is that you seem to like it."

Johnny opened a bag of cashews. He took out a handful and passed the bag to Dom. Then, he sat on the couch next to Joe.

"Hey, you'll never guess who I just saw," Johnny said. "I was driving down Second Avenue, and I caught Captain Clancy ducking into this old dilapidated building."

"You know, Clancy's is now Bill Brannigan's manager," Joe said. He glanced at Dom, and Dom lowered his head.

"Yeah, but do you know which building he went into?" Johnny said. "It was the same building where they had that cat house when we were kids."

"Peggy's?"

"Yeah, ain't that a pisser?

"I heard Peggy's closed a few years back," Joe said. "I also heard one of the wiseguys from the West Side turned it into a fag joint. Maybe Clancy is shaking them down."

"That's not in his jurisdiction," Johnny said. "That's the Ninth Precinct's territory. Clancy is in charge of the Fifth."

"Who the fuck knows?" Joe said "But Clancy's got big balls. Maybe he's putting the bite on them anyway."

Dom stood up from his chair.

"I think I'll visit the ladies upstairs," he said.

Joe smiled. He turned to Johnny, and said, "He's not even engaged yet, and already he's henpecked."

Johnny handed Dom the paper bag filled with the nuts and chocolates.

"Give this to the girls," he said to Dom.

Dom opened the bag and peeked inside.

"Will do," he said.

Then, he turned and exited the apartment.

Joe poured himself another scotch. He took a sip, and then he said to Johnny, "You know, the more I think about Clancy handling Brannigan, the more I don't like it."

"How could he hurt us?" Johnny said.

"I don't know," Joe said. "But Clancy's a real Irish prick who's got a hardon for us Italians. He could refuse to have Brannigan fight you, just on principle. And he's a cop, a freaking Captain for Christ's sake, so Carlo can't touch him."

"They can't put me on ice too long," Johnny said. "When the public sees that I continue to win fights, knocking guys out, they'll clamor for the fight. An Irishman against an Italian for the world heavyweight title. We'd sell out Yellowstone Park. But I'm in no rush. Every month I get better, and every month Brannigan gets older."

"You've got the right attitude, kid," Joe said. "You're good, but you need at least another year working with Ray Brown. Brannigan's a cutie, but in another year or two, with Ray teaching you the ropes, he won't be able to stay in the same ring with you. You'll walk right through him."

"Damn right. I'll know when I'm ready," Johnny said. "I don't quite have my timing down yet, but it's getting there."

"By the way, I hope you're not too pissed I cut out the liquor for you on New Years' Day," Joe said. "No booze for you for a while. That means no wine, or beer too. It saps your energy. And stay away from all those soft drinks like Coca-Cola or Manhattan Special. The sugar in that stuff can kill you."

"Don't worry," Johnny said. "Rita won't even allow any liquor in the apartment."

"She's a good girl, your wife. She's the best thing that ever happened to you. She keeps you in line."

"Well Joe, you see, Rita doesn't like this boxing business any more than we do," Johnny said. "But she knows it's our ticket out of this neighborhood. We'll rake in the big bucks, and then we can buy a house in Brooklyn, or maybe even on Long Island. And I'll even be able to buy my own car. This neighborhood is starting to change anyway. The Chinese are starting to buy up all the buildings. Pretty soon, there will be no more Little Italy. It will be all Chinatown."

"You're right about that, Johnny," Joe said. "Already the Italians are moving out of Little Italy. They're going to Knickerbocker Village in the 4th Ward where they have elevators. They want to be what people call 'upwardly mobile.' No more walking up five flight of stairs. No more tiny bathrooms with no tubs. No more garbage in the streets. We all want a better life."

"That's what keeps me going, Joe," Johnny said. "I know I got the talent to get to the top."

"And another thing," Joe said. "Your job is to train and fight. My job is to take care of guys like Carlo and Clancy. The title is going to be ours, and there's nothing either of them can do to destroy our dreams."

Chapter Sixteen

It was New Year's morning, and the sunlight peeked through the blinds in Carlo Russo's hotel room which caused him to wake up angrier than usual. His eyes still closed, Carlo swept his right hand across the satin sheets, and he ascertained that the warm, soft female body next to him was still sleeping.

New Year's Day was nothing special to Carlo. It was just another day, and he did what all the gangsters in Little Italy did daily: try to figure who they were going to rob and scheme, and how they were going to rob and scheme them. Money was God to men like Carlo, and Carlo always subscribed to the maxim that if some dope was not strong enough to hang on to something, it was Carlo's duty to take that something away from them. If Carlo didn't do it, some other tough guy would, and that would be a signal that maybe Carlo wasn't so tough himself.

Both of Carlo's parents had died when he was still a teenaged crook stealing hubcaps. Carlo always felt that his father was a sucker, working like a dog in the Fulton Fish Market, until the extreme weather, both cold and hot, combined with the backbreaking job of lugging hand trucks filled crates of fish, had ground him down to the nub. His death from a heart attack at the age of fifty was inevitable. 11 months after Carlo's father had passed, his mother did the same. The official cause of her death was also a heart attack, but family and friends agreed that she died from a broken heart.

Carlo had an aunt and two uncles living on Long Island, and Carlo knew they were glad he never visited.

A gangster in the family! What would the neighbors think?

Carlo's only real family was his brother Dom, and that nitwit was spending the holidays with the Italiano family, a clan whom Carlo hated with a passion.

To Carlo, New Year's Eve was a booze-induced blur. The last thing Carlo remembered he was humping the hell out of a giggling, big-titted blond, who was presently sleeping next to him and sawing enough wood to build Noah's Ark.

At least the giggling had stopped.

Carlo smacked Marilyn twice on her shapely derrière, and then he said, "Hey Marilyn, turn over, will ya. Your snoring is driving me crazy."

Marilyn stopped snoring for a second and purred sexily. Then, she wiggled her behind, gasped for air, twice, and then commenced snoring.

Carlo sighed, and then, as silent as a little mouse, he eased himself off the bed. He slipped into the bathroom, where he had hung his clothes. He had neglected to close the bathroom door, and as he started to put on his pants loose change fell out of his pants pocket and clanged onto the tiled floor. Carlo could hear Marilyn groan, and then her snoring started to splutter like she was drowning. But then it resumed its former rapid cadence.

Fully dressed, Carlo went back into the bedroom, and he pulled a pen and a small notepad out of the night table's single drawer.

On the notepad, he scribbled, "Thanks for everything. I'll call you soon. Here's cab fare. Happy New Year!"

He paced the note on the night table and covered it with five twenty-dollar bills; enough money for Marilyn to take a cab to Philadelphia if she desired.

Carlo slipped out of the hotel room and took the elevator to the lobby. He exited the hotel and hailed a cab.

"The corner of Mulberry and Canal," he told the cabby.

As the cab sped down Broadway, Carlo glanced at his wristwatch. It was 11 am, and he didn't have a damn thing to do.

Carlo hated the holidays. He considered them as a season for sentimental suckers. Buying Christmas presents was a waste of time and money; just a scam to make the store owners rich.

Still, deep down in his heart, Carlo envied the suckers who had loved ones to enjoy the holidays with. Carlo had no one; not even his stupid bother Dom.

The cab stopped at the southwest corner of Canal and Mulberry. Carlo paid the cabby, and then he slipped into Tony's Drug Store and Soda Fountain, which was always open just in case someone needed an emergency pack of Trojans. Carlo hoofed it to the phone booth in the back of the drugstore. He closed the door, picked up the phone, deposited the required dime, and phoned Captain Clancy's unlisted home phone number.

After three rings, a woman's voice appeared on the other line. She had an Irish brogue you could cut with a meat cleaver.

She said, "Happy New Year! This the Clancy residence. Who's calling, please?"

Carlo sharp intonation contrasted with the woman's melodious tones.

"This is Carlo Russo," he said. "If Captain Clancy there?"

"One minute," she said. Her voice became distant, but Carlo could still hear her say, "Honey, it's for you. Some fellow named Bosco, I think."

Clancy's ham-fisted voice conflicted with the woman's pleasant timbres.

He said, "Captain Clancy speaking. Who *is* this?"

Carlo said, "Hello Captain. This is your old pal, Carlo Russo. I hope I didn't make your hangover worse. Knowing you, you must have put on some load last night."

Clancy tried to speak, but instead, he started to choke. After hacking a full ten seconds, he finally managed to say, "How the fuck did you get my home number?"

Carlo heard glass shattering in the background, and he heard Clancy say, "Holy Shit, Molly! Get the mop and broom! I dropped the bottle of Jameson's!"

After Clancy got back on the phone, Carlo said, "Why, isn't your phone number listed? Or maybe a little birdie gave it to me."

"Cut the crap, greaseball!" Clancy said. "Now, what is the meaning of this intrusion?"

"Captain, I have a deal for you that can put bigtime bucks in your pocket."

"I don't do business with scumbags like you."

"Captain, since when is it against your nature to make some serious coin? I'm talking some real cash here. Meet me anyplace you want. An hour from now would be fine. Maybe we can start off the New Year by being friends. We sure as shit ain't making any money being enemies.

Clancy didn't speak for a full 30 seconds.

Then, he said, "All right. Meet me by the park benches on the Baxter Street side of Columbus Park across from the court buildings. I'll be there in an hour.

Carlo Russo stood in the dense fog by a park bench on the Baxter Street-side of Columbus Park. He was hatless, and, as he waited for Captain Clancy to arrive, he stuck his hands deep into the pockets of his pricy beige camel-hair coat.

After about a ten-minute wait, Carlo spotted Clancy parking his unmarked Plymouth in front of the Criminal Court Building across the street from the park. Clancy exited the car, and Carlo noted that he wore a wrinkled tan trench coat that looked like Clancy had just slept in it. A brown fedora sat slanted on his head. With the fog enveloping the police captain as he approached, Carlo thought Clancy looked like Humphrey Bogart in the last scene of *Casablanca*.

When Clancy arrived at the park bench, Carlo extended his right hand, but Clancy just looked at it like it held a dog turd.

Carlo withdrew his hand and said, "All right Captain, if that's the way you want it, then so be it. I'll be brief so that you can go home and finish embalming yourself in that fucking Irish whiskey of yours."

Carlo sat on the bench and motioned for Clancy to sit next to him. But the captain refused the invitation.

"Fuck you and your attitude," Carlo said. "I'll get a stiff neck with me sitting and you standing. Either sit next to me, or I'm standing up, too. Besides, we'll be less conspicuous sitting."

Reluctant, Clancy sat next to Carlo. The two men faced each other, with their legs crossed, and while Carlo stared straight into Clancy's eyes, Clancy glowered over Carlo's right shoulder, trying his best not to make eye contact.

Carlo still saw Bogart, but it was a different movie: *The Caine Mutiny*. Clancy was surely as paranoid as the squirrelly Captain Queeg.

Carlo noticed that Clancy's right hand was inside his outside coat pocket, indicating he might be fingering a gun.

"Stop fiddling with your cannon," Carlo said. "You might get nervous and blow off your kneecap. Besides, if I wanted to kill you, you'd be dead already. So, stop this nonsense. We're here to talk turkey. And I don't mean Wild Turkey."

Clancy took his right hand out of his coat pocket, and he folded his hands on his lap.

Suddenly, a stiff wind behind Clancy blew the Captain's breath into Carlo's nostrils, causing Carlo to cringe. After an awkward pause, he persevered.

"Here's the deal," Carlo said. "You have an aging Irish champion who's half-a-drunk. And I have a young Italian contender, clean as a whistle, who Jim Norris's International Boxing Club has just ranked number ten, making him eligible for a title fight. It's only a matter of time before my guy takes the title away from your guy."

"Only if I give you a shot at the title," Clancy said. "I have Jim Norris in my back pocket, and he'll do as I say."

Carlo reached into his inside coat pocket and fingered a pack of Camels. Clancy quickly shoved his right hand back into his coat pocket causing Carlo to freeze.

Carlo's voice went up two octaves when he said, *"Take it fuckin' easy, for Christ's sake. I'm only getting a smoke."*

Carlo produced his pack of butts, took one out, and inserted it between his lips. Then, he said, "Now, I'm going into my pants pocket for a light. Don't get crazy."

Clancy's mouth twisted into a smile that looked more like a grimace.

"Make it nice and slow," Clancy said. "Or I'll put six holes in the fine coat you're wearing."

Carlo took out a gold Zippo from his pants pocket, and he lit his cigarette. He tried to blow the smoke away from Clancy, but the wind had different ideas.

After Clancy disgustedly waved the cigarette smoke away, Carlo continued: "Look Clancy, a fight between Johnny and Brannigan is the biggest money fight around. An Italian heavyweight against an Irish champion will sell out Yankee Stadium, forget Madison Square Garden. It's the perfect marriage, and you need it as much as I do."

Clancy spat out the words, "Like hell, I do,"

"Just listen to what I have to say," Carlo said. "Because of Johnny's inexperience, Brannigan will be a big favorite; maybe as high as 5-1. And If Johnny looks lousy while training, the odds will go even higher."

"I'm listening," Clancy said. "Spit it all out."

"So, I'll make sure Johnny looks horrible in training, and you make sure Brannigan takes a dive on the night of the fight. We'll bet big on Johnny with the out-of-town books and make a mint."

Clancy's right hand went back to his concealed pistol.

"I ought to plug you right now," he said. "Bill's the champion, and he stays the champion. *See*?"

"No, you *see*," Carlo said. "After Johnny wins the title, we'll have a return match right away. Don't you get it?"

"No, spell it out for me."

"All right. Now Johnny's the champion. Brannigan looks washed up in training. The odds will go sky-high in favor of my fighter. So, we switch our bets and go big on Brannigan, This time, Johnny goes into the tank, and we make another killing. The third fight will be on the level. No more deals. Whoever wins, wins. So, at the very least, we'll both make three big paydays."

By the look on Clancy's face, Carlo knew he had been converted to the faith. Carlo could almost see the wheels spinning in Clancy's skull.

"I'll think it over," Clancy said. "Call me tomorrow."

"That I will certainly do," Carlo said.

Both men stood. Clancy hurried back to his car, and he burned rubbed going south on Baxter Street.

As Carlo strode out of Columbus Park, he figured it was at least 3-1 that Clancy had taken the bait; hook, line, and fuckin' sinker.

Chapter Seventeen

Captain Clancy violated most of the city's driving regulations as he propelled his unmarked Plymouth sedan uptown. In less than five minutes, he arrived at his favorite tenement building on 12th Street near Second Avenue. He parked by a hydrant and put his police identification on the dashboard so he wouldn't get a ticket. As he exited the car, Clancy's penis pulsated in his pants. He ducked into the building and his long legs negotiating the steps two at a time to the third floor.

He knocked on the door to apartment 3A, and the blond twink opened the door.

"I have someone in the next room who's waiting to meet you," Leo told Clancy.

"Do I know him?" Clancy said.

"Yes, we did a threesome a few weeks ago,"

Clancy followed Leo into the bedroom. A husky hairy man wearing women's stockings lay spread-eagled on the four-poster bed. His muscular arms and legs were tied to the bedposts with pink satin pillowcases. Clancy spotted wet sperm dripping down both sides of the man's legs.

While Leo sucked the prisoner's cock, Clancy undressed like Superman in a phone booth. Ready for action, Clancy snatched the prisoner's massive member from Leo, and then he slowly licked the prisoner's balls, moving upward until his mouth entirely enveloped the bulging prize. In the meantime, Leo took hold of Clancy's throbbing member and using one hand, then two, he jerked his hand up and down in a blissful cadence.

After minutes of mutual ecstasy, the prisoner opened his mouth.

"Shove your big cock down my throat," he said to Clancy.

Clancy obliged him, and in seconds, Clancy shot his load, in three hard bursts, saying, *"Happy New Year, my lovely wop!"*

Butch Salerno eagerly swallowed every drop.

Chapter 18

January 2nd at three pm sharp, Ray Brown shuffled slowly into Stillman's Gym. He climbed the stairs in the back to the second floor, and he knocked on Johnny Italiano's dressing room door. Joe Italiano opened it, and Ray Brown slipped inside.

Ray spotted Johnny sitting on the bench tying his black leather workout shoes. He was wearing grey sweatpants and a grey long-sleeve sweatshirt, as was his brother Joe.

"What's with the heavy sweatshirt and sweatpants?" Ray said to Johnny. "You'll get dehydrated wearing that shit. From now on boxing shorts and a tee shirt are the uniform of the day. Capisce?"

Johnny was not pleased.

"But I always train like this," Johnny said. "It's the middle of freaking winter, and this joint is freezing."

"If you work out properly, the cold don't mean a Goddamn thing," Ray said. "From now on you dress the right way. Around here, as long as I'm in charge, everything is going to be done the right way. My way."

Joe dug deep into his locker under a mound of pungent sweat clothes, and he pulled out a cotton tee shirt and black boxing trunks. He handed them to Johnny.

"What about you?" Johnny said to his brother. "If I can't wear sweats, you can't either."

"I'm keeping my sweats on," Joe said, winking. "You're in training, not me. I'm retired. Remember?"

Reluctantly, Johnny took off the sweatpants and sweatshirt, and he donned the tee shirt and black boxing trunks.

When Johnny finished, Ray turned to Joe, and said, "What's your brother's normal training routine?"

Joe said, "Johnny usually does four rounds jumping rope, four rounds on the heavy bag, four rounds on the speed bag, and four rounds of sparring."

"That's no good," Ray said. "Not enough sparring. I need more rounds to work with him on technique. I want six, and maybe eight rounds of sparring a day. We'll cut one round off the other three to make up the time. That way we won't kill the kid."

"You're the boss," Joe said.

"You got that right," Ray said. "Now, let's forget the speed bag and the rope jumping for today." He turned to Johnny. "Let me see how you hit the heavy bag."

The three men exited the locker room and rambled down the steps to the ground floor. They headed to the far corner toward one of three heavy bags: oblong objects filled with horsehair and suspended from the ceiling by a 12-inch metal chain.

Ray watched as Johnny pounded the bag with his full arsenal of punches: left jabs, straight rights, left hooks, and an occasional right uppercut.

Ray liked what he saw.

Ray was especially impressed with Johnny's straight rights, which exploded on the heavy bag like dynamite, shaking it violently from the force of the blows. Johnny's left hook looked good, too. It came straight from the shoulder with no wasted movement. The left jab was okay, but the right uppercut needed work.

But what impressed Ray the most was Johnny's foot movement. He moved like a ballet dancer, just like his brother Joe did when Ray was training him. But Joe was a middleweight, and Johnny was one of the big boys. He didn't trip over his feet like most of the hulking heavyweights. He had perfect balance, and his punches flowed like water down a sparkling stream. The kid looked like a real thoroughbred. But Ray knew from years of experience that any fighter could look good hitting the heavy bag, which didn't punch back, and still look terrible in the ring against a live body that did.

What Ray needed was to see Johnny in action to assess how much, and what kind of work, was needed to be done to make Johnny a finished product; which he clearly wasn't at the present time.

Ray turned to Joe, and said, "Who are the sparring partners Johnny usually works with?"

"They're decent heavyweights," Joe said. "Both pros. Junior Rhodes and Mike Barrett. They're always training for their own fights, so they're serious in their sparring."

"No good. We need new sparring partners," Ray said. "What are you paying those guys anyway?"

Joe said, "Pay them? I don't pay them anything."

"Well, you're getting what you paid for - nothing," Ray said. "Those two guys are heavy bags with heads. They move like the Statue of Liberty, only not as quick. Johnny needs to spar with guys who move side to side and back and forth. Bill Brannigan ain't going to stand and let Johnny punch away. Get me a good middleweight and pay him twenty bucks a day. It will be worth every penny."

"*Twenty bucks?*" Joe said. "Carlo will have a coronary. He's footing the bills."

"Don't worry. Carlo's got the cash," Ray said. "And I'm sure he wants his fighter to become a finished product; not some stumblebum who will make Carlo look bad with his buddies in the Mafia."

"But Johnny punches too hard for a middleweight," Joe said.

"I don't want Jonny loading up on his sparring partners anyway," Ray said. "Beating up on sparring partners teaches a fighter nothing."

"Okay, you're the boss," Joe said.

"Will you stop saying that?" Ray said. "Of course, I'm the boss. I wouldn't have it any other way. Now, get me a middleweight, or even a blown-up welterweight. Johnny needs to work on his timing, and it's best to do that with a quicker fighter."

Joe scanned the gym, and he spotted Chico Valdez taping his own hands. Valdez had won the Golden Gloves title the previous year as a welterweight. But now, at 20, he was already growing into a middleweight body.

Joe yelled across the crowded gym, "Hey Valdez. Veni ca. I want to talk to you."

Valdez stopped taping his hands, and he sauntered over.

"Hey, Joey man. What's up?" Valdez said.

Ray Brown gave Valdez the once-over, from head to toe, and he liked what he saw. The kid had to be six feet tall and maybe even taller. His body was chiseled with muscles, and he looked like the typical hungry fighter from the ghetto. Now, if only the kid could fight.

"Ray, I want you to meet Chico Valdez," Joe said. "He's a Golden Gloves champion, and he's just turning pro.

The old trainer shook the young fighter's hand. The kid had fingers like steel.

"How would you like to make twenty bucks a day?" Ray said.

It was like asking a drowning man if he wanted a life preserver.

Valdez smiled, and said, "Twenty bananas? What do I have to do? Rob a bank?"

"No, kid," Ray said. "All you have to give me is six three-minute rounds a day in the ring with Johnny Italiano."

"For that kind of money I'd spar with King Kong," Valdez said. Then, he stared at Johnny's bulging muscles. "But if this big fuck hurts me, I'll lay for him outside and part his hair with a crowbar."

Johnny showed Valdez all 32 of his sparkling white teeth.

"I ain't kidding with you, man," Valdez said. "I mean it. No rough stuff. I got a career ahead of me."

"If Johnny tries to hurt you, I'll crack his skull myself," Ray told Valdez. "I want Johnny to work on his speed and on picking off punches. I want you to give him a lot of side to side movement. Use your legs. Dance behind your left jab. I want to see plenty of left jabs."

After the men entered the ring, Ray ordered Joe to apply Vaseline to Valdez's face. Ray did the same to Johnny. Vaseline allows the punches to slip off a fighter's face, significantly reducing the chances of getting cut. Even with the fighters wearing headgear during sparring sessions, cuts happen all the time.

With both fighters greased and ready for action, Ray called them to the center of the ring.

"Listen to me, guys," Ray told them. "In the first round, I want both of you to go nice and easy. Jab and move; jab and move. Soft right hands, easy left hooks. I want to see what you both got. But no rough stuff."

Ray shoved a mouthpiece in Johnny's mouth, while Joe did the same to Valdez.

Ray stood outside the ring and rubbed his chin as the fighters went through their paces. Joe stood next to him.

It was almost too good to be true. Johnny Italiano was the quickest heavyweight Ray had ever seen. Valdez was one quick son-of-a-bitch, but Johnny matched him step for step and almost punch for punch. The sleek Puerto Rican had slightly faster hands, but that was good. Johnny would have to hustle and contrive to land and avoid punches.

In the second round, Valdez landed his left jab repeatedly on Johnny's mug. Even though both fighters wore sparring headgear, Johnny's face was starting to redden in exposed areas.

Ray yelled through cupped hands, "Slip the jab, Johnny. Move your head up and down, and side to side. Not straight back. Bob and weave faster."

Still, Valdez's sharp left jab rocketed in like radar.

"*TIME!*" Ray yelled.

The fighters stopped punching.

Ray turned to Joe and said, "Wipe down Valdez. I'll take care of Johnny."

Ray motioned for Johnny to meet him in the corner of the ring. The smaller man reached up and wiped Johnny's face with a towel. Then, he removed Johnny's mouthpiece.

"Not bad, kid," Ray said. "But we gotta work on your head movement. This kid's faster than any heavyweight you'll ever see, and that's good. When you face a real heavyweight in the ring, you'll rip him to pieces. It'll be like the bum is fighting in molasses."

Ray slipped the mouthpiece back into Johnny's mouth, and said, "The first thing you have to learn is to never, never move your head straight back to avoid a punch. When you do that, the punch can still land. The trick is to move your head side to side, and back and forth at an angle. Not straight in and out like you were doing. Make your opponent miss his jab, and then you can counter with any of your punches. Left jab, right cross, left hook. What good is it if you make your opponent miss, and you don't make him pay for it? One thing I never want you to do is counter from the outside with an uppercut. That's for amateurs. Uppercuts are for inside fighting."

Ray pushed Johnny back into the center of the ring.

"That's all I want today," Ray said. "Slip and counter. This kid's a middleweight. He can't hurt you, but he's as fast as lightning. Make him miss, and pay him back. But easy on the punches. Good sparring partners are hard to come by."

The two fighters met at the center of the ring and touched gloves, and Ray yelled, "*TIME!*"

Valdez bounced up and down, circling to his right. He flicked out three left jabs, followed by a straight right that detonated on Johnny's nose. Johnny shook his head and smiled through his mouthpiece. Johnny circled to his left, flicking out his own left jab. Valdez fired another right cross. It smashed on Johnny's nose; the sound of the blow reverberating throughout the gym. A small trickle of blood seeped from Johnny's nose.

Ray shook his head. This was not according to plan.

Valdez tried another straight right, Johnny absorbed in on the chin, but he kept moving forward. Once inside the middleweight's reach, Johnny fired two left hooks to the right side of Valdez's body, stopping him in his tracks. Valdez slumped to one knee, and he spit out his mouthpiece, gasping for air.

Ray slipped between the ropes, and yelled, "*TIME! For Christ's sakes! Friggin' time!*"

Valdez slowly crept to his feet and bent over, trying to breathe.

"Good for you, stupid," Ray said to Valdez. "What the hell were you loading up on your punches for?"

Valdez shook his head. "I don't know. I guess it was just a reflex action. I'm not used to pulling my punches."

Ray approached Johnny, who was smiling while laying against the ropes with his arms folded. The old man slapped the heavyweight hard across the chest.

"And you fuck-face, what are you smiling for?" Ray said. "I told you to work on slipping punches. I told you no rough stuff."

"Yeah, but you told me when he misses to pay him back," Johnny said. "So, I paid him back."

"Wiseguy," Ray said.

Ray brought the two fighters to the center of the ring, and he said, "Okay ladies, now let's go through his again."

He turned to Valdez, and said, "You okay, kid?"

Valdez took a deep breath and nodded his head in the affirmative.

"Okay, it's time to get back to work," Ray said. "And this time no fucking around."

The fighters resumed their sparring, while Ray and Joe stood outside the ring.

Joe softly put his arm around the old man's shoulder and whispered into his ear, "Nice going, you old tiger. That's what my brother needed. Someone to crack the whip. When I try it, he just laughs in my face. You, you're the freakin' Gestapo."

Ray stared straight ahead and watched the fighters go through their paces. Suddenly, he turned and winked at Joe, and a tiny smile creased his weather-beaten face.

Chapter Nineteen

Captain Clancy arrived at the Silver Coin at precisely 12 noon. It was Monday, Sergeant Rubenstein's day to make his weekly collections, but Clancy decided to make this particular pickup himself. Carlo Russo wanted to make a deal for a heavyweight championship fight. Clancy decided to agree, but only on his terms.

As several customers drank short beers at the long bar, Clancy spotted Carlo, who was sitting in the back at his usual table. As Clancy approached, Carlo stood at attention, like a marine recruit when a superior officer enters the room. He shot Clancy a military salute.

"At ease," Clancy told Carlo. "And give me a hundred pushups."

Carlo smiled, but he didn't offer his hand.

"My good friend, Captain Clancy," Carlo said. "To what do I owe the honor of your presence?"

Carlo slapped Clancy's back, a little too hard for the Captain's liking.

"Don't you ever put your hands on me again," Clancy said. "I'm not the type of fellow to play games with."

Carlo sat down, and Clancy took the chair opposite him.

Frankie Fish sauntered over to take Clancy's drink order. He sported one black eye, with a bandage covering a cut over on his eyebrow, and both his lips were split and swollen.

"What'll it be?" Frankie said.

"Crown Royal, straight up. Water on the side," Clancy said.

"Nothing for me," Carlo told Frankie. "Bring the bottle over for the Captain. He can serve himself."

Frankie departed the table to do as he was told.

"What happened to the bartender's face?" Clancy said.

"I don't know," Carlo said. "Maybe he banged his head into a door frame."

"Or maybe someone banged his head for him," Clancy said.

"Maybe he was stealing from the till," Carlo said. "Besides, what do you give a fuck for?"

"I don't. What you do here is your business," Clancy said. He smiled broadly. "As long as the envelopes keep pouring in every Monday."

Carlo reached into his inside suit jacket pocket. He removed a white envelope and placed it on the table in front of Clancy.

Clancy gobbled up the envelope and shoved it into his inside coat pocket.

Frankie arrived with a tray containing a bottle of Crown Royal, a bucket of ice, two glasses, and a pitcher of water. He placed the tray in front of Clancy.

Clancy poured a hefty helping of Crown into one glass. He filled the other glass with water and ice. After chugging down the Crown in one gulp, he washed it down with two gulps of the iced water.

Then, he said, "Okay Carlo, I'm here to make a deal. I'll give you what you want if you give me what I want. Understand?"

"Let's get specific," Carlo said.

"Alright, I'll be specific. You said you want a shot at the title. Three fights. You win one. I win one, and the third fight is on the level."

"That's right."

"Well, I'll agree to all that. Now, you have to give me what I want. I want twenty grand as reparations for Hank Kelly's death. Ten grand for my sister Lucille, and ten grand for Hank's widow Katie. He was married you know."

Carlo scratched his head in thought, and then he said, "Your sister, she gets the ten grand. Hank's widow, too. Is that all?"

"Not quite," Clancy said.

"I was afraid of that. You agreed to my deal too quick."

Clancy poured himself another Crown, but this time he just took a sip.

"As I told you before, your weekly payments aren't enough," Clancy said. "You're making a ton of money with the gambling. But what about the drugs you're dealing? You forget, we're partners on everything."

"Alright, partner. Let's hear the numbers," Carlo said.

"You're paying me a hundred a week for the gambling. I want another C-note a week for the drugs. I think that's a fair price, considering all the money I'm allowing you to make."

"And if I don't increase the payment?"

"Carlo, you're not that stupid," Clancy said. "What if your Mafia bosses found out about your drug dealing? I know as well as you do that dealing drugs is forbidden in your organization."

Clancy had played his trump card well. Even though the profits for dealing drugs were off-the-charts, Carlo was the only wiseguy on the Lower East Side involved in selling babania - heroin. His connection with the blacks in Harlem was just too good to pass up. The order from the higher-ups in New York City was no drug dealing; no exceptions. The penalty for disobeying this law was a permanent residence in the East River. But Carlo also knew this ban did not extend outside New York City. Wiseguys all over the country were raking in big cash selling drugs in the black neighborhoods, and sometimes even to the lily-whites.

"Alright, Captain. We've got a deal," Carlo said.

Clancy was overjoyed. He had won this battle, and he felt he would eventually win the entire war.

"Now, let's talk about the purses for the three fights," Clancy said. "I've already spoken to the people over at Madison Square Garden. There's a $500,000 pie for us to split. Bill's the champion, so we get 75% and you get 25%."

"Agreed," Carlo said.

"The next fight we split fifty-fifty."

"No good."

"What do you mean, no good?" Clancy said.

"What's fair is fair," Carlo said. "For the first fight, *you* get 75% because Brannigan's the champion. In the second fight, Johnny's the champion, so *we* get the 75%."

Clancy smiled, and said, "You forget, I have the champion now, and if I say no to you, you're out in the fucking cold."

"Bullshit!"

"It's fifty-fifty on the second fight or no deal on any fight."

Carlo's intense glare bore a hole into Clancy's forehead. He settled his nerves, and then he calmly said, "The purses for the fight don't mean dick anyway. We'll make our real killing betting on the actual fights. I can lay off the bets with out-of-town bookies who can't say shit when they lose. They gotta pay; no matter what. And get this - you don't have to put up a dime. I'll cover all your bets up to $50,000 a fight."

"You'll put up fifty grand of your money for me to bet the on the fights?"

"Sure, why not? We can't lose. We both control our own fighters. Right?"

"Yeah, that's damn right," Clancy said.

"So, look at it this way," Carlo said. "You give me 75% of the split for the second fight. But you're guaranteed a fifty grand winning bet on the first two fights. In both fights, the odds will be in our favor. If Brannigan is a 3-1 favorite in the first fight, which, because Johnny is green, he should be, you make a cool $150,000 without putting up a penny. In the second fight, Johnny will most likely be favored. We bet the other way, and make a second killing."

Carlo looked hard into Clancy's face and said, "Remember this. My ass is doing this for you. My ass and my balls. If you bet on your own with the New York City books, and they even smelled a fix, you'd be a dead man. You may not like me, you Irish prick, but this Dago is going to make you a lot of money."

Clancy's brain started working in overdrive. After a few seconds of self-deliberation, he hated to admit it, but Carlo's deal was golden. The two managers couldn't lose, and they would both make a mint. And most importantly, he didn't have to put up a penny of his own money, and, because of Carlo's stature in the Mafia, payment was guaranteed."

"Okay, you win," Clancy said. "As long as you guarantee my two fifty-grand bets."

"Done," Carlo said.

The two men shook hands. Then, Clancy stood and exited the Silver Coin.

He stepped lively to the pay phone located on the north-west corner of Canal and Mulberry. He punched in the right number, and after a few rings, a husky voice said, "Yeah."

"Butch, meet me over on 12th Street in exactly one hour," Clancy said. "I just completed some business that I have to mix with pleasure."

"I can't. I have pickups to make," Butch said.

"Just do as I say," Clancy said. "*BE THERE!*"

That said, Clancy slammed down the receiver. He hustled back to the Fifth Precinct, and he donned his civilian clothes.

As he was dressing, Clancy smiled. His plan was right on course.

Captain Clancy had Carlo's top man, that faggot Butch Salerno, in the palm of his hand. It's was his revenge against all those wop wiseguys on Mulberry Street.

Finished dressing, Clancy exited the Fifth Precinct, and he hopped into his unmarked Plymouth sedan parked on Elizabeth Street. As he put his car into gear, Clancy smiled again.

Because of his right-on strategic planning, thrown in with a little luck, the toughest wop on Mulberry Street would soon be sucking his dick, and then, hopefully, taking it up the ass.

It was the perfect time for Clancy to put his plan B into motion.

Chapter Twenty

Carlo Russo's cab arrived at Stillman's Gym just as Ray Brown was stepping into another taxi. Carlo slipped into the gym, and he spotted Pee Wee sitting at his desk by the front door.

"Where's the Italiano brothers?" Carlo said.

Pee Wee spat into the metal spittoon sitting on the floor next to his desk. Without looking up, he pointed to the back of the gym. Then, he spat into the spittoon again.

"Disgusting fuck," Carlo said.

Carlo headed to the back of the gym where he spotted Johnny Italiano beating a mean tattoo on the speed bag.

When he got there, he said, "Hey, boys. I've got some good news for you."

Johnny kept hitting the speed bag, as he said to his brother, "Hopefully, this cocksucker's got rectum cancer."

"Hey, watch your fuckin' mouth," Carlo said. "I ain't deaf. I heard what you said."

Johnny kept hitting the speed bag as he said, "Like I give a fuck."

Joe Italiano decided to clip his brother's insolence in the bud. What they didn't need right now was an angry Carlo Russo.

"Carlo, don't mind my brother," Johnny said. "When he's in heavy training, he doesn't start his brain before he puts his mouth into gear."

Carlo patted himself on the chest and said, "Now, I'm going to show you what a great manager I am. We're fighting Brannigan for the title sometime in March at the Garden. It's too cold in March for Yankee Stadium."

Johnny just shook his head and kept punching, but Joe couldn't hide his astonishment, and his jaw dropped three inches.

"Jesus, Carlo. That's great news," Joe said. "But the timing just ain't right. Ray Brown's only been working with Johnny a little over a week. We need more time. Johnny's doing just great under Ray's tutelage, but I don't want to rush him. Get us a tune-up fight at the Garden in late March. And then schedule Brannigan to defend his title against a dead body on the same card. When they both win convincingly, the interest for their fight will increase tenfold. By the end of summer, August, or September at the latest, we'll be ready to take on the champion. But not before then."

"Fuck you, and fuck your brother," Carlo said. "I'm calling the shots here. I'm not taking any chances that either fighter gets beat before they face each other. The fight is set for March, and that's it!"

Johnny stopped hitting the speed bag, and for an instant, it looked like he ready to attack the Mafiosi, a transgression in the Mafia punishable by death.

Joe saw the look in his brother's eyes, and he said to Johnny, "Go upstairs and take a shower. I'll handle this."

Johnny stared at Carlo like he wanted to bite off the mobster's head.

"I ain't going nowhere," Johnny said. "This little shit-ass ain't telling us what to do. No matter what it says on a fucking piece of paper, he ain't my manager. You are. So, he can go fuck himself. I ain't fighting Brannigan in March."

Carlo's hateful eyes bore into Johnny's. He said to the heavyweight, "That filthy mouth of yours is going to get you in trouble someday. Now, go do what your brother said. Go upstairs and take a fucking shower. And wash out your mouth with soap while you're at it."

Carlo pointed to the steps leading to the second floor and yelled "GO ON! *GET THE FUCK OUT OF HERE BEFORE I GET REALLY MAD!*"

Johnny started to charge Carlo, but Joe was quicker. He grabbed his brother from behind in a bear hug, and he dragged him kicking and screaming to the stairs in the back.

When they got to the bottom of the steps, Joe said, "Let me handle this. Maybe I can push the fight back a few months. Worse comes to worse, and we'll say you hurt your back in training. I got a doc who will confirm anything for the right price. Again, let me handle this. I know how to deal with this prick."

Joe went back to where Carlo was standing, and he could almost see the steam shooting out of Carlo's ears.

"Listen, Carlo, Johnny won't be ready to fight in March," he said. "His back ain't feeling so good. We might have to take time off until the back feels better. By the end of the summer, we should be ready to go."

"Fuck you, and fuck his back," Carlo said. "You think I'm stupid enough to fall for that bullshit? We have to fight when the Garden and Brannigan are available. Not when you and your asshole brother are good and fuckin' ready. The deal is already made, and *that's that!*"

Joe knew better than to argue with Carlo when Carlo was this angry; not when Carlo had every Mafioso in existence on his side and ready to take action. So, Joe took the path of least resistance. He lied.

"Okay, let me talk to Johnny about this," Joe said. "I'll see what I can do to convince him."

"Yeah, sure," Carlo said with contempt in his voice. He might as well as have said, "Fuck You!"

Carlo lit a dollar cigar with a gold plated Zippo lighter. He blew the smoke over Joe's head.

"Now there's something else I'm going to tell you," Carlo said. "Starting next week, Johnny ain't training in this shithole. I've made arrangement to have you, Dom, Johnny, Ray Brown, and your sparring partners stay at the Long Pond Inn in Greenwood Lake. They have a fancy gym there, and that's where Johnny is going to be training. Max Baer and Joe Louis trained there. And Sugar Ray

Robinson, too. My friend owns the joint, and he owes me a few favors. We're going first class on this all the way."

Carlo took a few more puffs on his stogie, and then he continued: "Up in Greenwood Lake, I'll arrange for all Johnny's workouts to be private. Nobody, and I mean nobody, is going to be allowed to see his workouts unless they have been cleared by me. Capisce?"

"Why all this hocus-pocus?" Joe said.

"Okay, here's the setup," Carlo said. "The Garden will arrange for a bus trip for all the New York boxing writers to come up to Greenwood Lake to see Johnny train. It will probably be about a week before the fight. When they arrive, I want Johnny to look like shit. I don't care how you do it, but you make sure Johnny looks like an amateur when the press arrives. When the New York papers start writing about how bad Johnny looks, the odds will shoot up like a skyrocket in favor of Brannigan. We'll bet big on your brother, and we'll make a mint."

"I don't bet anymore," Joe said. "You know that. I'm through losing my pants to the bookies."

"Have it your way," Carlo said. "But don't fuck this up. You'll be fucking with my money if you do."

That said, Carlo did an about-face. He headed for the exit of Stillman's Gym as Joe Italiano seethed.

Thirty minutes after Joe's annoying encounter with Carlo, he sat wearily on a bar stool at Gilhooly's. He told Lefty the bartender to give him a double Johnny Walker Black on the rocks and to be quick about it.

After Lefty placed the drink in front of Joe, he said, "Boy, things must be bad for you to be drinking scotch doubles. I never saw you order anything stronger than a beer."

"If you only knew, Lefty," Joe said. "If you only knew."

As he sipped his drink, Joe contemplated what Carlo had just told him.

Joe thought to himself, "We finally got a shot at the heavyweight title; something me and Johnny have been praying for, but something's wrong. Carlo's acting like Johnny's a cinch to win, which he's not. Sure, Johnny is faster and hits harder than Brannigan, but Brannigan is too cute to get hit with any solid shots. Johnny needs a few more month's work with Ray Brown in order to be able to deliver his punches accurately and with authority. The way Carlo is talking, it looks like he may have gotten to Clancy, and Brannigan is going to take a dive for the long money they could make betting on Johnny."

Three double Johnny Walkers later, Joe spotted Bill Brannigan stagger through Gilhooly's front door. He looked like a drunken sailor on a three-day leave. He slipped past Joe like Joe was Claude Rains – the Invisible Man - and he took a seat at the end of the bar. Joe watched as Brannigan ordered a double Jack Daniel's with a Ballantine Ale chaser; a combination drink called a "Boilermaker" that someone usually orders with the sole intention of getting drunk.

Joe got up and ambled over to where Brannigan was sitting. He plopped into the empty bar stool next to Brannigan.

"Hi Bill, what's the good word?" Joe said.

"There is no good word," Brannigan said. "And if you don't mind, I'd like to sit alone."

"I just found out we're fighting you in March at the Garden for the title," Joe said. "Do you think you should be drinking like this with the fight only two months away."

"Why do you give a fuck what I do?" Brannigan said. "I'm going to walk right through your little brother. He's not in my class."

"If you keep hitting the sauce, Johnny will knock you silly," Joe said.

"I ain't that stupid," Brannigan said. "This is my last day of drinking before I go into some serious training. When I'm in shape, Johnny doesn't stand a chance."

"Bill, you don't hit hard enough to hurt my brother, so how are you going to win?" Joe said.

"I'll box his pants off, that's how," Brannigan said. "I'll bust him up so much, both to the head and the body, he'll be begging to quit."

Joe stood from the bar stool, offered his hand to Brannigan, and said, "It's going to be a great fight, Bill. And may the best man win."

Brannigan took Joe's hand and squeezed it just a little too hard.

"I'm the best man, and I'm going to win, easily," Brannigan said.

Joe just nodded and went back to his bar stool. He thought to himself, "Well, Brannigan isn't talking like the fix is in. But all his drinking has got to work in our favor. He's been banging the bottle real good for years now, and with him in his thirties, that might tip the scale in Johnny's favor."

Joe finished his drink, left Lefty a healthy tip, and exited Gilhooley's.

Joe swaggered down Eighth Avenue with a spring in his step.

He said to himself, "Yeah, all of a sudden, Johnny is looking damn good. My baby brother has a damn good chance of becoming the heavyweight champion of the world."

Joe knew something just didn't add up. But at the present moment, he wasn't too interested in doing the math.

Chapter Twenty-One

Joe Italiano hiked up the four flights of stairs to his brother Johnny's apartment. Puffing like a choo-choo train, he knocked on the front door. Rita answered, and the smell of fish from the kitchen hit Joe like a damp smack in the face. Rita was wearing an apron, and she held a cast iron frying pan menacingly in her right hand. Rita's red, watery eyes flashed angrily, and Joe sincerely hoped her eyes got that way from peeling onions.

As soon as the door closed behind Joe, Rita snapped, "What the hell is wrong with my husband?"

"Nothing's wrong," Joe said. "We just got ourselves a title shot, and we're finally going to make some serious cash."

"Then, why did he go out of his way to pick a fight with me as soon as he walked through the front door?"

"Who knows? Maybe he's just got a headache from all your nagging."

As soon as the words left Joe's mouth, he knew he had made a grave mistake.

Rita lifted the frying pan and said, "How about if I crack you on the head with this frying pan?"

As Rita swung the pan in a wide arch, hitting nothing but the fish-contaminated air, Joe hurried to the opposite side of the kitchen table.

"Hey, easy with that pan!" Joe said. "You might hurt somebody."

"No shit, Sherlock," Rita says.

"So, what happened to make you like this?"

"I tell Johnny I was making him a steak," Rita said. "I bought it today at Louie the Butcher, that creep with his thumb always on the scale. That thieving bastard charges me a freaking dollar-fifty a pound, and I know half the weight was his freaking fat thumb."

Again Rita swung the pan, but this time it was apparent she was doing just it to make a point and not to part Joe's skull. Joe watched until the path of the pan had run its course, and then he pushed the kitchen table into Rita's stomach, just to be safe.

"So, now my husband says he don't want no steak, he wants me to cook fish," Rita said, still brandishing the pan. "So, I look in the refrigerator, and I see this fish you gave us yesterday; you know the fish that fell off your hand truck in the Fulton Fish market like it does every Friday. I start cooking, and then he tells me he don't like the smell. So, he storms out of the apartment and tells me he's eating downstairs at your place."

She laid the pan down. Then, she turned around and grabbed the hot pan on the stove by the handle containing the guilty fish. And in one motion, she flung, not the pan, but the fish across the table. Joe caught the hot fish against his chest; ruining a damn good brown suede jacket.

"Nice catch," Rita said. "Now eat the sucker."

Joe took the fish by the tail and deposited into the brown paper bag on the floor that served as a homemade trash can.

Joe sat at the kitchen table, and Rita sat across from him, quietly sobbing.

"Listen," Joe said, "It's that asshole, Carlo Russo. Carlo got us a title shot against Brannigan without consulting with us first. Johnny got real pissed, and so did I. But now that I've thought it over, maybe it's for the best. It would be nice if Johnny had more time training with Ray Brown, but Ray still has two months to mold Johnny before the fight."

"When's the fight scheduled for?"

"March, but maybe I can move it back a month or so."

"Are you sure my husband is ready for someone like Brannigan?"

"He's almost ready."

"That's like being almost pregnant," Rita said. "Either Johnny is ready, or he's not. I don't want my husband getting hurt."

"He won't get hurt," Joe said. "I'll leave it to Ray Brown. If in six weeks Ray doesn't think Johnny is ready to fight Brannigan, we'll fake an injury. What's Carlo going to do? We ain't cancelling the fight. Just postponing it a few months."

Joe grabbed Rita's hand, and said, "Rita, this is our big money shot. When Johnny wins the title, the money will come rolling in. Then, you can move into that big house in Brooklyn you always wanted to buy but couldn't afford."

"Screw Brooklyn, we're moving with you and Nancy to Florida," Rita said.

Joe's mouth fell open.

"Who told you that?" he said. "It was supposed to be a secret."

"We girls don't keep secrets very well," Rita said. "Nancy told us all about your plans. The only one who doesn't want to move to Florida is Mary, but we're working on her. She'll eventually cave."

"Well, now I'll tell you another secret, but this one you gotta keep," Joe said. "Dom bought Mary a nice diamond ring on Canal Street yesterday. This Sunday, we're all having dinner over at my place. Dom's going to give Mary the ring and pop the question right after dinner."

"Well, it's about time," Rita said. "Mary was beginning to worry if Dom really cared, or if he was feeding her a line of bullshit."

"Dom cares," Joe said. "I'm starting to really like him. Get him away from his brother Carlo, and Dom's a completely different person."

"But will Dom be keen on moving to Florida with Mary after they are married?"

"I'll start dropping some hints to Dom," Joe said. "You keep working on Mary. If things work out according to plan, the six of us will be down in the Sunshine State in three years, at the latest. Besides, I'm sick and tired of this whole neighborhood, and I'm sick and tired of working in the freezing weather at the Fulton Fish Market. And more than anything, I'm sick and tired of the wiseguys and their greaseball attitudes; looking to kill anyone who they *think* has stepped out of line. Not to mention that the Chinese are moving in in droves and taking over the neighborhood. At Transfiguration Grammar School, half the students are Chinese already."

"What do you want? Chinatown is part of this neighborhood, and it has been for 50 years when they called it the Five Points."

"Yeah, I know. But that doesn't mean I have to like it."

"Well, anyway, our long-term strategy is starting to shape up pretty good," Rita said. "Let's stick to our game plan. And don't worry about Johnny and the title fight. I'll tell my husband if he throws away this big payday, I'll never speak to him again."

Joe stood up, and he headed towards the front door of the apartment. But before he got there, he turned around, and said, "Don't tell Johnny that. If you do, he'll *never* fight Brannigan."

The frying pan hit the closing door as Joe fled the apartment.

Chapter Twenty-Two

It was the night before the big fight when Johnny Italiano would battle Bill Brannigan for the World Heavyweight Title, and Johnny, Rita, Mary, and Nancy kept loose by playing open-poker with a dime-a-bet limit. Rita was the big winner, almost five dollars to the good. But money was not paramount, keeping Johnny loose was their primary objective.

Rita won another hand, and after raking in a big pot, she rubbed her hands together like Scrooge on Christmas Day.

"Keep the money coming, kiddies," Rita said. "With all this cash I'm winning, I'm going to buy myself a nice, sexy negligee." She planted a sharp elbow into Johnny's ribs. "Six weeks with no sex, but after tomorrow night my favorite song is going to be 'Back in the Saddle Again.'"

Two flights below, Joe Italiano sat in the living room slouched in an easy chair with a snifter of Remy Martin on the end table next to him. Now quite calm, he contemplated the events of the previous week. Carlo had read Joe the riot act after all had not gone according to Carlo's plan at Press Day in Greenwood Lake's

Long Pond Inn. But at this moment, Joe could care less. Johnny winning the fight was the only thing that mattered.

The bus filled with boxing writers had arrived five days before the fight. They were there to assess the chances of the young Italian heavyweight from Little Italy against the seasoned champion, Bill Brannigan from Hell's Kitchen. On the 1 ½ hour ride, which started in front of Madison Square Garden to Greenwood Lake 60 miles north of New York City, not one writer had given the young challenger a chance. The accepted wisdom was that Brannigan was too seasoned, too wily, and too strong for the upstart Johnny Italiano. In fact, some boxing writers thought it was a mistake for Carlo Russo to throw his young fighter to the wolves before he had a chance to become a seasoned pro. But after Johnny's impressive display before the press, some scribes sang a different tune on the trip back to New York City.

While the writers watched with mouths agape, Johnny exhibited speed and power, and an uncanny ability to slip punches. He was in the ring with two season pros, Mitch McGinty and Solomon Thompson, both of whom at one time were ranked among the top ten heavyweights in the world. Johnny went through them like Grant went through Richmond, knocking both down several times, while wearing over-sized 16-ounce gloves, which were like pillows compared to the 10-ounce gloves they would use for the title fight.

Joe had warned Johnny that Carlo would be livid if Johnny didn't adhere to Carlo's game plan: look lousy in the ring and look lousy even when hitting the speed and heavy bags. Carlo had also gone as far as ordering Johnny to screw up his rope-jumping routine.

"Trip over the fucking rope a few times," Carlo had told him. "Make it look like you have two left feet."

Johnny had yessed Carlo to death, but he never intended to obey a single word. And he told Joe so.

"What's the big deal if you look terrible just for one day?" Joe had told him. "Carlo's betting a ton of money on you, and he wants the odds as high as possible favoring Brannigan."

"Fuck Carlo where he breathes," Johnny had told Joe. "I wasn't born to make that ugly fuck rich. I want the people to know how good I am, even before I get into the ring. To me, there's no honor in trying to deceive the public. If you can't see that, I'm ashamed to call you my brother."

As Joe expected, Carlo's face had turned three different shades of red when he saw Johnny impressing the press with his tremendous display of superior ring generalship and awesome punching power. As Joe also expected, he would have to take the brunt of Carlo's anger instead of Johnny. And he did, when Carlo smacked him, hard, three times across the face. Joe bit his bottom lip not to return the favor. But he knew he would not have to deal with Carlo much longer. After Johnny won the title, the big paydays would follow. In two years, three years tops, they would have enough dough to move the entire family to Florida, where Johnny would officially announce his retirement, and, like Johnny had said, "Fuck Carlo where he breathes."

Joe could open his own gym in Florida and train young fighters. And he could use Johnny's fame, as the undefeated former heavyweight champion of the world, to draw the young boxing talent to the gym.

While most New Yorkers flocked to cities like Miami on the east coast of Florida, Joe favored the west coast of Florida on the Gulf of Mexico.

Tampa. Sarasota. Fort Myers. Or maybe even Naples sounded like good places for the Italiano family to settle for the rest of their lives.

Money wasn't God to the Italiano family like it was for Carlo Russo. They needed just enough money to live comfortably. Carlo, with his ambitious greed, could never earn enough money. No matter how much cash he would accumulate, he always wanted more. Men like Carlo are never satisfied, and some experienced reduced life expectancies because of their greed. At best, that unalterable fact guaranteed Carlo Russo a life of anger, frustration, and murder; maybe even his own, which to Joe would be the best of all possible outcomes.

Joe finished his cognac, and he decided it was time to join his family upstairs. Just as he stood from his chair, he heard a knock at the front door. Joe answered the door, and he came face to face with Frankie Fish, the bartender at the Silver Coin. Frankie boozed-up breath hit Joe in the face like a crowbar. Frankie wore a lopsided grin on his craggy face, and his body was bent forward, at a 45-degree angle, like he was carrying the weight on Mulberry Street on his back.

"May I come in?" Frankie said.

After Joe let Frankie inside the apartment, Frankie said, "I'm sorry to bother you this late, but I have something very important to tell you."

"Do you need any more tickets to the fight?" Joe said.

"No thanks," Frankie said.

"Well then, what's on your mind?" Joe said.

"Joe, I overheard a conversation at the bar a few months ago, and I think you should know about it," Frankie said. "It was between Carlo and Captain Clancy from the Fifth Precinct."

"Go on," Joe said. "Let's hear it."

"Well it was a couple of days after the New Year, and Clancy came to the bar to speak to Carlo," Frankie said. "I made believe I wasn't listening, but I got the gist of the conversation. Carlo and Clancy made a deal. Tomorrow night, Brannigan is going into the tank. Both Clancy and Carlo are betting big on Johnny."

"Are you sure about the part about Brannigan throwing the fight?" Joe said. "Johnny is going to win anyway. With the way he has looked in training, I wouldn't be surprised if he knocked Brannigan out."

"Yeah, I'm sure. And that ain't the best part of my story," Frankie said. "There's going to be a return match as soon as possible, and this time Johnny is going into the tank. Both Carlo and Clancy will then bet big on Brannigan."

"That's fucking impossible," Joe said. "Johnny would never willingly throw a fight."

"Then, after the second fight where Brannigan wins, there's going to be a third fight that will be on the level," Frankie said. "Three big fights. Three big paydays. That's what they said."

"Frankie, why are you sticking your neck out like this?" Joe said. "You're a dead man if Carlo finds out you blabbed to me."

"Joe, you and your brother are swell people," Frankie said. "I know you wouldn't agree with any shit like that. Besides, I can't take any more of that fucking Carlo. I'm leaving town right after the fight, and where I'm going, he'll never find me."

Joe didn't know what to think. Until he saw Brannigan drunk at Gilhooly's, Joe figured Brannigan was tanking the fight. But the way Brannigan spoke that day, Joe had changed his mind. One thing for sure, Frankie was definitely planning to leave town, or he would never have spilt his guts to Joe tonight.

But was he telling the truth, or was his just a delusional drunk who had his fill of Carlo Russo's bullshit?

Joe and Frankie Fish shook hands, and Frankie exited Joe's apartment.

Frankie staggered down the steps, and as he was exiting the building, he ran right into Carlo Russo.

"What the fuck are you doing here?" Carlo said. Spittle flew from the gangster's mouth as he spoke, and a few droplets hit Frankie flat in the face

"I just came to wish Johnny good luck," Frankie said, his heart beating like Big Ben.

"Just make sure you're at work on time tomorrow," Carlo said. "And go home now to sleep it off. Your breath smells like a brewery."

"Sure thing, boss," Frankie said.

As Carlo tramped up the stairs, Frankie scurried down Bayard Street towards Mulberry Street like a scared rabbit.

After climbing the four flights of stairs, Carlo knocked on Johnny's apartment door. Rita answered.

"Look who's here, Mr. Sunshine," Rita said.

Carlo forced a smile, but it looked more like a grimace.

"I just came to wish Johnny good luck," Carlo said.

"You can come on in, but make it quick," Rita said. "You're holding up our card game, and I'm beating their pants off. I was killing them at poker, and now I'm killing them at rummy. Pretty soon, they'll want to play blackjack, which is my best game."

Carlo entered the apartment. Johnny spotted him and said, "What do you want? It's ain't Halloween, you know."

"I just wanted to wish you luck in tomorrow night's fight," Carlo said.

"Ten of spades," Johnny said.

He picked up the discarded ten and inserted into his hand, making it three tens and three sixes. Then, without looking up, he said to Carlo, "Thanks, you can go now."

"You looked real good when the press came up to our training camp a few days ago," Carlo said.

"Our training camp?" Johnny said. "What do you have a cockroach in your pocket or something? It's *my* training camp. And yeah, I looked real good just like you wanted me to. I heard the odds on the fight are almost even money now."

Three weeks before the fight, the odds were 4-1 in favor of Brannigan. But after Johnny's impressive showing on Press Day, the odds in the morning papers had it down to 7-5 in favor of Brannigan. Johnny figured, with any luck, it would go down to even-money by fight time. Carlo' big bet would not bring him the consideration he had previously counted on.

"You're a real wise kid, but I like you," Carlo said. "I just hope in the future you'll listen to your manager more carefully."

Johnny picked the discarded six off the table, making it three tens and four sixes.

"Rummy!" He said.

Then, he slammed the cards on the table, stood up, glared at Carlo, and said, "Who gives a fuck what you like or don't like?"

Then, he brushed past Carlo and headed out of the kitchen, saying, "Goodnight ladies. I'm going to get some shut-eye. The sudden smell in here is killing me."

Carlo's face turned a bright red. He spun around and rushed out of the apartment, slamming the door behind him.

"Every time I see that guy, he's slamming doors," Nancy said.

"He's just an asshole," Rita said. She locked the front door.

"You think you guys got it bad?" Mary said. "That asshole is soon going to be my brother-in-law."

Joe exited his apartment on the second floor just as Carlo barreled past him and down the steps without saying a word. Joe didn't like the look on Carlo's face.

When he arrived upstairs at Johnny apartment, he turned the knob, but the door wouldn't budge.

Rita screamed from inside, "Who's is it?"

"It's me!" Joe said. "Open the damn door!"

After Rita let him inside, Joe said to her "What's with Carlo? He hurried past me on the stairs like he had the runs."

"He's got the runs, alright," Rita said. "I call it diarrhea of the mouth."

Joe turned to Nancy, and said, "Okay, *you* tell me what happened."

"It was typical Johnny showing he don't give a damn for anybody," Nancy said. "He abused Carlo so bad; I almost felt sorry for Carlo."

Joe's stomach tightened. This was not good.

"Someday my smart-ass brother is going to get all of us in trouble," Joe said. "Why can't he just be civil with Carlo, and leave it at that? Carlo is dangerous. Can't Johnny see that?"

"I have as much control over my husband as Dom has over his brother Carlo," Rita said. "Johnny's just a thick-headed bastard."

Joe glanced at Mary, who sat petrified, and it seemed as if she was about to cry. He sat next to her, put his arm around her shoulder, squeezed her tight, and said, "Look, we're all family here, including Dom. Unfortunately, he's Carlo's brother. God gives us all crosses to bear. Carlo's our cross. We have got to learn to live with Carlo just a little while longer. When the time's right, we'll drop him like a bad habit."

Chapter Twenty-Three

The brightly lit marquis flashed on top of the entrance to Madison Square Garden:

15-ROUND HEAVYWEIGHT CHAMPIONSHIP FIGHT TONIGHT! BRANNIGAN VS ITALIANO

As the boisterous New York City sold-out crowd bulled its way through the turnstiles, an usher wearing a bright-red uniform and navy-blue hat speedily tore the ticket stubs in half. He turned to his partner at the next turnstile and said, "This is the biggest fight crowd I've seen since the end of the Second World War. It there's a bad decision tonight, God forbid, they'll be the Third World War, and we'll be right in the middle of it."

His partner nodded and said, "We're lucky the fight won't go the distance, I'm betting the kid won't last ten rounds with Brannigan."

"Ten bucks says you're wrong," the first usher said. "I like the kid to box rings around the old geezer."

"You're on!"

The press room on the 50th Street side of the Garden was total chaos. Local scribes from the New York area thirteen daily newspapers, in addition to boxing writers from around the United States, jockeyed with sharp elbows for spots around the Western Union teletype machines where they sent their advance copies concerning the upcoming fight to their respective rags.

A sportswriter from Los Angeles sat dejectedly on the floor in a corner. It was his first time in New York City, and while he rode the subway, a light-fingered connoisseur in the art of pickpocketing had deftly removed his wallet from his back pocket, containing all his identifications, fifty bucks in cash, and his newly issued Diners' Club Card.

"How could it be I never felt a thing?" he wailed.

A New York scribe told the out-of-towner, "You should know better. This is New York City; not LaLa Land where all you jerkoffs have your heads up your asses. We locals always carry our wallets in our front pants pockets."

"You should have told me that yesterday."

"What am I, your frigging babysitter?"

A sportswriter from the *Herald-Tribune* spoke quietly on one of the dozen phones situated on a long table sometimes used for buffet dining. His right hand cupped the mouthpiece so that he couldn't be overheard by men from competing newspapers.

"I'm not kidding," he whispered to his sports editor. "The word on the street in front of the Garden is that Brannigan is going to take a dive. The smart money's on the kid. And now the odds are even-money; 6-5 either way. By rights, Brannigan should be a huge favorite. If Brannigan throws the fight, instead of a heavyweight title fight, I'll be covering the biggest riot here since the New York City Civil War Riots of 1863."

He hung up the phone and removed a roll of twenties from his pants pocket.

"Does anyone want Brannigan?" he yelled to the swarm of newspapermen. "I'm giving 7-5 in favor of Italiano!"

Thirty minutes before fight time, Joe sat in one corner of Johnny's dressing room assembling the wares he would bring into the ring with him.

Bucket. Water bottle. Round-pointed scissors. Q-tips. Jar of Vaseline. Cotton balls. A shiny new fifty-cent piece, that he used to reduce the swelling around the eyes, was placed in ice and sat in a covered plastic container. And most importantly, his lucky rabbit's foot that an unlucky rabbit had contributed to the cause.

Joe was ready but not as ready as his brother.

Joe had never seen Johnny so loose before the fight. While he was shadowboxing in another corner of the dressing room, Johnny showed as much emotion as if he was going for a jog around Columbus Park. It's like he *KNOWS* he's going to beat Brannigan.

Joe said to himself, "There's no way I'm going to let anybody tarnish my brother's win. No fucking way!"

Joe walked over, tapped Johnny on the shoulder, and said, "I'm going into the arena and see if the girls are seated. I'll be back in five minutes."

Johnny stopped throwing punches at the air, and he said, smiling, "Are you sure you aren't going to throw up in a stall in one of the public bathrooms?"

"Very funny," Joe said. "See you in five."

Joe exited Johnny's dressing room, and he marched down the long gray hallway which led to the dressing room of the champion. Joe knocked on Brannigan's dressing room door, and Captain Clancy opened the door.

"What do *you* want," Clancy snapped.

With one hard kick, Joe knocked the door and Clancy backwards, propelling Clancy onto the floor in front of the seated Brannigan.

"Bill, I want to speak to you alone," Joe said.

Clancy clamored to his feet, and he said to Joe, "You get out of here this instant, or I'll have you arrested!"

"I knew you didn't have the balls to arrest me yourself," Joe said. "But if anyone gets arrested, it will be the captain of the Fifth Precinct."

Joe watched as Clancy's face drained of all color.

"All right, Joe, I'll speak to you alone," Brannigan said.

He led Joe into his private bathroom, the size of a closet. As soon as Brannigan closed the door behind him, Clancy put his ear to the door.

"Bill, how long have you been champion?" Joe said.

"Five years," Brannigan said. "And I've been a good champion. I took on all comers, and I never ducked anyone."

Joe turned on the cold water on the sink's faucet and said, "See this water going down the drain? Well, if you fuck up tonight, your legacy is going down the drain just like this water."

Joe poked Brannigan's chest with his forefinger, and then he continued.

"Yes, you've been a damn good champ. But, if you throw this fight, all anyone will ever remember after this fight about you was that you were a tank artist, not a great champion. Just like Jake LaMotta. One bad move and your entire career goes kaput."

Brannigan lowered his head in shame, but he didn't speak.

So, Joe did all the talking.

"Two months ago, I didn't want this fight," Joe said. "I felt my brother just wasn't ready to fight someone like you. But he's improved so much since then I've changed my mind. He can beat you, and he will beat you tonight in a legitimate fight. But last night I found out you're in the bag. In front of twenty thousand people in the Garden tonight, plus those watching it on TV and listening on the radio, you're going to disgrace yourself and my brother, too."

"What do you mean you only found out about it last night?" Brannigan said. "I thought you were in on the deal from the beginning."

"That's bullshit," Joe said. "Don't you remember what I told you after they killed Hank Kelly? *I told you that me and my brother don't want any setups*! I don't care what kind of deal Carlo has with that rat bastard who's listening at the door."

Joe banged his fist, hard, on the door, in line where he figured Clancy had positioned his head. He was right, and Clancy recoiled backwards, covering both ears with the palms of his hands.

Joe continued to Brannigan: "Now, you can go out there and disgrace yourself. Or, you can go out there like a man, like a true champion, and try your best to win. Like I told you before, don't worry about Carlo. I have an ace in the hole to handle him. But if you throw this fight, I'm going right to the press and spill the beans about everything. And then there will be a huge scandal with you right in the middle. Is that what you want?"

Brannigan just stared downwards and didn't answer. But Joe knew he had made his point.

Joe quickly opened the bathroom door, and Clancy fell face-first to the floor, half in and half out of the bathroom.

Joe stepped over Clancy, and, after resisting the urge to kick the cop in the face, he stormed out of Brannigan's dressing room. Clancy picked himself off the deck, and one look at Brannigan told him the fix was off.

Clancy burst from the dressing room, and he sprinted down the hall and into the main arena of Madison Square Garden. He spotted Carlo sitting at ringside. Butch Salerno was seated to Carlo's right, and there was an empty aisle seat belonging to Clancy on Carlo's left. Clancy hurried to Carlo's row and plopped his ass down on the vacant seat.

"Carlo, we need to cancel our bets on the fight," Clancy said.

"Are you crazy?" Carlo said. "The bets are already in."

Carlo turned around in his seat and pointed to two men sitting two rows back. He said, "See those two men? They're bookies from Harlem who I made the bets with. They're in on the fix, and they already laid off the bets with out-of-town bookies who can't say shit. The out-of-town books have to pay no matter what. They ain't connected to no one we have to worry about. So what's the fucking problem?"

Clancy pulled a handkerchief from his inside jacket pocket and wiped the sweat dripping down his forehead.

"Carlo, we've got big trouble," Clancy said. "Joe Italiano just came into Bill's dressing room. He told Bill, if Bill takes a dive, he'll blow the whistle to the press. Bill's not going to cooperate with us anymore. Johnny Italiano is going to have to beat Bill fair and square."

Carlo jumped from his seat like he had just sat on a thumbtack.

"Are you fucking kidding me?" Carlo screamed.

"No, Carlo. Bill's going to fight his heart out tonight," Clancy said.

"What are you guys worrying about?" Butch said. "I saw Johnny in training. He's going to kick Brannigan's ass."

Carlo sat back down and said, "Well, I'll tell you this, Captain Clancy, if Johnny doesn't win this fucking fight, the streets are going to be littered tonight with at least two dead Irishman."

As Joe Italiano, accompanied by Ray Brown, led his brother Johnny down the aisle to the ring, the Madison Square Garden crowd screamed uproariously. It was so loud Joe could not even hear himself think. As they passed Carlo and Clancy, Joe winked at them and smiled.

Incensed, Carlo screamed at Joe, "Puttana sarà tua madre!"

Joe, turned and screamed back, "No, puttana sarà *tua* madre!"

"No use bringing mothers into this," Butch said. "Let's just sit and enjoy the fight. I'm telling you, Johnny's going to beat this Irish bastard's brains in."

Now, it was Brannigan and his entourage's turn to make the trip towards the ring. The crowd roared, but not as loud as it did when Johnny had just made the same trip.

As they passed Carlo and Clancy, Carlo said, "That donkey son-of-a-bitch! If he fucks this up, I'll cut his balls off and shove them into his mouth before I slit his Goddamn throat."

Clancy's face turned red. Then, he turned towards the aisle and lost his dinner onto the concrete floor.

Carlo, sickened, said under his breath to Clancy, "Disgustoso maiale."

Clancy stood and wiped his mouth with the sleeve of his jacket. Then, he stepped over the mess he had just created and hurried to Brannigan, who was just ready to climb the steps into the ring.

He put his hand on Brannigan's shoulder and said, "On your mother's grave, Bill, don't turn on me now. If you do, we're both dead."

Brannigan shrugged off Clancy's hand and said, "Worry about yourself. I'm going to do the right thing here tonight."

That said, Brannigan climbed the steps and into the ring.

Clancy trudged back to his seat. Carlo noticed that both Clancy's right and left temples were beating like a frog's throat.

"Tell those guys behind us the bets are off," Clancy said.

"Fuck you," Carlo said. "Those out-of-town sucker books gave us 2-1 favoring Brannigan. Sit back and enjoy the fight like Butch said."

In the ring, Johnny's face exploded into a massive smile as Joe removed Johnny's red, white, and green satin trunks, the colors of the Italian flag. The Mulberry Street wiseguys inhabited the ringside seats, but the legitimate neighborhood people could only afford to sit in the nosebleed seats in the balcony. Ignoring the mob guys up front, Johnny waved to his friends in the balcony.

In the opposite corner, a reflective mask clouded Brannigan's face. His muscled body seemed to be in great shape, but the appearances were deceiving. Knowing he was throwing the fight, Brannigan had not trained with the same intensity that he had for other fights. In addition, countless boilermakers, at home and in bars, had drained Brannigan's endurance. Brannigan knew he could not last the scheduled 15 rounds, so he had to take out his opponent quick.

Butt him. Elbow hit. Hit him low in the family jewels.

Brannigan knew he had to use every trick he had learned in 15 years of professional boxing, and that's what he decided to do.

Brannigan glared across the ring at his opponent. Johnny looked relaxed, but his body contained nary a drop of sweat. That meant that Johnny had not warmed up properly in the dressing room. Brannigan decided that he would have to jump on this kid fast. He figured a quick blitz would catch Johnny off guard.

Brannigan also knew that this was the only strategy by which he could win the fight.

The ring announcer Johnny Addie stood in center ring and waited for the microphone to descend from the rafters into his hand. Addie, a smallish man with a cherub's face, wore a black tuxedo, white shirt, and black bow tie. As he prepared to announce the fight, Addie could pass for a Maître D is a fashionable New York restaurant.

The microphone firmly in hand, Addie tilted his head slightly upward and said in his booming tenor voice: *Ladies and gentlemen. Welcome to Madison Square Garden. The next contest is 15 rounds for the heavyweight championship of the world!*

Introducing in the red corner. The challenger. From Little Italy on the Lower East Side of Manhattan. Wearing white trunks. Weighing in at a trim 195 pounds. With a record of 21 wins and no losses, with 16 knockouts. The Mulberry Street Mauler. Johnny Italiano!

The crowd roared with gusto, and a slight mingling of boos barely dented the cheers.

Johnny bowed, once in succession, to the four corners of the ring. He spotted Rita, sitting petrified in a ringside seat in between an equally nervous Many and Nancy. Johnny brought both of his gloves to his mouth, and he blew the ladies a double-barreled kiss.

Rita woke from her trance and jumped to her feet.

"*Beat his brains in, honey*!" she screamed.

Nancy grabbed Rita's arm and pulled her down into her seat.

Mary sat immobile like she was afraid to move; her eyes almost giving way to tears. She held her boxing program so tight, he hands had turned a light shade of red. To comfort her, Rita wrapped her arm around Mary's shoulder, and said, "Why the sour puss? In a few minutes, your brother is going to be the heavyweight champion of the world."

Mary forced a smile that looked more like a grimace.

Johnny Addie continued: *And in the blue corner. From Hell's Kitchen on the West Side of Manhattan. Wearing black trunks.*

Weighing in at 215 pounds. With a record of 45-2 with 20 knockouts. The Champion. The Irish Assassin. Bill Brannigan!

The Madison Square Garden howled again. But this time the boos dominated the cheers. The crowd was obviously favoring the challenger.

The referee Ruby Goldstein called the fighters to the center of the ring for the pre-fight instructions.

"You men are both professionals," the ref said. "I went over the rules with you in your dressing rooms. I want a good clean fight. When I say 'break,' I want you to break immediately. This is for the heavyweight championship of the world. God bless the both of you. Touch gloves now. Go back to your corners, and wait for the bell."

After the fighters touched gloves, Johnny stared directly into Brannigan's craggy mug, and said, "Good luck."

Brannigan stared straight ahead at Johnny's chest, showing no emotion, He nodded slightly, then he did an about-face and headed to his corner as Johnny did the same.

Joe inserted Johnny's mouthpiece, and said, "Alright kiddo. This is for all the marbles. Remember, slip his left jab and come right over the top with the right. And plenty of left hooks to the body. With all the booze Brannigan's been drinking, bodywork is a prime investment. No way he can take it downstairs for a long period of time."

The two brothers hugged, and then Joe kissed Johnny on both cheeks.

The bell rang signaling the start of the fight.

Chapter Twenty-Four

Brannigan came out of his corner warily, and he circled slowly to his right, away from Johnny's vaunted overhead right cross. Brannigan had not studied films of Johnny's previous fights, but he knew Johnny's right was his homerun punch. He flicked out his left jab, hard. One, two, three times; with his left thumb extended. Johnny's left eye caught Brannigan's thumb all three times, and he began blinking; seeing three Brannigans instead of the one standing in front of him.

The ref pushed Brannigan away and yelled, "Hey watch that thumb! Close your fucking fists!"

As the crowd booed lustily, Brannigan just nodded.

Johnny pawed at his left eye with his left glove. He glanced at the glove, but he saw no blood. His vision was still blurred, so Johnny decided to get in close where he could at least feel his opponent. After Johnny dug both hands into Brannigan's body, he grabbed the champ in a bear hug.

Brannigan had the kid where he wanted him. He lowered his head onto Johnny's chest, and then he thrust it upward, nailing Johnny on the point of his chin.

The fight was barely thirty seconds old, and Brannigan had already used two tools in his arsenal of dirty tricks.

Joe screamed from his corner, "Hey, ref! Watch his fucking head!"

The referee jumped between the fighters. He pushed Brannigan away and said, "This is your second warning. Next time, I'm taking a round away."

As the crowd's booing intensified, Brannigan just nodded and put the ref on his pay-no-mind list.

Brannigan continued circling to his right. When he had positioned himself so that the ref was standing directly behind him blocking his view, he threw a short left hook, followed by a sharp left elbow. Both landed directly on Johnny's blurry left eye. Johnny fell to one knee, holding his glove to his left eye. Before the ref could move, Brannigan stepped in and fired a right directly on Johnny's jaw, depositing Johnny flat on his back.

The Garden crowd was now becoming quite ugly, and fights broke out in the stands between the rival factions.

In his ringside seat, Carlo grabbed Clancy's elbow. He squeezed it, and said, "If your fighter does that again, I'll shoot him from right here. And I'll plug you, too."

Carlo pulled back his suit jacket just a bit to show Clancy that he indeed had a gun.

As Johnny stood and shook his head to clear the cobwebs, the ref scolded Brannigan for hitting Johnny when he was down. Then, he informed the two other judges at ringside that it was a knockdown but that he was taking the first round away from Brannigan for hitting a downed fighter.

Brannigan stood in a neutral corner and smiled. He said to himself, "Fuck taking the round away from me. This fight ain't going to the scorecards anyway."

Johnny faced Joe in his corner, and Joe wiped the blood from Johnny left eyebrow with a towel.

Joe screamed at the ref, "It was an elbow that caused the cut!"

The ref came over and told Joe, "I didn't see no elbow. I took the round away from Brannigan for hitting your brother when he was down."

"How do I look?" Johnny said to Joe.

"Like a movie star," Joe said. "But I think it time for you to start fighting dirty, too. Kick him in the balls if you have to. He's fouled you three times already. The ref ain't going to disqualify you now no matter what you do."

Johnny's head had started to clear. His vision was still cloudy, and his eyebrow was cut, but he was not otherwise badly hurt. As the ref waved him to the center of the ring, Johnny decided it was time for him to make his move and take control of the fight.

Brannigan charged Johnny, trying to finish him off, but Johnny was ready. Brannigan forced an overhand right with bad intentions, but Johnny slipped the punch by leaning back and slightly to the side like Ray Brown had taught him. Then, he fired a right hand of his own that caught Brannigan clean on the left temple. Brannigan's legs quivered, and he grabbed Johnny in a clinch to stop from toppling to the canvas.

Ray Brown yelled to Johnny from outside the ring, "He's hurt. Push him off! *Push him the fuck off!*"

Ray looked up at the ringside clock. It said there were only ten seconds left in the round.

The ref needed a crowbar to separate the fighters, and since none was available, the battlers stood stuck together chest to chest until the bell rang ending round one.

In the corner between rounds, Joe went to work on Johnny's damaged eye. After wiping off the blood with a towel, he pressed the frozen fifty-cent piece directly above the cut over Johnny's left eye to try to reduce the swelling. Then, he applied Vaseline onto the cut and smacked his brother's face.

While Joe was doing the dirty work and Dom Russo wiped a wet sponge dipped in ice on Johnny's neck and back, Ray Brown told Johnny, "Start throwing the left hook to the body. And stay out of the fucking clinches. This guy's a surgeon with his elbows."

"But my right eye is fucked up," Johnny told Ray. "I keep seeing three of him."

"Then, hit the one in the middle," Ray said.

"You're a fucking genius," Johnny said.

Just then, the ref and the ring doctor visited Johnny's corner to assess the damages. They didn't like what they saw, but the doctor said the fight could continue, at least for a while.

"If the bleeding keeps up, I'll have to stop the fight," the ref told Joe.

"But it was an elbow that caused the cut," Ray said.

"I already told, Joe, I didn't see any elbow," the ref said.

"You didn't see any legal punches from Brannigan either," Ray said.

After the ref and the ring doctor had departed their corner, Ray told Johnny, "The cut's bad, kid. You got one, maybe two more rounds."

When the bell rang starting round two, Johnny rose to his feet. He yelled at no one in particular, "This fucker is finished!"

Brannigan charged from his corner, and Johnny rushed from his; two thoroughbreds chomping at the bit.

Brannigan fired a wild right which Johnny sidestepped. Then, Johnny shot a left hook to Brannigan's exposed belly than made Brannigan grimace like he had been stabbed.

As the crowd roared, Carlo yelled from his seat, *"Finish him off, Johnny. He's ready to go."*

Clancy was too petrified to say a word. He just nodded his head up and down like a lunatic in an asylum.

Rita stood from her ringside seat, waved her handbag over her head, and yelled, *"Kick his ass, Johnny! Kick that Irish bastard's ass!"*

Nancy ducked the handbag, and then she pulled Rita back into her seat.

Mary, who hadn't seen a punch since the fight had started, was crouched in her seat with her hands over her eyes.

Brannigan tried to grab Johnny in a clinch, but Johnny just pushed him away like Brannigan was a little child. Brannigan stumbled backwards, and Johnny charged at him looking to do some serious damage.

The ref stopped Johnny with a stiff arm in the chest and said, "No pushing."

Johnny ignored the ref and continued to charge forward.

Brannigan attempted two soft left jabs, but Johnny slipped them, and he fired a left-right into Brannigan's body. Brannigan tried another clinch, but Johnny was too strong. He pushed Brannigan off and fired two left jabs which caught Brannigan's nose. An overhand right landed on the side of Brannigan's head, and his legs looked like overcooked spaghetti. Johnny's left hook followed the right, and Brannigan fell flat onto his back.

Johnny sprinted to a neutral corner as the ref began his count over the fallen champ. Johnny stared into his corner for instructions. Ray Brown cupped his hands and screamed, "Hook to the body! Right to the head! Then, another hook to the head!"

Brannigan pulled himself to his feet at the count of nine. He stood in mid-ring like he was three sheets to the wind.

Johnny charged him.

Bad mistake.

Brannigan was playing possum. He suddenly came alive and fired a straight right that caught Johnny coming in on the point of his chin. Johnny stopped in his tracks. He had absorbed Brannigan's best punch, but he was still standing and barely hurt.

"Is that all you've got?" Johnny yelled at Brannigan. "My wife hits harder than you."

Johnny waved Brannigan towards him with both arms, inviting the champ to mix it up.

Brannigan nodded, and he trudged resolutely forward.

The crowd's uproar reached a crescendo.

Johnny got off first with a left hook to Brannigan's body. Brannigan fired a wild overhand right. Johnny saw it coming, and he moved his head slightly to the right, causing the punch to miss by an inch. With Brannigan off balance and bent forward, Johnny fired a short chopping left hook that detonated on Brannigan's jaw.

Almost in slow motion, Brannigan started to topple face-forward towards the canvas. Johnny nailed him with another chopping left hook on the way down for good measure, and Brannigan was unconscious before his face hit the floor.

The ref tolled the final countdown:

EIGHT...NINE...TEN...YOU'RE OUT!

Johnny Italiano was the new Heavyweight Champion of the World!

Madison Square Garden looked like an absolute nut house. Italians hugged each other in the seats and in the aisles; while the Irish cheered the bravery of Bill Brannigan.

And money changed hands throughout the arena.

But no one mentioned a fix.

Inside the ring, Joe and Dom hugged the new champion, while Ray Brown stood proudly outside the ropes on the ring apron and watched the celebration.

Rita climbed into the ring and kissed her husband on the lips. Standing in front of their seats, Nancy embraced Mary to keep her from fainting.

A few rows back at ringside, Carlo, Clancy, and Butch all cheered loudly. Then, Carlo grabbed Clancy by both shoulders and said, "You are one lucky Irish cocksucker."

"When do I get paid?" Clancy said.

"How about right now?" Carlo said.

Carlo nudged Butch with his elbow. Butch spun around and nodded to the two bookies from Harlem standing two rows back. The taller one, a huge smile spread across his face, skipped down the steps and placed a large envelope in Butch's jacket pocket. Then, the two bookies left the arena without saying a word.

Butch handed the envelope to Carlo, who tore it open. In full view of anyone who was watching, Carlo counted out the money, and then he gave Clancy his share, saying, "Here's your cut I promised you, you fuckin' asshole. Fifty fucking grand, no thanks to you, you prick."

That said, Butch and Carlo exited the area. Clancy waited a few minutes to be safe, and then he did the same.

Chapter Twenty-Five

The Heavyweight Champion of the World!

These words hummed in his head as Johnny Italiano drove Dom Russo's borrowed white Cadillac into Virginia Beach, a honeymoon haven 300 miles south of New York City. Rita slept in the passenger seat; her head nestled on her husband's shoulder.

Four years earlier, their honeymoon had consisted of two nights at the seedy Broadway Central Hotel on Broadway, just east of Greenwich Village, and not exactly the Plaza Hotel. They were one of the few couples checked in not paying by the hour. But with all the Italianos milling about, it beat 104 Bayard Street Bayard by a country mile. Plus, the Broadway Central had a real shower, and the tub was not in the middle of the kitchen like it was at 104 Bayard Street.

Because Johnny had won the title, and they were now rolling in dough, Rita decided a belated honeymoon was in order. In Virginia Beach, they would experience one entire week of romantic bliss; making love while swaying to the rhythm of the waves beating upon the beach.

As Johnny directed the Caddy into the town of Virginia Beach, he spotted a sign that said: *WELCOME TO VIRGINIA BEACH! VIRGINIA BEACH IS FOR LOVERS!*

As if on cue, Rita awoke and said, "See that sign lover-boy! We're in for a very physical week. I hope that stupid fight didn't drain away all your energy."

"If we get tired, we can always watch television in our room," Johnny said.

Rita sat up straight in her seat and punched Johnny playfully on the shoulder. She said, "If you ever put on that television when I want to do something else, watch how fast I throw my shoe through the screen."

Joe Italiano skipped down the steps of the Bowery Savings Bank, a Roman classical-style architectural wonder with Corinthian columns that was designed in 1895 by famed architect Sanford White. Joe wore a massive smile on his face.

Joe's mission had been accomplished. For a change, he had made a hefty deposit in the bank instead of a painful withdrawal, usually for the purpose of paying off his gambling debts. Johnny's purse had been $100,000, and after deducting Carlo's one/third managerial cut, and after giving Ray Brown a seven grand bonus, there was a whopping 60 grand left. Joe took out his agreed-upon ten grand cut, which left Johnny with fifty grand to do with what he pleased.

Hell, Joe was more than satisfied. Ten large was more than Joe had made the previous two years, combined, hauling fish at the Fulton Fish Market.

Before Johnny and Rita had left for their second honeymoon, the Italiano family met for dinner to discuss their future in greater detail. At this get-together, Mary and Dom agreed to a double-wedding in June, that would also include Joe and Nancy tying the knot. Pete Romano had insisted on paying for the entire extravaganza. That did not sit well with Carlo Russo. Not that Carlo actually enjoying spending his cash, but it didn't look good for Carlo in the mob to allow someone else to pick up his brother Dom's wedding tab.

Unfortunately for Carlo, Pete Romano was his boss, and what Pete said was golden.

"What about Sarasota, Florida for the honeymoon?" Joe had asked Dom. "I was there last year, and the place is gorgeous."

"What about the heat?" Dom had asked. "Ain't it hot in Sarasota in June?"

"New York City is hot in June," Rita said.

"That's because you're always blowing hot air," Johnny said, smiling.

After seeing the look on Rita's face, Johnny decided that was his last contribution to the conversation. He looked to Joe for salvation.

Joe obliged by saying, "Everything's air-conditioned in Sarasota. It's ain't like New York City, where you have to go to an air-conditioned movie theater to stay cool in the summer."

"Sounds good to me," Dom said. He turned to Mary, and said, "How about you, sweetheart? Does Sarasota sound good to you?"

"Whatever you and Joe decide is fine with me," Mary said.

"Whoa, take it easy," Nancy said to Mary. "Don't give these baboons the idea that they are calling all the shots." She thought for a moment, then she smiled and said, "But I say Sarasota, too. That way, for at least one week in June, we won't have to sleep on the roof or on the fire escape to keep cool."

Joe said, "Besides, I think it's a good idea for us to scout Sarasota as a final resting place for the six of us after Johnny wins a few more fights. Little Italy is starting to suck, especially with Carlo up our asses all the time. The further we get from him, the better."

The foursome also decided that it was Joe, no matter what Carlo Russo said, who would be the architect of their future. He was the oldest and the wisest, and it was up to him to move the pieces on the chessboard of their future.

No matter how much hate emanated from Carlo, the Italiano's knew that strength, with unity and love, conquers all.

After he left the Bowery Savings Bank, Joe headed for Nancy's apartment on Hester Street. When he arrived, Nancy was sitting at the kitchen table mending holes in her father's socks.

"Where's your father?" Joe said.

"I finally convinced him to go see his doctor for a checkup," Nancy said. "He's been puffing like a locomotive lately, and he can barely make it down the block without stopping to breathe."

At fifty-five years of age, Pete Romano health was that of a man 15 years older. Pete inhaled pasta and all the other calorie-rich Italian foods, and he now tipped the scales at 250 pounds, fifty pounds more than he had weighed just five years earlier. With his excess baggage, Pete found it extremely difficult to negotiate the four flights of stairs up to his apartment. And most dangerously, his blood pressure had zoomed into the stratosphere.

Dr. Depasquale, the family doctor since Hippocrates, had read Pete the riot act.

The good doctor said, "You better lose at least 30 pounds, or you'll be residing at Calvary Cemetery within a year."

"You worry too much, doc," Pete said. "You sound just like my daughter. I'll tell you the same thing I told her: only the good die young. What I need is a B-12 shot and some other vitamins. That's why I came to you in the first place."

"What you need is a complete overhaul with your diet, not vitamins," the doctor said. "Have pasta just once a week, on Sundays. The rest of the week eat only chicken and fish. And plenty of fruits and vegetables. No red meat. All the red meat you'll need will be in the meatballs you eat with your pasta on Sunday. And no sausages. Too much grease."

"Okay, so I'll diet a little," Pete said.

"No, you've got to diet a lot," Dr. Depasquale said. "And stop smoking those Camels like a chimney."

"I'm already down to two packs a day."

"Two packs a day? That's insane!"

"Okay, I'll go down to one pack a day."

"My God, Pete. If you can't do it for yourself, do it for your daughter. Imagine how you'll look in the wedding pictures. Like a stuffed elephant! If you even make it to her wedding."

"Alright," Pete said. "I'll go on a diet, and I'll stop smoking. Happy now?"

"Yes, I'm very happy," Dr. Depasquale said. "But not as happy as your daughter will be. I didn't want to tell you, but she phoned me yesterday. She begged me to convince you to do the right thing."

"I'd do anything for my daughter, you know that doc," Pete said.

"Good. I'll call her back and tell her about our little conversation. I know it will make her feel much better to know that I got through to you."

Carlo Russo sat at his customary table at the Silver Coin, content as a fatted cow. He was presently the manager of the heavyweight champion of the world, with all the respect that comes with it. Carlo was now a big shot it the neighborhood and, in the Mafia, but Pete Romano still treated him like shit.

With Joe Italiano soon to be Pete's son-in-law, things could get really uncomfortable for Carlo in the near future. Carlo liked Joe as much as he liked getting syphilis, and Carlo knew the feeling was mutual. Soon, Carlo's dim-witted brother Dom would be a part of the Italiano clan, which was strike number two. Carlo knew the time was near for him to do something to improve his lot, but now he had something more important to worry about.

Family disputes would have to wait.

When Captain Clancy rested his feet on the massive desk in his private office at the Fifth Precinct, official folders fell aimlessly to the floor. Clancy could care less. Right now, police business was the last thing on his mind.

What Clancy needed to do was to get the heavyweight title championship belt around Bill Brannigan's waist as quickly as possible. That was the deal from the start. Johnny Italiano wins the first fight. Brannigan wins the return match. The third fight would be up for grabs for the better man to win it.

That was all well and good, except that Clancy had no intention of allowing the third fight ever to take place.

Johnny Italiano proved in the last fight that he was, without a doubt, the better man in the ring. Plus, Brannigan had shown he was basically a shot fighter, and he would have to be matched properly with amateurish stumblebums to allow him to keep the heavyweight title after Johnny went into the tank.

It made no difference that Brannigan had not trained properly for the first fight with Italiano. Brannigan's advanced age, combined with his fond love for a bottle of booze, had swept away his talent on the magic carpet ride of empty whiskey bottles. Once Clancy got the title back for Brannigan, Carlo Russo could stick his finger up his ass.

What was the greaseball going to do anyway?

Call the cops?

Kill him?

No, Carlo had more brains than to murder a police officer, let alone the chief commander of the Fifth Precinct, which patrolled all of Little Italy. If Carlo ever did anything so downright stupid, if the law didn't get him, his cronies in the Mafia certainly would. Killing cops brings the heat; the one thing the Mafia can do without.

And Clancy was ready to bet his life that his theory was correct.

Clancy took his feet off the desk. He grabbed the phone and dialed the number of his favorite shyster lawyer, Bill "The Swindler" Schlindler. Schlindler was a criminal attorney in every sense of the word. Yet, his unorthodox style made him very useful to Clancy.

When a person was needed to grease the proper palms, Schlindler was the man. Is blackmail your game? Then Schlindler's the name. And to use Schlindler's expertise, for Captain Clancy the price was always right. Clancy had a secret file on Schlindler big enough to give Charles Atlas a hernia. And if Schlindler didn't work for Clancy at a reasonable fee, and sometimes for free, he could bet his ass that he would soon be administering his talents behind bars.

Schlindler answered on the first ring like he had been sitting on the phone. Clancy knew that Schlindler's busty negro secretary had quit the week before because she had resisted his attempt to pay her in inches instead of good old United States currency.

"William Schlindler's office," he said.

"How come you're not out chasing ambulances?" Clancy said.

"Why Captain Clancy, it's a great pleasure."

"I guess the fact that you're answering your own phone means you must be hard up for the cash to hire a new secretary," Clancy said. "Do what I say, and you'll have enough money to hire another secretary and a white one to boot."

"I happen to like Negro women," Schlindler said.

"Well, like they say in here in Little Italy: 'Sauseech his own.'" Clancy said. "But what I need you to do is to set up a meeting with Carlo's Russo's attorney. What's his name? Ruffino?"

"No, that's the wine," Schlindler said. "His name is Raffo. And what's the purpose of this meeting?"

"I want to arrange the return bout for Brannigan as soon as possible," Clancy said. "So, set up a meeting for me and Carlo for tomorrow morning."

Schlindler was in a bind. A rich and very crooked banker he had done business with had suffered an unexpected fatal heart attack. Schlindler had planned to attend the banker's funeral the following day to get close to the widow, with the purpose of redirecting some of the banker's ill-gotten gains into Schlindler's own bank account.

"Sorry, I'm tied up tomorrow morning," Schlindler said. "Can't we make it the following day?"

"Well, then get un-tied up," Clancy said. "I'm not waiting another fucking day."

Schlindler hated Captain Clancy's guts. But Clancy was a man Schlindler could not afford to make an enemy. Besides a dossier

Schlindler knew Clancy kept on him, he also needed the good captain to keep on alerting him when one of Schlindler's clients' numerous gambling houses were being ticketed for a raid.

"For you, Captain, I'll cancel my appointment," Schlindler said. "I have a copy of the contract in my files, and if my memory serves me correctly, we were guaranteed a rematch within six months."

"That's right," Clancy said. "I want to move it up to four months. The quicker, the better. Of course, they'll be the usual remunerations for your services when all this is settled."

Schlindler knew, that since he had not gotten a plug nickel for drawing up the original contract, Clancy was going to stiff him again.

"Okay, sir. I'll get right on it," Schlindler said.

"Well then what are you waiting for?" Clancy said. "Get off the fucking phone and contact that dago, Raffo."

"Aye aye, sir."

The sound of the dial tone summarily dismissed attorney Bill Schlindler.

Chapter Twenty-Six

Attorney Bill Schlindler dialed fellow attorney Mario Raffo's phone number.

Some people questioned Raffo's honesty, but no one doubted his work habits. Raffo worked long hours protecting organized crime figures from being put behind bars. He charged astronomical fees, but Raffo got results. Facts and minute details were Raffo's obsession. Schlindler barely knew how to spell the words. That was another reason Schlindler feared the smallish Italian attorney.

Raffo himself answered on the third ring.

"Mario Raffo's law office," he said.

Schlindler couldn't contain the glee in his voice, when he said, "Mr. Raffo, when are you going to hire yourself a secretary? You certainly have the cash."

"Well, well," Raffo said in his thick New York accent. "If it isn't Schlindler, the world's most crooked attorney. As for my secretary, she's working for me on a case that needs my immediate attention."

"You sure she isn't on her knees under your desk working on your knob?"

"That's you, shit-face. My secretaries actually work. Yours are too busy running from your lecherous advances. Now get to the point. I'm a busy man."

"Okay, I'll get to the point," Schlindler said. "I'm calling to expedite the return match between my client's fighter and your client's fighter. We wrote the return bout clause into the original contract. Remember?"

"Sorry counselor," Raffo said. "But that contract is invalid."

Schlindler almost choked on his own tongue.

"What do you mean the contract's invalid?" he said. "A deal is a deal, so stop fucking around."

"I'm not, as you say, fucking around?" Raffo said. "If you had done your job properly and did your due diligence, you would have known that return-bout contracts are invalid in the state of New York. The New York Boxing Commission instituted that exact rule to prevent what your client, Captain Clancy, was trying to do - fix fights in order to have return matches."

"What the fuck are you talking about?" Schlindler said. Sweat poured down both sides of his face. "*We have a contract!*"

"You can wipe your ass with that contract," Raffo said. "By law, Johnny Italiano will have to defend his title against someone else, preferably the number one contender, before we can even entertain the idea of Johnny fighting Brannigan again. Besides, with Brannigan looking so washed-up when Johnny kicked his ass, the public is hardly clamoring for a return match. Brannigan will have to work his way back into contention by beating another top contender, which I doubt he can do."

Schlindler decided to play the only trump card he had.

"You're asking for trouble," Schlindler said. "You forget, as a high-ranking police officer, Captain Clancy can cause your client and his pals a lot of grief."

"Stuff the threats, Schlindler," Raffo said. "There's nothing anyone of us can do to alter the situation. Even if we agreed to the fight, which we won't, the New York State Boxing Commission would never sanction it until Johnny had at least one defense of his title."

"So, we'll move the fight to another state," Schlindler said. "Or maybe even to a different country; like Italy, or Ireland. That fight would sell great in either country."

"Now, you're talking like an asshole," Raffo said. "Both Johnny and Brannigan are from New York City. No way would we permit that fight to take place somewhere else."

Schlindler wiped the sweat from his face with a hanky.

"You knew about that anti-return bout rule all along, didn't you?" Schlindler said. "How could you fuck me like this?"

"I didn't fuck you," Raffo said. "You fucked yourself by being lazy. Maybe if you hadn't been chasing your secretary around your office, eight hours a day, you would have done the research necessary to learn that a return-bout clause would never fly."

"But Raffo, please," Schlindler said.

The phone line went dead.

Schlindler wracked his brain for a few minutes, and he came to the conclusion he had only two choices. He could tell Clancy the truth: that he had been outsmarted by a better attorney. Or he could take the quarter million dollars he had in a safety deposit box, and watch New York City getting smaller in his rearview mirror until it completely disappeared.

Schlindler could do what he always wanted to do: open a small antique shop in some far-away wilderness, like the Poconos, or maybe even Canada, and live comfortably like a country baron for the rest of his life. Schlindler knew that Raffo was right. He just didn't dedicate himself to his chosen profession like a professional is supposed to do.

After careful consideration, Schlindler decided what he had to do.

He phoned Clancy at the Fifth Precinct, and Clancy answered the phone in his usual gruff manner.

"Okay, what time do we meet tomorrow?" Clancy said.

"We don't. There's a problem," Schlindler said.

"What fucking problem?" Clancy said.

"We got fucked, plain and simple," Schlindler said.

And then he told Clancy about the New York State Boxing Commission's ban on immediate return bouts.

"Well, there must be some way around this," Clancy said.

"Sorry, but there isn't," Schlindler said. "And to tell you the truth, I really don't care."

"*You don't care!*"

"No, I don't," Schlindler said. "Next time hire yourself a good lawyer, a lawyer that you actually have to pay, and maybe you'll get better results."

Schlindler didn't remember the last time he had felt so much pleasure hanging up the phone.

Angry like a lion with a thorn in his paw, Captain Clancy hurried into the private men's room reserved for the higher-ups at the Fifth Precinct. He busted into a stall and slammed the stall door behind him. He unzipped his fly and proceeded to induce a mighty erection, which he yanked with a vengeance.

He thought to himself, "*I'll get even with that Guinea bastard Carlo Russo if it's the last thing I do.*"

Suddenly, just as he was about to abort completion, as usual, Clancy heard someone entering the stall next to him. He tried to shove his penis back into his pants, but it was too late. With Clancy moaning in half despair and half ecstasy, oceans of hot cum burst all over his neatly-pressed blue police pants.

"Son of a bitch!" Clancy said, a mite too loud.

A familiar voice in the next stall boomed, "What's going on in there? I sincerely hope that someone doesn't have a girl in there with him."

Clancy reached for the toilet paper, but only two sheets were left; hardly enough to clean up his mess. He opened the stall door hoping to use the paper towel dispenser by the sink, and he came nose to nose with Chief Inspector Riley. Inspector Riley's eyes quickly shifted from Clancy's face to Clancy's desecrated police trousers.

"Dear God!" Inspector Riley bellowed. "Don't you get enough at home, man?"

Clancy was too terrified to speak. He tried to say something, but only short gurgles came from his parched throat.

"I think a visit to the Police Chaplin is what you need, son," Inspector Riley said. "In fact, I'm going to order it. Do you understand?"

Clancy nodded yes like a zombie.

After washing his hands, Inspector Riley, his face a mask of disgust, exited the private men's room.

Clancy rushed back into his office, thinking, *That fucking Carlo! I'll make him rot in hell for this!*

Clancy reached for the phone and dialed Butch Salerno's phone number.

"Meet me at 12th Street in half an hour," Clancy told Butch.

"I can't. I have an appointment," Butch said.

"Fuck your appointment, you dago queer," Clancy said. "Do what I say, or I'll spill your little secret all over Mulberry Street."

"Settle down, Clancy," Butch said. "Make it an hour, and I'll be there."

"All right. I'll give you an hour, but not a minute more," Clancy said.

An hour later, Butch used his private key to open the door to apartment 3A at 250 East 12th Street. He opened the bedroom door, and he spotted Clancy naked and flat on his back with the young blond Leo giving him an expert blowjob.

Seeing Butch, Clancy pushed Leo's head back, and said, "Get away, kid. Let Butch finish the job."

Leo turned around and smiled at Butch. Then, Leo turned back to Clancy and resumed sucking.

Clancy said, "Hey kid, you deaf?"

Suddenly, Leo bit down, hard, on Clancy's rigid member.

"*MY DICK!*" Clancy yelled as blood dripped down the sides of Leo's mouth.

The first bullet from Butch's gun dislodged Clancy's right eye. The second caught Clancy in the mouth, and the third dotted the middle of Clancy's forehead. He was dead before he fell off the bed, his bloody head clunking on the bedroom's shag-rugged floor.

"I've got the morgue bag in the closet," Leo told Butch. "Julio will be here any minute with the van. He'll take care of the body."

"Make sure it disappears," Butch said. "No body, no murder. And get this rug cleaned."

Butch pulled a wad of hundred dollar bills wrapped in a rubber band from his pants pocket.

He counted out fifty, and said, "Here's five grand, kid. Give Leo what you think is right. But make sure Clancy's body disappears."

Butch turned to leave, then he spun around and kicked Clancy once in the head and four more times in the body.

Giggling like a madman, Butch spat on Clancy and said, "You were a lousy blowjob anyway."

Chapter Twenty-Seven

Thirty minutes before the scheduled double-wedding, 104 Bayard Street was a madhouse.

In apartment 4F, the men tried to discover the best method to squeeze themselves into their white three-piece tuxedos without damaging important parts of their body.

Downstairs in apartment 2F, the ladies were even more disorganized.

Rita gritted her teeth as she struggled to pull up the zipper in the back of Mary's wedding gown.

"How much weight did you gain since they measured you for this gown?" Rita said.

Mary inhaled as Rita's struggle continued.

"Ten pounds," Mary said. "I've been so nervous about making the final arrangements, I ate everything in sight, including the linoleum."

Rita smiled, and said, "Don't worry, you'll work off those ten pounds on your honeymoon."

In the closet-sized bathroom, Nancy pressed her face against the mirror, trying to put the finishing touches on her makeup. While Nancy penciled in her eyeliner, her rear end was pressed against the bathroom door behind her. That is until Rita pushed the door from the outside, which buried the doorknob in the small of Nancy's back.

Nancy screamed twice: first at the sudden pain and then at her reflection in the mirror.

The sudden thrust from behind forced Nancy's black eyeliner to manufacture a long, thin, squiggly line down the right side of her face.

Spotting the distortion on Nancy's face, Rita burst out laughing.

"Don't change a thing," Rita said. "You look like *Dracula's Daughter.*"

Mary confirmed that three is a crowd when she pushed herself inside, saying, "Give me the red lipstick in the medicine cabinet."

Nancy opened the medicine cabinet and extracted the red lipstick. She tried to hand it behind her to Mary, but her extended elbow cracked Rita in the jaw.

Rita peered over Nancy's shoulder into the mirror to assess the damages to her face. Seeing none, she screamed, "That's it! I'm going upstairs to my apartment to finish dressing. I'm not the one getting married, so I'm allowed to see the grooms before the wedding."

Rita exited apartment 2F, and she trudged the two floor up to her apartment. She turned the knob on the front door, but the slip chain in place impeded her entrance.

Johnny, who was the best man at both weddings, peeked through the crack in the door. He spotted his wife and said, "We don't want whatever you're selling."

Then, he shut the door and locked it from the inside.

With the palm of her hand, Rita banged on the door hard, twice.

Then, she said, "Let me the frig in before I kick this door off its hinges."

"What will you give me to open the door?" Johnny said.

"It's what I won't give you," Rita said. "*Now open the goddamn door!* I need to put on my makeup. Downstairs, I don't have room to scratch my behind."

Johnny said, "With the size of your behind, you'd need the Grand Canyon anyway."

Johnny opened the door, fully expecting a right cross to the jaw. But Rita just barged inside and passed her husband like he was a ghost. She spotted Joe struggling to pull his pants all the way up. She also spotted red material behind Joe's open zipper.

"You jerk," Rita said. "You still have your red bathing suit on that you wore at Coney Island this morning."

"Red bathing suit?" Joe said. "Shit. I must have put it back on instead of my skivvies after I took a shower."

Hearing a scream from Dom in the bathroom, they rushed to the bathroom, and they spotted Dom with his shirt over his belt and his zipper halfway open. The reason his zipper wouldn't close was because the flesh of his uncircumcised penis was stuck in the teeth of the zipper.

Dom's face looked as red as Joe's bathing suit.

Johnny and Joe froze in a mix of shock and horror. But Rita was not so squeamish.

"Get me the butter from the refrigerator," she told her husband.

Johnny did as she requested, and after he handed the butter to his wife, he grabbed her wrist, and said, "You're not going to do what I think you're going to do, are you?"

"Of course, that's what I'm going to do," Rita said. "You guys don't have the balls to do it, and Dom is getting married in less than an hour. He can't walk into church the way he looks now."

Both Johnny and Joe watched in horror as Rita knelt down in front of Dom, whose face had now turned from a bright red to a dark purple.

"Don't move, kiddo," Rita said to Dom. "One wrong move and your honeymoon goes out the window."

Rita moistened the stick of butter with her tongue. Then, she smeared the butter on her right forefinger and applied it, up and down, to Dom's zipper, while holding Dom's flaccid penis in her other hand, away from the zipper.

Ever so gently, Rita pulled the zipper up while pulling Dom's penis in the opposite direction. In seconds. Dom's ordeal was over, and his penis was only slightly damaged in the process.

Rita stood, and she said to Joe and Dom, "You grooms aren't nervous, are you? One guy wants to get married in his red bathing suit, and the other almost castrates himself. I'm going back downstairs. It's crazy down there, but not as crazy as this looney bin."

At ten minutes to five, Dom spotted two black limousines pulling up to the curb in front of 104 Bayard Street. Dom turned to the Italiano brothers and said, "Our ride's here. We gotta move."

Joe turned to Johnny and said, "You've got the rings, right?"

Johnny looked at Joe like Joe had a third eye in the middle of his forehead.

"What rings? I don't have any rings," Johnny said. "The last I remember, Rita had them yesterday."

The three men raced out of the apartment and sped down the steps to the second floor. They spotted Rita standing outside of apartment 2F with the two wedding rings in her right hand.

"Forget something, fellas?" Rita said. She handed the rings to her husband. "You guys are worse than the Three Stooges."

Johnny grabbed the rings, kissed his wife's cheek, and followed Joe and Dom down the steps. They got into one black limo, and after that limo was safely out of sight, Rita, Nancy, and Mary exited apartment 2F and took the other limo to Transfiguration Church on 29 Mott Street, one block east and one block south of 104 Bayard Street.

The double-wedding went smoothly.

Well, Almost.

While the two brides were heading down the aisle to organ music, accompanied by Pete Romano, Johnny burst out laughing. Pete Romano's tuxedo jacket was open, as were two buttons on his shirt, exposing his ample belly.

Johnny turned to Joe, and said, "Pete looks like Fat Stuff in the Smilin' Jack comics."

Father McLaughlin, the church's pastor, did not take kindly to Johnny's blasphemous departure from church decorum.

The priest bellowed, loud enough to be heard over the organ music all the way to the back of the church, "*DON'T YOU REALIZE YOU ARE IN THE HOUSE OF GOD*?"

All eyes in the church were riveted on Johnny, whose face was red from his uncontrollable fit of the giggles. But as soon as Johnny spotted Rita shooting him the evil eye, his sniggering suddenly stopped.

Father McLaughlin turned to Johnny, and while fanning the air with the sign of the cross, the priest said, "May God forgive him."

At precisely 5:30 pm, Father McLaughlin pronounced Joe and Nancy Italiano, and Dom and Mary Russo as husbands and wives.

Finally.

Chapter Twenty-Eight

More than five hundred people were jammed into the Jade Manor Catering Hall in Bensonhurst, Brooklyn. The reason for the wedding reception relocating to Brooklyn, and not Manhattan, was because Pete Romano owned a piece of the place.

The guest list for the double-wedding reception looked like "Who's Who in the Mafia." The big-shot racketeers who were unable to attend sent underlings with fat envelopes containing cash to give to the newlyweds.

Contrary to his doctor's orders, Pete Romano consumed an enormous amount of alcohol at the reception; enough to get two men drunk. During his customary visit to each of the fifty tables, Pete refilled his glass with whatever sort of booze he could get his hands on. Then, he toasted the bride and groom, saying, "Today I get drunk. Tomorrow I rest in bed. Salute! I thank each and every one of you for coming here to honor my lovely daughter and her handsome husband. And may God bless all of you."

Conversely, Carlo Russo spent the entire reception in a sour mood. It was his brother Dom's wedding, and his brother had disgraced him in front of the top mobsters in New York City by allowing Pete Romano pick up the entire tab.

Carlo even overheard one drunken mobster say to another, "Carlo must be a brokester to let Pete pay for everything. I'm surprised he even showed up, the cheap bastard."

Even worse, Dom had picked Johnny to be his best man instead of Carlo. That would mean, according to Italian custom, that Johnny would be the Godfather to Dom's first-born child. Dom did ask Carlo to be an usher in his wedding party, but Carlo refused. If Carlo couldn't be Dom's best man, anything less prestigious would amount to a double insult. Carlo had seriously considered not attending the wedding at all, but harsh warning words from Pete Romano convinced Carlo such actions would be hazardous to his health.

Carlo swore that the time would come when he would settle the score with everyone who had insulted him. Carlo also vowed that the time for the score-settling would come sooner rather than later.

The voluptuous Marilyn had accompanied Carlo to the wedding. But the dress she had poured herself into looked more suitable for the chorus line at the Copacabana. The black low-cut number Marilyn wore was so tight it increased the blood pressure of every red-blooded male in the joint and a few female switch-hitters, too. Marilyn had big breasts, to begin with. But this particular dress compressed against her boobs, making her cherry-sized nipples look like two derringers ready to explode.

To add insult to insult, Carlo sat in the back of the ballroom at a table of ten, six of whom he hated with a passion. If it were Yankees Stadium, his seat would have been in the far reaches of the Bleachers. Only Butch Salerno, accompanied by a mousy girl fifteen years his junior, said a word to Carlo all during the reception; that is until all hell broke loose.

It started when Pete Prelli, a competing neighborhood bookie and more than a little drunk, wrapped his arm around the back of Marilyn's chair.

"Hey, you!" Carlo screamed at him. "Get your arm off the back of my girl's chair. Who the hell do you think you are? Rudolph Valentino?"

"I was just talking to the lady," Prelli said. "What's the big deal?

Even Butch Salerno had to smile. Calling Marilyn a lady was like calling Bluebeard a gentleman.

Mona Prelli, Pete Prelli's wife, added fuel to the fire when she said to Carlo, "Leave my husband alone. He ain't doing nothing anyway. I got my eyes on him." She jumped to her feet, put her face inches from Carlo's and said, "If it don't bother me, why should it bother you?"

As blood bulged the veins in Carlo's neck, he stood and said to Mona, "Because you're a putana, that's why!"

Mona Prelli hurled her vodka martini, glass and all, into Carlo's face.

Marilyn got into the act by emptying her Manhattan onto Mona's borrowed wig.

Before any of the men could move, Mona got Marilyn in a headlock, squeezing her head so tight in her arm that Marilyn's makeup, including her lipstick, smeared all across her face and onto Mona's arm.

While the two females engaged in a wrestling match more suited for Madison Square Garden, Carlo's two hands engulfed Pete Prelli's neck, forcing Pete to emit short choking sounds.

The melee did not go unnoticed from the dais.

Dom, spotting the commotion, dashed from the dais and headed towards the scuffle, thinking, "Carlo's got no right to make a scene at my wedding. Brother or no brother, this is the last time Carlo will ever make a fool out of me."

But before Dom got there, Butch had broken things up, and Carlo was headed to the men's room to clean up, with Dom in hot pursuit.

Joe, sitting at Pete Romano's table with Nancy, spotted Dom rushing towards the men's room. He jumped up, and Nancy grabbed his arm.

"Don't get involved," Nancy said.

But Joe just ignored her, and he rushed towards the men's room.

Inside the men's room, Carlo was stooped over the sink washing the liquor stains from his black shark-skin suit, with Butch standing next to him like the trusty bodyguard he was. Dom surged inside, and without saying a word, he spun his brother around and slapped him, hard, across the face. Butch just froze, startled and surprised by the usually-timid Dom Russo's actions.

Fury creased Carlo's face. He quickly pulled out the .38 caliber revolver he carried in a sling under his left armpit. But before he could pull the trigger, Joe barged into the bathroom. He lunged into Carlo like a linebacker sacking the quarterback, and the gun slid across the marble floor.

Dom bent down to retrieve the pistol, but before he could grab it, Butch nailed him with a wicked chopping right cross off the side of his jaw. Gore spurted from Dom's mouth and all over his white tuxedo. He fell face-down to the floor, out cold.

Now, it was two against one, but Joe still liked the odds.

As Carlo reached down to retrieve his rod, Joe unleashed a left hook into Carlo's kidneys. Carlo groaned like a wounded animal, and Joe finished the job with a right cross to Carlo's jaw, depositing him onto his back.

From the corner of his eye, Joe spotted Butch launching a dangerous right of his own. Joe ducked the blow, and then he fired a right uppercut into Butch's belly. As Butch held his gut in agony, Joe put out his lights with a left hook to the jaw.

Behind Joe's back, Carlo crawled on all fours towards the gun. Carlo's hand had barely touched the handle when Johnny Italiano raced into the bathroom. He kicked Carlo in the right temple. Carlo fell backwards, and he hit his head on the marble floor.

The ref could have counted to a hundred.

The men's room now resembled the Roman Coliseum after the lions had battled the Christians. Blood was splattered all across the mirrors, the floors, and the urinals. As Johnny contemplated what to do next, Joe sprinted from the men's room. He returned in seconds with a pitcher of water he had grabbed off a back table. He bent down, lifted Dom's head off the floor, and he slowly poured the contents of the pitcher over his new brother-in-law's face.

Revived somewhat, Dom whimpered softly.

Johnny decided to use more primitive methods to revive the other two goons.

By the back of their collars, he dragged Carlo and Butch, one at a time, and deposited them in neighboring bathroom stalls. Then, one at a time, he shoved their heads into the bowls. Four flushes revived Butch, but it took six flushes to return Carlo to consciousness.

Within seconds, people of both sexes had crammed into the men's room. Mary bent over Dom, and she sobbed softly as she cradles her husband's head in her arms. Tears dripped down the sides of both their faces.

"From now on I have no brother," Dom told Mary. "You and your people are my only family."

Pete Romano entered the men's room last. He noticed that Dom's face looked like it had been hit by a Mack truck.

"What's going on here?" Pete said, in a voice slurred by too much wine.

Pete spotted Carlo Russo staggering out of a bathroom stall.

"Hey you, disgraziato! Did you start this trouble?" Pete said to Carlo.

Carlo lowered his head, but he did not say a word.

Pete backhanded Carlo across the face. Then, he smacked him again, this time with an open hand. Carlo sank to one knee, and Pete buried his right knee into Carlo's chin. Then, Pete grabbed Carlo by the hair and flung him towards the bathroom door.

"Now, get out of here," Pete said. "And don't let me see your face again in the neighborhood until I send for you. If I see you before then, you're a dead man. Capisce?"

Carlo staggered towards the bathroom door. Joe held it open for him, and for an instant, their eyes met. Extreme hate flashed back and forth.

Pete turned to Butch Salerno, who had just emerged from the bathroom stall, and said, "From now on, you work for me. Now, go home and stay there. I'll call for you in a couple of days."

Butch nodded in the affirmative. Then, he, too, exited the men's room.

In seconds, the bathroom had emptied, and the party continued in the main ballroom. While the band played "Begin the Beguine," Pete asked the bandleader for the microphone.

"Everyone, please stay and have a good time," Pete said into the mic. "The night is still young, and the trouble is gone for good. Please stay and enjoy my daughter's wedding."

The celebration continued until the wee hours of the morning. And no one who had attended would ever forget the double-wedding or the horrible tragedy that ensued.

Chapter Twenty-Nine

At six a.m., the remaining guests exited the Jade Manor, and most of them were not able to walk a straight line. It was a good thing that certain woman had abstained from drinking and could still drive un-intoxicated. Otherwise, they would have, most surely, had to call a bus to take them all home.

After serving the partygoers a breakfast consisting of Eggs Benedict and assorted Italian pastries, the Maître D stood at the door and gave each of the departing guests a copy of the Sunday Edition of the *New York Daily News*.

As the final revelers staggered into the nearly-empty parking lot, Pete Romano brought up the rear, accompanied by his daughter Nancy and her new husband, Joe Italiano. Joe put his arm around Pete's shoulder, which helped keep Pete upright. Dom, Mary, Rita, and Johnny snuggled into the back seat of the stretch limo, followed by Nancy and Joe, who sat facing them in the jump seats.

Pete Romano startled everyone when he opened the driver's door and ordered the chauffeur to vacate the limo.

"Here's the keys to the Red Buick behind us," Pete told the chauffeur. "I'm driving the limo; you take my Buick back to the city.

I'll meet you at the corner of Bayard and Mulberry in about an hour. And I'll give you a big tip for your troubles."

"Dad, are you crazy?" Nancy yelled from the back seat. "You've had too much to drink. Sit in the front seat next to the driver. You can pick up your car tomorrow."

"Come on. Let me enjoy myself a bit," Pete said. "I'm dropping you all off at the Plaza Hotel, where I reserved three rooms for two nights. I took care of the bill, and Monday morning a limo will pick you all up and drive you to the airport for a trip to Las Vegas for a week. You're compted for everything. They'll even be three grand in cash waiting for you in Vegas for you to gamble."

Pete snatched the hat off the limo driver's head, and said, "How am I going to drive this limo without wearing a hat? That would be un-American. Communist even."

With no one in the limo having the guts to countermand Pete's order, he started the limo, and minutes later, he glided it onto the Belt Parkway heading back to New York City.

As the early morning sun peeked through the horizon, the nearly-deserted Belt Parkway's roadway was streaked with yellow and orange beams of light. Pete's red Buick had already sped past them, and Pete, sticking to the speed limit, never noticed the White Cadillac that was following them from the moment they had left the Jade Manor.

Pete was too busy serenading his passengers with bastardizations of his favorite Italian songs.

Pete sang, a little too loud, "O sole mio. O ravioli..."

Nancy had her hands over her ears in the back seat.

"Hey, Dad. Cut it out!" she said. "You're killing my ears."

Pete continued. "Return to Sorrento...la-la-da-da-de-dum..."

"Oh, frig it," Nancy said.

The black limo weaved a crooked line in the middle lane, while the white Caddy maintained its speed about 100 feet back.

Suddenly, the white Caddy accelerated, until it was about 10 feet in back of the limo. Then, the Caddy started flashing its high beams off and on.

Pete waved his left arm out the open window, and yelled, "Come on. Pass me up!"

Joe peered out the back window, trying to decipher the inhabitants of the Caddy. Suddenly, a cold chill ran down Joe's spine. He leaned forward and whispered to his brother, "I think that's Carlo following us. He drives a white Caddy."

Johnny nodded in a semi-inebriated stupor.

Finally, the white Caddy swerved into the left lane and picked up speed.

"It's about time," Pete Romano said.

As the white Caddy eased up alongside the limo, it suddenly swerved to the right forcing Pete into the right lane and then off onto the shoulder of the road.

As the muscles tensed in the back of his neck, Joe yelled, "Pete, watch yourself. It's Carlo and Butch."

As Pete glanced quickly to his left, pain shot through his upper torso. As he grabbed at his chest, Pete let out a soft moan. With his left hand on his chest and his right hand on the wheel, Pete guided the limo to a stop onto the grassy knoll on the shoulder of the road.

The white Caddy screamed to a halt about thirty feet in front of the limo. Carlo and Butch emerged and sprinted towards the limo, guns blazing.

Johnny Italiano sprung from the limo first and was met by searing hot lead. The first bullet caught him in the right shoulder. The second hit him right in the heart, and he was dead before he fell face-first onto the grass.

Joe jumped out of the limo next. Butch Salerno fired twice, and both bullets buried into Joe's stomach. He crumbled to the ground and onto his back, clutching his belly.

Nancy rushed out of the limo and knelt by her husband, cradling his head. Joe's blood drenched her white wedding dress.

"*You son of a bitch!*" she screamed at Carlo.

Carlo smiled and calmly fired two bullets into Nancy's right breast. She fell on top of her husband, and neither moved.

Dom crawled out of the rear driver's door. On his knees, he opened the front door of the limo. The now-deceased Pete slumped out of the car; his right hand still clutching the steering wheel.

Dom reached inside Pete's tuxedo jacket searching for Pete's gun. Finally, Dom fingered the cold steel, but before he could remove the gun, Carlo killed him with two bullets into the back of his skull.

Then, Carlo aimed into the back seat at Rita and Mary, and he pulled the trigger, twice. But all he heard was two hard clicks.

Carlo heard a siren blare in the distance. He growled like an angry bear, and then he kicked his dead brother twice in the ribs.

Carlo and Butch dashed to the white Caddy. They got inside, and the white Caddy sped off into the dawn.

A police car ground to a halt behind the limo, and Police Officer Sparrow, his gun drawn, burst from the police car in a crouch.

Rita staggered out of the limo, dragging Mary by the hand behind her. As Mary bent over Dom, she cried hysterically. She pulled his head to her chest, and the screams became muffled.

One by one, Officer Sparrow search for heartbeats in each of the four men, but he could not find any.

Rita knelt beside Nancy and Joe's bodies. She placed her face onto Nancy's back, sobbing softly.

Officer Sparrow put his hand on Rita's shoulder and said, "Do you know who did this?"

Rita shook her head and said, "Two men. But I never saw them before."

"Can you give me a description of the two men involved?"

"No. It was too dark. It happened so fast."

The first ambulance arrived ten minutes later. Then, two more.

When the sun shined a few minutes later, only the pools of red blood soaking the wet grass gave evidence to the terrible carnage that had occurred.

Chapter Thirty

Johnny Russo 1984

Growing up on Mulberry Street was no walk in the park. For Johnny Russo, it was tougher than for most.

His father Dominick Russo had died before Johnny was born. His mother, the former Mary Italiano, passed away when Johnny was in knee pants. So, Johnny's Aunt Rita, the wife of the tragic heavyweight champion of the world, Johnny Italiano, inherited the burden of Johnny's upbringing.

Aunt Rita, always vague when discussing her dead relatives, had told Johnny many times since he was a kid, "Stay away from your Uncle Carlo and his son, Vinny. They're bad people. If you bother with them, you either wind up dead or in jail."

Bad People? How could that be?

Uncle Carlo wore huge diamond rings, and everyone bowed down to him like he was a King. Uncle Carlo was a man of respect, and as his nephew, everyone treated Johnny with that same respect, too.

What did aunt Rita know? She was just an old woman; a second-class citizen on Mulberry Street. It was ingrained in Johnny by his Uncle Carlo that woman existed only to cook, clean, and satisfy their husband's sexual needs. Johnny felt that Aunt Rita only spoke badly of Uncle Carlo because he was a man; envied and respected by other men.

When he was only twelve-years-old, Johnny started running errands for his Uncle Carlo. That was Johnny's first mistake.

"Hey, Johnny Boy," Uncle Carlo would say. "Do me a favor. Bring this package to Harlem for me."

Uncle Carlo would give Johnny the address, cab fare for the trip and back, plus another hundred bucks when Johnny returned home, and the project was completed.

Johnny was unaware that the package he was carrying contained heroin. But who cared anyway? Some married men in the neighborhood didn't make that much money in a hard-working week.

Every five years, or so, the New York City Police Department, usually under a newly-elected mayor, decides to get tough on illegal gambling. When that happens, the bosses like Carlo make sure the small-time bookies take the fall. Out of the goodness of his heart, Carlo would pay the sucker's legal fees and donate a few bucks a week to the poor sap's family. When the dupe finally got out of prison, he was fortunate enough to get his old job back. That is until the NYPD got ambitious again.

After a brilliant amateur boxing career and ten straight wins as a pro, Johnny spent two years at Riker's Island after being convicted on a bookmaking charge. Uncle Carlo paid for Johnny's lawyer, and the state of New York provided free room and board.

The first commandment in the Mulberry Street jungle is that shit flows downhill, and woe to the jerks at the bottom.

In prison, Johnny had plenty of time to ponder his future. Finally realizing his Aunt Rita was right, Johnny understood that working for his Uncle Carlo was a losing proposition. Johnny hit the weights every day, toning his body for his return to the fight game after he was released from the can. Driving a limo would pay the bills until his boxing career took off like his Uncle Johnny's had more than 25 years earlier. Fighting was in Johnny's genes, and not being a world champion was not an option.

Uncle Carlo was not too happy with the change in Johnny's career choice.

"Why do you want to be a flunky?" Uncle Carlo said. "You like opening doors for people? You enjoy some drunken bum puking in the back seat of your limo? You are my nephew. What you are doing is a disgrace to the family name. I demand your loyalty. Come back and work for me, and I'll make sure you'll never go behind bars again. You broke your cherry by going to prison. Just stick with your Uncle Carlo, and I'll make you a rich man."

Johnny told him. "Uncle Carlo, I don't mean any disrespect, but I have to run my own life. I want to be champion someday, and I don't want to do anything that might put me back in prison. Please, give me your blessing."

"I'll give you nothing," Carlo said. "I won't stop you, but don't expect any help from me ever again. You made your bed, now sleep in it. Imagine, my nephew the flunky. What a fucking disgrace."

Aunt Rita wholeheartedly agreed with Johnny's change of direction.

"Fuck Carlo Russo," she told her nephew.

Johnny sat in Benny Bastone's office at Prestige Limousine, and he pondered the events of the previous night when he took one ride too many.

After what he considered a full day's work, Johnny's sleek black limo had glided on the Belt Parkway headed towards the Brooklyn Battery Tunnel. The glare from the early evening summer sun had forced Johnny to lower his sun visor. Johnny had been so busy with work the previous two days he never had the chance to phone his girlfriend Linda. Johnny decided to give her a ring when he was safely back in his Mulberry Street apartment.

One hundred yards from the Brooklyn Battery Tunnel, Benny's voice had screeched through Johnny's two-way radio, "Hey, Johnny Boy. Do you read me?"

"Yes, Benny I read you," Johnny said. "What do you want? I took that Mrs. Banks ride at seven this morning, and I'm exhausted."

"Listen, I need a solid from you," Benny said. "I have that beautiful chick that Mario had last week, and I have no one to take the ride."

"How long does she want the limo for?" Johnny said. "I'm really bushed. It's been a long day."

"Johnny, the ride came in 'as directed,'" Benny said. "That could mean one hour, and it could mean all night long. You know how it goes."

"No way can I last all night long," Johnny said. "I'm ready to fall asleep as it is."

"Look, Johnny, I'll make a deal with you," Benny said. "If this broad keeps you out past midnight, you won't have to report to work until six tomorrow evening. I'll even give you the entire day off if that's what you want. But this girl is with lots of important people who give us loads of business. We can't refuse this job. It will be bad for business, and that affects us all. Business is bad as it is. I might even have to lay off some drivers if this lull continues."

Johnny knew what Benny was implying, and he knew Benny was right: business was terrible. If Johnny lost this job, he would be without a steady income as he proceeded on his boxing career. He might even have to go back to work for his Uncle Carlo; perish the thought.

"Okay Benny, I'll do the dirty deed," Johnny said. "I need the cash anyway to buy an engagement ring for my girl, Linda."

"Thanks, kid," Benny said. "Maybe, if this broad makes a long stop somewhere, you can get some shuteye in the limo."

Johnny paid the toll. Then, he drove past the toll booth and pulled over to the shoulder of the road. He grabbed a pen and paper and said to Benny, "Okay, shoot. What's her name, and where's the pickup?"

"Thanks, Johnny, you're a real gem," Benny said. "Her name is Diane Hamilton. She's at the Beverly Tavern on Lexington Avenue between 39th and 40th Streets. I'll call her there, and let her know you're on the way."

"Ok, I should be there in half an hour," Johnny said. "It's according to the midtown traffic."

"Great kid," Benny said. "And to show my appreciation, I'll even put in a chit for you to pay for dinner for you and your girl for whenever."

"Yeah, that could be in a week or in a month the way I'm going," Johnny said.

"Don't worry," Benny said. "I'll make it an open-ended chit with no expiration date."

Johnny smiled, and said, "You know Benny, you ain't such a bad guy. No matter what everyone says about you."

Chapter Thirty-One

After Johnny's limo had exited the Brooklyn Battery Tunnel, a severe New York City-traffic jam cracked him right in the face. After fighting cabs, trucks, and nutty drivers for 45 minutes, Johnny double-parked the limo in front of the Beverly Bar on Lexington Avenue, just south of 40th Street.

Johnny read the neon sign on the front bay window before he entered that said: ***Drinks half-price for ladies from 5 pm until closing.***

Johnny didn't know the Beverly Bar from a crowbar, but he had a funny feeling this joint was a hangout for hookers.

Johnny slipped into the dimly-lit pub, and he peered into the darkness trying to decipher the situation. After his eyes adjusted to the lack of light, he spotted creatures of the female species slithering from bar stool to bar stool trying to drum up action from well-dressed and mostly-inebriated rubes. Johnny knew full well how these low-class cocktail lounges operated.

The scam was this: The hookers were on establishment's pad, and their job was to entice the male customers into buying them drinks. When they girls ordered champagne, it was usually ginger ale poured from champagne bottles. Single malt scotch could be celery soda, or any number of other non-alcoholic beverages;

the same with any top-end cognac. But the customers paid upwards of ten bucks, and sometimes twenty bucks, for a drink not even worth a dime. Every time a girl conned a mark into buying her a drink, the bartender handed her a poker chip worth two bucks. At closing time, the girls cashed in their chips and walked out with a nice piece of change.

Sometimes these slinky dames even left before closing time, accompanied by one of the drunken male fools, whom they would charge as much as $200 for a quick roll in the hay in a sleazy hotel, or as much as fifty dollars for a blowjob in the front or back seat of a car. The bartender took note of who left and with whom, and the following day, the girls had to kick back 50% of their night's take to the bosses. They were, of course, on the honor system as to how much they had made the previous night. And the girls knew if they ever were caught shorting the boss, usually a made-guy from Little Italy, Greenwich Village, Italian Harlem, or the Italian sections of Brooklyn, they would either be roughed up, put in the hospital, and in extreme cases, deposited right into the morgue.

To stay in the game, and to keep healthy, most of the hookers toed a straight line with the Mafia.

Johnny scanned the room which consisted of a long mahogany bar that extended on the left-hand side of the long narrow establishment. On the right, a row of booths disappeared into the darkness. And on the jukebox, Frank Sinatra said there used to be a ballpark here.

Johnny counted ten people sitting at the bar; five sluts attending to five suckers. Judging by the scowl on his face, the bartender looked like he just had spent ten years in Sing Sing. As he tried to look busy, his bald head glistened in the dim red Tiffany light fixture that dangled from a chain attached to the ceiling.

Johnny bellied up to the bar and waved at the bartender, who looked like he was annoyed a being interrupted from basically doing nothing.

"I'm looking for a Diane Hamilton," Johnny said. "She called for a limo."

The bartender yelled toward the back of the room, "Hey, Diane. Your ride is here."

A tall, leggy woman, wearing a black velvet V-neck dress that ended three inches above her knee, emerged from the darkness in the back. Black mess stockings encased her lusciously long legs. Her breasts tilted up like they were the front bumper of a 1958 Buick, and a cigarette dangled from her sensuous lips like Lauren Bacall in "To Have and Have Not." As she sashayed closer, Johnny decided that Diane Hamilton was, indeed, not a bad-looking broad, but not in the same class as his girlfriend, Linda.

When they were face to face, Diane eyed Johnny up and down like she was examining a side of beef. Then, she smiled, and said, "So, you're my driver for the night. What a big improvement! The last driver they sent me looked like a refugee from a bocce court. His body stunk of garlic, and when he opened his half-toothless mouth, I smelled death."

Johnny detected a slight accent, but he couldn't discern the origin. Diane Hamilton could be anything from a classy French dame to a Puerto Rican prostitute.

"Are you ready to leave?" Johnny said. "Or should I wait in the limo?"

"No, I'm ready to blow this popsicle stand," she said.

She snatched the cigarette from her mouth, flung it to the ground, and stomped on it with a twist of her foot.

She turned to the bartender and said, "Hey, Joe. Put what I owe you on my tab. I'll settle up later." She handed him a twenty and said, "This is for your troubles."

Diane led the way out the front door, and Johnny wearily followed.

Johnny opened the back door of the limo for Diane to slip inside. And when she did, she exposed just enough leg to get Johnny's attention. As soon, as Johnny hit the ignition, Diane leaned forward and said, "Take Park Avenue uptown. I know a great Indian restaurant. I just love Indian food. Don't you?"

Without taking his eyes off the road, Johnny said, "To tell the truth, I never tried it."

"The restaurant is on the right side of Park Avenue; just past 63rd Street," she said. "It's called 'The Far East.'"

Johnny eased the limo in front of a hydrant 30 feet past the entrance canopy of "The Far East." He got out of the limo, walked to the back passenger door and opened it. Diane slid out of the limo, and her eyes met Johnny's.

She said, "I hate eating alone. Why don't you join me?"

Normally, Johnny would have rejected the offer. From experience, he knew all too well that it was not a good idea for a chauffeur to get too chummy with the customers. All kinds of situations could arise, and most of them were bad. But Johnny was starving from being on the Mrs. Banks' ride all day long without eating a decent meal. So, he reluctantly accepted the offer.

As Diane waited by the front entrance, Johnny backed the limo directly in front of the restaurant. He exited the limo, and he handed the doorman the keys, wrapped in a ten-dollar bill.

"Take care of this for me, okay Buddy," Johnny said.

The doorman palmed the ten-spot and nodded in the affirmative.

Johnny followed Diane into "The Far East." Fighting hard not to, Johnny's eyes became glued to her shapely rear end and her knockout pair of legs.

Something told Johnny Russo he was making a terrible mistake. But one more glance at Diane Hamilton's rear end and that feeling suddenly disappeared.

Chapter Thirty-Two

A tall, gangly Sikh wearing a white turban and sporting the nose of an eagle greeted Diane Hamilton at the front door of "The Far East." His cheerless eyes seemed to be set three feet back into his head, and his hooked jaw was thrust out almost as far as his nose. But his most distinguishing facial feature was his piano-key-sized pearly white teeth, complete with razor-sharp incisors.

"Table for two?" the Sikh said.

"Yes, Omar," Dane said. Her voice was somber like she was ordering a casket in a funeral home. She pointed to the back of the dimly-lit restaurant and said, "I'd like the table in the far right corner. And send the tarot card reader over at once."

With Johnny following, Omar led Diane to a large round table covered by a beige embroidered tablecloth. A gold candelabrum, containing four low-lit candles, stood in the center of the table. The table was set for four, and Omar removed two settings.

Johnny noticed that only one other table in the restaurant was occupied, which he felt was odd at this time of the evening.

After Johnny and Diane were seated, Omar said, "Shall I get you a cocktail, Madam?"

"Bombay Safire Martini on the rocks," Diane said. "And make it extra dry."

"I'll have a diet coke," Johnny said.

A few minutes later, a waif-like woman, dressed in what looked like a dirty tablecloth, arrived with the drinks. A purple veil covered the bottom of her face, and her beady eyes shifted from right to left and then from right to left, like Groucho Marks, as she set the drinks down on the table.

Then, she bowed and departed.

Johnny picked up his glass and said, "Here's luck."

Diane did the same, and as they clinked glasses, she said, "Luck's overrated. Give me the big bucks instead."

Seconds later, the tiny lady with the purple veil and shifty eyes returned. She sat at the table and produced a standard deck of cards.

She stared directly into Diane's eyes and said, "At your service, Madam. My name is Sasha. Omar said you wanted a card reading. Or would you prefer I read your palm?"

"A card reading will be fine," Diane said.

Diane gulped her drink down like it was tap water, and then she said to Sasha, "And another martini. And this time make it a double in a tall glass."

"For you, or for the gentleman? Or for both?" Sasha said.

Johnny let out a short chuckle, and said, "No Martini for me. I'll just have another diet coke."

Johnny glanced at Diane, and her face was still set in stone.

Sasha stood and snapped her fingers at a waiter standing on the opposite side of the room. Then, she shrieked in a voice a little too loud for Johnny's liking, "Double Bombay Safire martini in a tall glass for the lady! And another Diet Coke!"

Johnny couldn't put his finger on it, but something about this strange kabuki wasn't exactly kosher. Unfortunate, his hunger overruled his usual common sense.

Sasha produced a deck of cards. She spread the cards face down on the table in front of Diane, and said, "Please pick 13 cards from the deck at random."

Diane glared intently at the cards. She reached for a card, then quickly pulled back her hand. Then, she extended her hand a second time and removed 13 cards, one at a time, slow and agonizing, like she was plucking the toenails off her toes.

Sasha turned the cards Diane had selected face-up in the shape of a fan. Then, she stared through the cards like she had x-ray vision. She shook her head side-to-side several times, and her face looked deeply troubled.

She said to Diane, "Are you positive you want me to read these cards? They are very tired cards. They have already been used five times today. I cannot guarantee the reading. Shall I try a new deck, perhaps?"

"No, these cards are fine," Diane said. "I see the Queen of Clubs as the first card on the left. Is that my client card?"

"Yes."

"Then, proceed with the reading."

"As you wish," Sasha said.

Four jacks stood next to the Queen of Clubs, followed by the ten, nine, eight, and seven of spades. The three other sevens lay next. The last card on the right was the King of Diamonds.

Sasha continued her reading: "As you said, the Queen of Clubs is your client card. It represents you: a dark-haired lady. The four jacks next to the Queen of Clubs can mean two things. It can mean huge amounts of success, or it can mean you are about to quarrel with someone. Shall I proceed?"

A waiter placed Diane's double martini and Johnny's diet coke on the table. Diane took a slow sip of the martini, but her eyes never left the cards.

"Please continue," Diane said.

As his empty stomach grumbled, Johnny squirmed in his seat. He thought this might be a great time to visit the men's room, but he decided to stay and witness this weird scene to the end.

Sasha continued: "The ten, nine, eight, and seven of spades can only mean one thing: you are headed for unpleasant times. You will have much sorrow, failure, and misfortune. The King of Diamonds means a man of great power will be involved."

Johnny took a sideways glance at Diane's face. She looked horrified, and he figured the chances of him enjoying a much-needed meal was now going slowly down the drain.

He tried to lighten the situation by saying, "Hey, Sasha. Now, what about the bad news you were talking about?"

Johnny wore a big smile on his face. But after looking at the faces of the two woman seated at the table, he knew his little joke had fallen like a lead balloon.

Diane took her wallet out of her purse. She dug out a fifty-dollar bill and handed it to Sasha.

"Please tell the waiter to bring the check," she told Sasha. "I suddenly lost my appetite."

Sasha stood up and bowed to Diane. Then, she disappeared into the darkness at the back of the restaurant.

Johnny shrugged, then he said to Diane "What a depressing place. How about I take you to Chinatown for some Chinks?"

"Eat Chinks? I'm not a cannibal," Diane said.

"No. I meant for some Chinese food," Johnny said, "That's the way we talk in Little Italy."

The waiter returned and handed Diane the check. She handed him a fifty-dollar bill and said, "Keep the change."

Johnny figured the way Diane was flipping around fifties, at least he would get a good tip at the end of the night.

Diane stood, and Johnny did the same.

"I'm going to the ladies' room," she said. "Wait for me outside."

As Johnny exited The Far East, a light sprinkle started to fall. He took his car keys from the doorman, opened the trunk of the limo, and removed a large black umbrella.

He met Diane at the door, and as they strode to the limo, he held the opened umbrella over her head to block the rain. Johnny opened the back seat door, and Diane said, "I rather sit in the front seat with you. Is that alright?"

Johnny hesitated, and then he said, "It's not customary, But sure, why not?"

He opened the front passenger door, and Diane slipped inside. Johnny closed the door behind her.

Johnny walked around to the driver's side. The doorman opened the car door for him, and said, "Have fun."

'Have fun?" Johnny whispered to him. "I just want to get something to eat."

As Johnny guided the limo up Park Avenue, Diane placed her left hand on his right knee, and said, "Head towards Central Park. I love driving through the park at night."

Johnny made a left on 79th Street, and at Fifth Avenue, he drove into Central Park and headed north.

As Johnny drove with an impassive look on his face, Diane flipped on the car radio and searched for music to suit her mood. Finally, she located a station playing a soft melody. Then, she slid her left hand up Johnny's thigh, stopping when she reached his manhood.

"Pull over to the side of the road," Diane said. "I have some dynamite blow that'll make you hard in seconds."

Johnny did what she said and then he said, "Listen, lady. I have a girlfriend, and in fact, we're getting engaged. So, I think you should get into the back seat and tell me where to take you."

"Okay, if that's the way you want to play it," Diane said.

She was not smiling.

Diane stormed out of the front seat of the limo and slid into the back seat.

"Take me to Caruso's on West 44th Street," she said. "And make it snappy."

"Is that a final drop off?" Johnny said. "I've been on the road since early this morning."

"Too fucking bad," she said. "I'll tell you when I'm finished. You're just here to take me where I want to go. Now, shut the fuck up and drive."

Then, she lowered the limo's partition, cutting off Johnny before he could speak.

Johnny said to himself, "This broad a real wacko. I'd like to strangle Benny for conning me into taking this ride."

He continued driving through Central Park while keeping one eye on the back seat.

He didn't like what he was seeing.

Chapter Thirty-Three

Johnny stopped the limo in front of Caruso's, a dining and drinking establishment that catered to New York City's affluent theatre crowd.

Johnny got out of the limo and strolled over to the back seat passenger's door. He opened it, and Diane staggered out like she was drunk. Johnny knew the reason for that, since he clearly saw her snorting coke in the back seat, while intermittently swigging from a large flask of who-knows-what alcoholic beverage.

As Diane approached the entrance, she bumped into the doorman, who was dressed like a Royal Canadian Policeman waiting to be inspected. The doorman straightened his cap and cleared his throat. Then, he opened the front door for Diane to enter.

But before she made it inside, Johnny said to her, "How long will you be?"

Diane's dark eyes flashed. Then, she said, "You ask too many questions. Just be here when I come out."

As Johnny and the doorman just shook their heads, she tottered into Caruso's.

Once inside, Diane sashayed past the dining room towards the stairs in the back, which led to the second-floor bar. The place was packed, and Diane bellied up to the bar next to a well-dressed elderly gentleman who was half in-the-bag himself.

As she waited for the barrel-chested bartender to notice her, the elderly man eyed her up and down. He liked what he saw, and then he said, "Take my seat, honey. I don't mind standing."

Diane eyed him up and down, and she liked what *she* saw, too – MONEY.

"Don't mind if I do," Diane said.

Johnny sat quietly in the limo and silently cursed Benny. On the radio Lionel Richie was bellowing, "All Night Long...," and Johnny sincerely hoped Richie was not prophetic.

Twenty minutes later, as Johnny sat with his eyes closed, the doorman abruptly banged on the driver's side window.

Johnny lowered the window, and the doorman said, "You better get rid of that broad on the second-floor bar. She's causing a riot!"

As soon as Johnny entered the restaurant, he heard the commotion upstairs. It sounded like a jailhouse revolt. He rushed to the stairs in back, and he bounded up the steps two at a time. When he got to the bar, he spotted a crowd circling a fracas. But no one dared to intercede.

Inside the human circle, an elderly gent squatted on his haunches, while Diane rained smacks on his head with both hands. As he moaned and groaned, crimson trickled down both sides of the elderly man's panic-stricken face.

Finally, the bartender emerged from a back room. He busted through the human circle, and he grabbed Diane from behind by the waist. Then, he pulled her off the old man, while she screamed, *"Get your motherfucking hands off me, you big gorilla!"*

The bartender froze, and she yelled even louder, *"I'll call the cops and have all you degenerates arrested for rape!"*

The bartender backed off, and Johnny lifted Diane from under her armpits to her feet.

Diane spun around, and when she saw Johnny, her grimace turned into a big smile.

"Here's my buddy; here's pretty boy," she said.

She pointed to the elderly man who was now being helped to his feet by the bartender.

Diane said to no one in particular, "What do I need an old fuck like him for when I have a young stud like this waiting for me?"

An elderly woman, dressed in a mink and sprouting diamonds, climbed the steps to the bar and approached the elderly man. He told her, "I'm sorry dear. But I was just making conversation when she attacked me."

Diane snickered, "Is that your wife?"

The elderly lady said, "Yes, I'm his wife, and you've got some nerve putting your hands on my husband!"

Diane belched out a belly laugh, and, while pointing to his wife, she said to the elderly man, "See what you get for a hundred bucks, you cheap bastard!"

Diane picked up her purse by its strap and flung to over her shoulder.

"Come on, lover boy," she said to Johnny. "Let's blow this fag trap."

Diane marched down the steps on shaky legs, and Johnny followed.

Once outside, the doorman opened the back limo door for Diane, and she literally fell inside. Johnny started the limo, and he glanced into the back seat. Diane was sleeping like a baby, her long legs stretched out on the entire length of the black leather seats.

Johnny headed down Broadway, trying to figure out what to do next. If worse came to worse, he could always drive her to a police station and drop her off like the Pony Express dropped of mailbags during the Wild Wild West.

As Johnny made a left turn on Houston Street, Diane sprung to a sitting position, like a corpse in a casket suddenly coming to life.

She said in a slurry voice, "Take me to York Avenue and 61st Street. There a gambling joint there on the second floor."

"No, this night is *over*," Johnny said. "Tell me where you live, and I'll take you home."

He pulled over by a hydrant, and said, "Or you can get out right here. Take your pick."

Diane screamed, "I'll get you fired for this! I know your boss! When he finds out how you treated me, he'll fire your ass!"

"Listen, Diane," Johnny said. "What you need is a good night's sleep anyway. Let me take you home. Where do you live?"

"Fuck you! I want to go gambling. 61st and York. And make it snappy!"

Against his better judgement, Johnny made a U-turn on Houston Street and headed east. He figured the quickest way to York Avenue and 61st Street was to drive north on First Avenue to 59th Street, hang a right to York Avenue, and then make a left to 61st Street.

When he got to the Bowery, Johnny decided that the Fifth Precinct on Elizabeth just below Canal was much closer. No law that said a limousine driver had to put up with a loud, obnoxious broad with a penchant for violence. He decided the best thing to do was let the cops sort everything out. Besides, the Fifth was his home precinct, and he knew most of the cops. Maybe they'd cut him a break.

Just as Johnny turned south on the Bowery, Diane screamed, "Hey, jerkoff! You're going the wrong way!"

"No, I'm not," Johnny said. "I've had enough of your crap. I'm dropping you off with at the police station."

Diane pressed the button to lower the glass partition. Then, she sprang over the partition and clawed at Johnny's face. She barely missed gouging his eye.

Johnny leaned backwards and tried to push her onto the back seat. But she was too quick.

She bit down hard on his right hand. Then, she went for his face again.

Johnny jerked his head to the left, trying to avoid her sharp nails. She missed his face, but her hand raked across his neck, breaking his gold chain at the clasp.

The limo careened down the Bowery, and Johnny considered stopping the car and abandoning the limo with Diane Hamilton sitting in it.

Suddenly, he spotted a police car parked facing north on the Bowery. Two cops were sitting in it, and Johnny saw they were either sleeping or maybe resting their eyes. Either way, they were oblivious to Johnny's plight.

He jammed on the breaks; stopping the limo with a screech. He cut the engine, grabbed the keys, and sprinted from the limo towards the law.

But before he could get there, he heard the limo door slam behind him. He turned around just in time to see Diane duck into a Checker Cab that just happened to pull up behind the limo.

Johnny stood in the middle of the Bowery, his heart beating like a jackhammer. He started towards the police car, but neither cop had yet opened his eyes.

"Fuck it!" Jonny thought.

He felt there was no legitimate reason to wake up the two cops now. Besides, they might start grilling Johnny, like the cops did when he had been arrested years ago. What Johnny didn't need was the law peering into every facet of his life again.

Johnny did an about-face and watched as the Checker cab containing Diane Hamilton sped south on the Bowery. Johnny got back in the limo, started the engine, and headed back to his Mulberry Street apartment.

There were no parking spots available on Mulberry Street, so he parked by a hydrant on the corner of Mulberry and Hester.

Screw parking tickets.

Screw Benny.

Screw everybody.

This was a day Johnny hoped he'd soon forget.

Johnny trudged up the stairs to his apartment. But before he got even halfway up the first flight of stairs, a rat as big as Lassie scurried past him in the opposite direction. Johnny jumped back, and he almost fell backwards down the stairs.

Firggin' Rat!

Friggin' Chinese illegal immigrants!

Johnny figured that ever since the Chinese began taking over the neighborhood, buying every property in sight, the rat population in the neighborhood seemed to explode with the same propulsion as the influx of illegal Chinese immigrants into Little Italy. Johnny figured it was only a matter of time before Chinatown devoured Little Italy like the whale had eaten Jonas.

Johnny turned the key in his apartment door lock and let himself inside. He headed straight for the refrigerator where a bottle of Dewars sat on top.

He poured three fingers of booze into an empty Sau-Sea shrimp cocktail glass and downed it in one gulp. Warmth flowed though he body, but he was only a little less pissed-off than he had been moments before.

He slipped into the bathroom and stepped in front of the mirror to assess the damages to his neck.

It did not look good.

Three thick, jagged red lines ran across the right side of his neck, and there was no way to hide them unless he wore a turtleneck shirt or sweater, of which he had precisely none. Even though he had done nothing wrong, Johnny figured he'd have to lie and tell Linda he got the scratches sparring in the gym.

Beautiful and sweet Linda. How he wished he could hold her in his arms this very moment. Maybe he would tomorrow night; if Benny gave him the entire day off like he had promised.

Johnny poured himself another scotch. He figured if he didn't do the right thing soon and ask Linda to marry him, one day he'd wake up and find Linda gone. With that in mind, Johnny figured tomorrow morning would be a good time to get an engagement ring from his friend Louie Mingione, who ran a jewelry stand with his brother Johnny in the Bowery Jewelry Exchange, just north of Canal Street. Then, he would get down on his knees, show her the ring, and beg her to marry him.

Johnny knew he would never get rich driving a limo. But at least it was good honest work that could never get him into the trouble he had when he worked for his Uncle Carlo. Johnny figured, if he worked hard, in just a few years he could save enough money to buy his own limo and establish his own business, using clients that he had nurtured while working for Benny.

On the other hand, in boxing, Johnny knew he could make some fast hard cash in much less time. Boxing talent was in his genes. Johnny's uncle, Johnny Italiano had become the heavyweight champion of the world, and his other Uncle Joe Italiano, according to his Aunt Rita, was a damn good middleweight before a detached retina ended his boxing career.

It was just a matter of Johnny training hard when he wasn't driving a limo and living a clean life. What he needed was a few big paydays, and maybe even a shot at the heavyweight belt his uncle had won. If he won the title, Johnny figured he needed just a couple of defenses, and he was ready to get into the wind; maybe even retire to Florida and soak in the beautiful sun.

Johnny downed the rest of his scotch. No more liquor for him tonight.

Tomorrow, he'd sleep late, get in his roadwork, and then head for the gym. From now on, it was clean living. Early to bed. Early to rise.

No booze and no drugs; especially the cocaine all his friends were snorting like they were Hoovers.

Johnny slept with a peaceful smile on his face, with visions of Linda and winning the heavyweight championship title foremost on his mind.

It was the last good night's sleep he would enjoy for a long time.

Chapter Thirty-Four

Benny Bastone's boyish facial features were frozen in a frown as he examined the three long scratches on Johnny's neck. Prestige Limo was in danger of losing its best driver, and Benny was in danger of losing his best friend; possibly for 25-years-to-life.

"I'm surprised the cops ain't here yet," Benny said. "Listen to me. You have to lay low until we can figure out a way to get you off the hook."

Johnny shook his head. Then, he slouched into Benny's private bathroom and stared at the three scratches on his neck again in the bathroom mirror. Johnny knew those scratches were the last nail that would seal the coffin on his life as a free man.

Johnny slid back into Benny's office, and he spotted his pal scribbling on a scratch pad.

"What are you doing?" Johnny said.

"I'm trying to figure a way out for you," Benny said. "I think better when I write things down."

"What have you come up with so far?"

"Well, there one thing for sure," Benny said. "Everyone knows you wear a gold boxing glove on a gold chain around your neck. So, when the cops get here, I'll have to tell them the truth."

"Yeah, they've got me by the balls," Johnny said. "I was seen with Diane Hamilton at the Beverly Bar, the Far East, and Caruso's. The broad gets whacked, and my gold boxing glove and gold chain were found in her hand. Plus, my neck looks like it went through a meat grinder. Boy, someone set me up real good. Perry Mason couldn't get me out of this mess."

"Yeah, but you do have one thing in your favor," Benny said.

"What's that?"

"Motive. You have no motive. Cops aren't stupid. There's got to be a motive. You have nothing to do with the Palumbo and Miranda extortion trial."

"Yeah, but the cops also know I was mobbed up, and I did time for it," Johnny said. "They'll say it was a contract killing. Either that, or she attacked me, and then, in a fit of rage, I killed her."

Benny reached into his desk drawer and removed a flask filled with cognac. He handed it to Johnny. Johnny took a short swig and handed the flask back to Benny.

"One thing's for sure," Johnny said. "I'll have to go on the lam until I find a way to get myself out of this mess. Either that or the cops will do their job and find the real killer."

Benny jotted down a phone number on a post-it note and handed it to Johnny.

"That's the telephone number for the phone booth on the corner of Houston and Mott Street," Benny said. "Call me there tomorrow night at 8 pm, sharp. In the meantime, I'll contact your Uncle Carlo and see how he wants to handle this. He owes you big-time for the bit you did in prison because of him and his rackets."

"Yeah, make sure to contact my uncle right away," Johnny said. "He has connections over at One Police Plaza. Maybe he can pull some strings."

"Okay, go home and throw a few clothes in a suitcase," Benny said. "When the cops get here, I'll try to delay them. Take the limo. Then ditch it, and grab a cab. Or maybe even take the bus or subway. Check into some fleabag hotel, and stay out of sight. Pay cash. No credit cards. And don't forget, call me tomorrow night at 10 pm at the number I just gave you."

"No. I'm taking my car and heading out of town," Johnny said. "The further I get away from the city, the better."

"Okay, but make it fast," Benny said. "You don't have much time."

Benny stood and hugged Johnny. Johnny hugged him back, knowing full well that not many friends would put their necks on the line like Benny was doing for him now.

"You need money?" Benny said. "I have some petty cash in the safe. I'll just tell my uncle I needed it to pay for some repairs."

"Thanks, but I have some cash stashed away in my apartment," Johnny said.

"Great. Now get lost before the cops get here," Benny said.

Johnny kissed Benny on both cheeks.

He exited the garage and drove the limo back to Mulberry Street where he parked by his favorite hydrant.

Inside his apartment, he hung three pairs of sharkskin trousers and three silk shirts in a blue leather suit bag. Then, he stuffed underwear, socks, and assorted toiletries into a nylon carry bag, along with the half-empty bottle of Dewars.

He hurried to the refrigerator and took out a Maxwell House coffee can. Johnny opened the can and pulled out a huge wad of cash containing nothing but one-hundred-dollar bills. The last time he counted there was five grand there, but that was weeks ago. There must be close to six, or maybe even seven grand in there now. He stuffed the money into his inside suit jacket pocket. Then, he grabbed the two bags and exited the apartment.

Johnny's 1972 green Caddy Couple DeVille was parked in Bunny's Parking Lot across the street from his tenement building. He jumped inside, turned the key, and the engine sputtered to life.

Five minutes later, Johnny was on the FDR Drive heading north. The speed limit was 45 mph, and Johnny stuck to it all the way to the George Washington Bridge. After exiting the bridge, he took Route 4 West, to Route 17 north.

For the first time that day, Johnny felt safe from the law. New York City cops were notorious for not wanting to work with outside law enforcement for fear of not being given the proper accolades for the collar once one was made. They'd scour the city for Johnny first, then, only as a last resort, would they look for help outside their jurisdiction.

Johnny reached into his jacket pocket for a pack of cigarettes before he remembered he had quit smoking two years ago.

Old habits never die.

He snapped on his car radio and scanned the channels. He stopped at WCBS-FM where he heard Elvis singing "Jailhouse Rock."

Johnny sincerely hoped that this tune would not be his theme song for the next 25 years or so.

Chapter Thirty-Five

Johnny Russo's green Cadillac Coupe DeVille eased into a Mobile gas station on Route 17 West in New Jersey, 20 miles north of where his girlfriend Linda lived in Greenwood Lake, New York. Sooner or later the New York City cops would put two and two together and figure Johnny might be holed up near Linda, and he wasn't taking any chances until he could find a way to clear his name.

Johnny told the gas station attendant, who looked older than dirt, to give him ten dollars' worth of gas. Due to the new trend in self-service gas stations, this was one of the few gas stations where gas attendants actually existed.

"Where's your phone booth?" Johnny asked the attendant.

"Inside, next to the men's room," the attendant said.

The pay phone dangled from the wall next to the men's room door. It was a typical black Depression-style rotary antique, as old as the old man pumping gas into Johnny's car. All that was missing from the phone was the hand crank.

Johnny spotted a Yellow Pages phone directory on the floor. He picked it up and let his fingers do the walking until he reached the heading that said: "Motels." After flipping through several, he found one to his liking: the Parrot Motel in Monroe, New York, which was only 10 miles from Greenwood Lake. He pulled a pen from his inside jacket pocket and wrote the number down on the palm of his hand. Then, he dialed the number of his cousin Vinny

Russo, his Uncle Carlo's son, who owned a small bungalow in Greenwood Lake.

Vinny answered on the third ring.

"Vinny, it's me," Johnny said. "I'm in a shitload of trouble, and I can't talk on the phone. Copy down this phone number."

He waited until Vinny got a pen. Then he said, "Okay it's 586-3243. Call me there in an hour. It's a motel, and I'll be registered under the name of James Dunn."

"What the problem, cuz? You don't sound so good," Vinny said.

"I said I can't talk now. Just call me in an hour, and call from a pay phone."

Johnny hung up before Vinny could ask any more stupid questions.

Johnny paid for the gas outside, tipped the old man two bucks, and then he continued north on Route 17.

Ten minutes later, Johnny's Caddy reentered New York state near the entrance to the New York Thruway. Johnny passed the turnoff to Greenwood Lake, and he headed 15 miles further north to the Parrot Motel, a two-story dive that needed to get acquainted with a coat of paint.

At the front desk, a sign on the wall said a room for the night was $22, plus tax. The receptionist was a weather-beaten and big-chested nice-looking broad, maybe in her mid-50's and maybe ten years past her prime. Her straw-colored hair was done up in a 1960's-style bun; ala Sandra Dee, and she wore a sweater tight-enough to arouse a dead body.

She told Johnny to sign the register. He did as she requested, and then he handed her a $100 bill.

"This is for four nights," he said.

She took the C-note and then said. "But I still needed a credit card to keep on file in case of any damages."

"I don't have a credit card," Johnny said. "Will some more cash solve the problem?"

The lady smiled and said, "Cash always solves problems."

Johnny took out a wad of hundreds, peeled off five, and handed them to the lady.

The lady took the cash and said, "Do you need a receipt?"

"No receipt, lady," Johnny said. "You look like you've been around the blocks a few times. Now, look at me. Do I look like someone who likes to get screwed?"

"No, sir," the lady said.

"That's what I thought," Johnny said. "Now, where can I get some ice?"

"There an ice machine by the stairs on the right. If you need to purchase any alcoholic beverages, there's a liquor store down the road about a mile. It's open till midnight. They have beer and wine, too."

"Maybe tomorrow," Johnny said. "I have enough for tonight."

She handed him the key to room 221.

"Thanks," he said. "I may have company in about an hour or two. But don't worry. It's a guy, and I'm not a fag."

She eyed him up and down like he was a side of beef.

"I didn't think so," she said. "If I was ten years younger, you might like me."

Johnny grinned and said, without any malice, "If you were ten years younger, you'd still be old enough to be my aunt."

She let out a belly laugh, and then she said, "I knew you were a wiseass."

"Only kidding, lady," Johnny said. "You're still a good looker, even at your age."

"Does that mean you'd give me a tumble?"

Johnny shook his head. Then, he said with a crooked smile on his face, "Ah, no. You see lady, I'm about to be engaged. And I don't cheat."

"Just as I figured," she said. "All the good ones are already taken. I get stuck with the stiffs, the criminals, and the cheapskates. Like they say, 'Life sucks, and then you die.'"

Johnny leaned over the counter and gave her a peck on the cheek.

"You still have a lot of mileage left on your caboose," he said, "Stick with it, and soon you'll find the right guy."

That said, he spun around and headed up the steps to the second floor.

Room 221 had the bare necessities, plus the luxury of cable television, which a guest could watch only in black and white, not because the TV was faulty, but because it was a cheap black and white TV. Johnny figured he couldn't complain about a joint only charging 22 bucks a night.

Johnny unpacked his bags and put his clothes in the right places. Then, he poured three fingers of Dewars, neat, into one of the two plastic glasses that the establishment had provided for such occasions. He was too bushed to search for the ice machine.

He snapped on the television, and because the ancient TV had no remote control, he flipped through the stations by hand. He stopped when he saw "Cheers" bartender Sam Malone pour two beers for his regulars Norm and Cliff. Frazier Crane sat at the bar next to them, and before Frazier could annoy anyone, the phone rang in Johnny's room.

On the other line, Vinny said, "OK, Cuz. What's the problem?"

"Just meet me at the Parrot Motel in Monroe. I don't want to talk on the phone," Johnny said.

Thirty minutes later, Vinny knocked on the front door of Johnny's room.

Johnny handed him the other plastic cup with Dewars in it and told him to sit on the bed.

Vinny did as he was directed, and Johnny sat in the only chair in the room.

"Did you read the *Post* today," Johnny said.

"Yeah, what about it?" Vinny said.

"There was a story on page three about some broad getting whacked last night."

"Yeah. So what?"

"Well she was in my limo last night, and I was probably one of the last people to see her alive."

"What time did you get rid of her?" Vinny said.

"Yeah, and I had to get rid of her, too," Johnny said. "She was a real nut-case; drinking martinis and snorting coke like she was a Hoover. I told her I wanted to take her home, and she went wacko on me. She scratched my neck and broke my gold neck chain with the gold boxing glove on it. I saw a cop's car on the Bowery, and I jumped out of the limo to alert them to what the fuck was going on. The two copper fucks were sleeping in the squad car. But before I got to them, she jumped out of my limo and right into a cab. When they found her dead, she had my fucking gold chain and gold boxing glove clenched in her hand. It looks like I'm fucked."

"Yeah, you're fucked alright. What do you want me to do? My dad knows some good lawyers."

"Screw the lawyers," Johnny said. "I didn't do a fucking thing. I'm innocent of this whole mess."

"If you say so," Vinny said.

"What do you mean, "if I say so?'"

"Well, everyone knows you have a temper. And if that broad roughed you up, I could see you whacking her."

"But I *didn't* kill her," Johnny said. "It happened just like I said."

"Look, you plead guilty to manslaughter. The broad attacked you first, so you'll get off easy. Five years at the most."

"Five years! I ain't spending five years of my life in the can for something I didn't do."

Johnny stood up, and Vinny did the same.

"Look, Vinny," Johnny said. "Go talk to your father. Not on the phone. Drive into the city and see him in person. Tell him I need his help. He owes me big-time for the stretch I did in the can because of him and his illegal businesses. He has connections in the police department all over the city. Maybe he can pull a few strings. Or, at least get the cops off my back until I can find the real killer."

"Ok Cuz," Vinny said. "I'm on my way."

After Vinny closed the door behind him, Johnny picked up the phone and dialed the Greenwood Lake number of his closest friend, attorney Mark Marino.

Mark's voice appeared after the first ring.

"Mark Marino speaking," he said.

"Mark, it's me," Johnny said. "I'm in a shithole of trouble, and I need you to get me out of it."

"Okay. What can I do to help?"

"Did you see the newspapers today about the broad that got killed?"

"Sure, she was a rat. She was supposed to be the key surprise witness in the Miranda-Palumbo trial."

"Well, the cops think I killed her," Johnny said.

Johnny told Mark about his unfortunate encounter the previous night with Diane Hamilton; from start to finish, including the part about his lost gold chain and gold boxing glove.

"Damn, you're being framed," Mark said. "Stay where you are and don't move. I'll come to you."

Johnny gave Mark and address and phone number of the Parrot Motel.

"Ok, sit tight. And don't leave the room," Mark said. "I'll be there in a half-an-hour."

At eight pm sharp, Johnny dialed the number of the pay phone Benny had given him. Benny answered, also on the first ring.

"Did the cops come for me?" Johnny said.

"Yeah, they got here about an hour after you left," Benny said. "I reported the limo you were driving as stolen."

"Good thinking. They're probably scouring the city looking for the limo."

"Where are you?" Benny said.

Johnny told him.

"That's too close to your girl Linda's house," Benny said. "Maybe not today, but definitely by tomorrow, the law will check out the whole area around Greenwood Lake, including Monroe. Listen, I have an uncle who lives in Brooklyn. He went to Italy for a month, so his house is empty. The address is 1472 73rd Street. It's in Bensonhurst."

Johnny wrote the address down on a piece of hotel paper.

"Meet me there tomorrow night at around 8 pm," Benny said. "It might be a good idea to ditch your car someplace upstate. Grab a bus to the city and take the West End train to Brooklyn. The 71st Street stop."

"Okay. Will do," Johnny said.

Johnny hung up and dialed Linda's number in Greenwood Lake. Her brother David answered.

"Is Linda home?" Johnny said.

"She's sleeping," David said. "How are you? I sense you're in some trouble."

David McKay was a narcotics cop for the New York City Police Department. He lived with his sister Linda and their father in Greenwood Lake. Their mother had passed away a few years earlier. Most importantly, Johnny trusted David with his life.

"David, I'm jammed up," Johnny said. "I want to explain everything to Linda, and I want you to listen to the conversation on the extension line."

"It's the Diane Hamilton murder, isn't it?" David said.

"Yeah, how did you know?"

"Johnny, not many guys wear a gold boxing glove around their necks. Besides, that girl was dealing big-time babania. We had a tail on her, but we lost her a few days ago. She was the surprise witness in the Mafia case."

"David, I didn't kill her."

"I know you didn't. One of the mob guys did it. But with your background and criminal record, you might have to prove it. But I think I can help you out."

"Does Linda know anything?" Johnny said.

"No, she doesn't read the New York City newspapers. But she's mad because you haven't spoken to her in a few days. That's not like you. Where are you now?"

"I'm in a motel in Monroe."

"Okay. Meet me at Fisherman's Lounge on Route 17 in Monroe in an hour," David said. "And don't bring your cousin Vinny with you. We need to talk. You're in deeper than you think."

"How is that even possible?" Johnny said.

"I'll fill you in on all the details when I see you," David said.

Chapter Thirty-Six

Johnny's Green Caddy arrived in front of the Fisherman's Lounge, a one-story ranch-style saloon, fifty feet off Route 17 West and hidden behind a double row of trees. Attorney Mark Marino sat next to Johnny in the passenger's seat.

All the front parking spots were taken, mostly by vans, panel trucks, and F- Series Ford trucks; the chosen set of wheels for the upstate yahoos.

Unlike in Little Italy, there wasn't a Caddy in sight.

Johnny drove around to the back of the bar, and he spotted David's red Corvette parked in front of the side entrance.

Johnny turned to Mark and said. "David's here already. That's his red 'Vette."

"Judging by the rigs out front, the inside of this joint must look like a scene from *Urban Cowboy*," Mark said. "I bet the main attraction is a coin-operated bucking bronco with a drunken cowpoke mounted on top."

Johnny found a parking spot two cars away from David's car.

Johnny and Mark entered the front door, and they were immediately engulfed in a forest of cowboy hats. On the blaring jukebox, Pat Benatar was daring someone to hit her with their best shot, and Johnny wondered how long it would take for one of the local yokels, who, judging by the decibel level in the joint were already fired up, to take Ms. Benetar seriously and start throwing punches.

Johnny spotted David sitting alone in a booth next to the jukebox. He was easy to spot. No cowboy hat.

To fit in with the crowd, Johnny and Mark swaggered over to David's booth and took a seat opposite him.

"Hi, David," Johnny said. He extended his right hand across the table and David took it. "You remember Mark Marino, don't you?"

"Sure," David said. He extended his hand, and Mark shook it.

"If I knew what we were walking into, I would have dressed more appropriately," Mark said, fingering the jacket lapel of this three-piece suit.

Just then, Johnny Cash began railing about a boy named Sue. The noise from the jukebox was so loud; Johnny could barely hear himself think. He turned around and spotted an empty table in the back.

He pointed at the empty table and said, "Let's move back there before I strangle someone."

The three men vacated the booth and relocated to the back table. Johnny noticed that three other men immediately took their place. One was wearing a three-piece suit, another a simple shirt and tie, and the third was a round mound of flabby male flesh, wearing a brown jacket with tassels.

Johnny, Mark, and David ordered their drinks; nothing too fancy or they figured they might get roughed up and pitched through the front door.

"Three Buds," Johnny told the waitress, who had poured her size 16 body into size 12 Levi's. Her ample cleavage, bursting through her V-neck blouse, almost made up for it.

After each man took a sip of their brew, David spoke first.

"Ok, gentlemen, this is confidential information, so what I say here dies here," David said.

Both Mark and Johnny nodded in the affirmative.

David continued: "The police drug investigation taking place in Little Italy began almost a year ago. Because of my relationship with Johnny, I immediately told my supervisors that I had to recuse myself because of the conflict. They didn't like it, but finally, they acquiesced. Still, little by little I began hearing things that told me Johnny was involved, even if he didn't know it. So, I had my partner Hank Peters keep me up to snuff on the investigation. Of course, this is against police regulations, but me and Hank go way back, and we always have each other's backs."

Johnny nervously took a long swig of his Bud, and it almost gushed back up his gullet.

David continued: "These two men on trial, Miranda and Piazza, are just small fish in a big pond. In fact, they're guppies. The main man behind every drug deal in Little Italy is Johnny's uncle, Carlo Russo. Carlo's dealing more dope than anyone in town, and I mean heroin, too. The coke and pot he deals are not as profitable. He sells them mostly as an accommodation for his junkie customers."

Johnny couldn't believe his ears. Everyone knew dealing drugs was the Kiss of Death in the neighborhood. A man dealing babania, if he gets caught, is facing bigtime in the slammer. That's when the canaries start singing to save their asses. As a result, if a mob guy gets arrested for dealing drugs, and if he hits the street before trial, he's a dead man.

David continued: "Gregory Piazza, the guy who turned stoolie, is a sleazy nightclub owner who is hooked on blow. He used his uptown bar as a front for Carlo Russo to sell his drugs. That way, Piazza made a few bucks, and he kept his nose happy at the same time.

"Piazza made his first mistake about a year ago when he hired a new bartender. The guy just walked off the street looking for a job, and Piazza was so coked-up he didn't bother to check his references, of which he had none anyway. One day, about six months ago, Carlo walked into Piazza's joint near closing time to collect his junk money. Carlo spotted the new bartender, and he blew his top. Piazza said Carlo's eyes nearly bugged out of his head when he saw him. It seemed that this bartender, a Lower East Side guy named Frankie Fish, had screwed Carlo 30 years ago and had been on the lam ever since. There was no one in the joint except Carlo, Frankie, two waiters, and Piazza. Carlo ordered the waiters to leave, and as soon as they made it out the front door, Carlo put six bullets in Frankie's head and torso. Piazza said Carlo was still firing away after his gun was empty. Then, he dropped the gun and began kicking the dead body in the face and torso; like a total maniac.

"Carlo and Piazza rolled the body up in a rug and put him in the truck of Piazza's car. Then, they threw the body into the East River."

"Typical Carlo," Johnny said. "There's more dead bodies in the East River than dead fish."

"But here comes the most important part," David said. "What Carlo didn't know was that there was a broad holed up in the ladies' room when he started shooting. Piazza was banging this slut named Diane Hamilton. She was a high-class looking dame, but for enough nose candy, she'd suck a dick in Macy's window and give you an hour to draw a crowd. Knowing what she knew, she figured she had a score, and she began blackmailing Piazza and Carlo."

"So, you're telling us that the police already know Johnny's not involved in Diane Hamilton's murder," Mark said. "He's in the clear, right?"

"No, Mark," David said. "He's in deeper than ever."

Suddenly, two masked men burst through the front door of the Fisherman's Lounge. Both held two guns; one in each hand. They hurried up to the three men sitting by the jukebox and opened fire. Bullets smashed into flesh and bone as customers dived for cover. Others ran screaming out the front door. In seconds, the three men lay dead; their blood splattered over the tables, floor, wall, and the jukebox.

When the firing started, Johnny and Mark dove under the table. And as the murderers rushed towards the front door to exit, David jumped to his feet and pointed his police revolver at the two shooters.

He yelled, "Freeze! I'm a police officer!"

The two gunmen dropped their guns and put their hands up high over their head. As Johnny and Mark slipped out from under the table, the side door opened. A lone masked gunman aimed at David and fired several times. One bullet caught David over his right ear. He staggered two steps to his left, and then he fell face-first onto the floor.

The first two gunmen ran out the front door, while the third gunman slipped out the side door from which he had emerged.

Mark rushed over to David. He turned him over onto his back and put an ear to his chest. He heard nothing.

Then, he grabbed David's wrist, hoping for a pulse.

Still nothing.

Mark got to his feet and said to Johnny, "Let's blow this place. David's dead, and I have a feeling the three dead men by the jukebox are dead because someone thought they were us."

Mark and Johnny sprinted out the side door. They were met by gunfire. A bullet ripped into Johnny's right shoulder, and he fell onto the dirt road. As the firing continued, Mark dragged Johnny behind a parked car. They watched as the three gunmen fled in a gold Buick.

Johnny thought he recognized the car, but he wasn't sure.

He screamed in pain, "Son-of-a-bitch-bastard!" Then, he turned to Mark and said, "Are you hit, too?"

"No, you were the one they were after," Mark said. "Let me see your shoulder."

A red dot, the size of a dime, decorated Johnny's shoulder. There was no exit wound. His arm felt numb, but there was no significant bleeding.

"Let's get out of here before the cops arrive," Mark said. "And we're not going back to the hotel. Anyone could easily find us there."

"But I have several belongings there," Johnny said. "Clothes. Shirts. Pants. Things like that."

"You can buy new stuff," Mark said. "No use getting killed over a few silk shirts."

"And three sharkskin pair of pants," Johnny said. "I bought them at Al Kaplan's on Canal."

"The last I looked, Al Kaplan's was still in business," Mark said. "Now, let's get the hell out of here! I'll drive. You lay low in the back seat."

Seconds later, Johnny's green Caddy, Mark at the wheel, was cruising carefully on Route 17 West, right at the 55 mph speed limit.

Johnny lay flat on his back in the back seat. He lifted his head slightly and said, "Where are we heading?"

"I have a doctor friend in Albany," Mark said. He directed the Caddy onto the New York State Thruway heading north. "He spent some time in the can for fraud, so he can't legally practice medicine anymore. But he'll fix your shoulder so your arm won't fall off."

The full impact of what just happened hit Johnny like a left hook to the liver.

"I have to phone Linda," Johnny said. Tears streamed down both sides of his face. "It's my fault her brother is dead."

"Get a grip on yourself," Mark said. "David's dead, and there's nothing we can do about it. First, we'll take care of your shoulder. Then, I'll phone Linda. Remember, I'm your lawyer, and I'll handle everything from here on out."

"OK, I'll leave everything up to you," Johnny said. "I'm not thinking too straight right now."

"Johnny, one thing is quite clear," Mark said. "We're both supposed to be toes up right now. Someone fingered us when we walked into Fisherman's Lounge. So, either we or David were followed there. Someone then gave the word that we were sitting next to the jukebox. One of the men who took our place near the jukebox was even wearing a three-piece suit like I'm wearing. Now the question is: 'Who wants you dead?' David was just collateral damage. He was in the wrong place at the wrong time. The only answer I can come up with is your Uncle Carlo. I just don't know why."

"I think David was about to give us the answer when the shooting started," Johnny said. "I didn't think of it until just now, but David told me not to bring my cousin Vinny along with me tonight. But he didn't object to you being there. The gold Buick that fled the scene looked like Vinny's car. He drives a gold Buick, too."

"Does Vinny know where David lives?" Mark said.

"Sure, Linda lives with David and their father, and Vinny's been over several times," Johnny said.

Mark took the next exit, and he parked next to a pay phone booth in a Merritt gas station.

Mark turned to Johnny, and said, "Give me Linda's phone number."

Linda answered on the fifth ring. She sounded like she had been sleeping.

"Linda, I'm sorry to wake you, but this is Mark Marino, Johnny's friend," Mark said. "Remember me?"

"Sure, I remember you," Linda said "You're an attorney. Is anything wrong with Johnny?"

"Linda, listen carefully to what I have to say," Mark said. "We don't have much time to talk, but you're in grave danger. Johnny is here with me. He's been shot in the shoulder, and I'm taking him to a doctor. He'll be alright, but your brother David has been shot, too, and I'm sorry to say, he's dead."

Mark heard a loud shriek on the other end of the phone.

"Linda, please don't panic," Mark said. "Just get dressed as fast as you can and drive to this address in Albany." He gave her the address and phone number.

Just then, Johnny staggered out of the back seat of his caddy and grabbed the phone from Mark.

"Listen, sweetheart, do exactly what Mark just said. And do it quick. We'll be in Albany waiting for you. I'll explain everything when I see you. Is your father home?"

"No, he working the night shift. He won't be home until early morning."

"Leave him a note, but don't tell him where you are. Just tell him you'll be in touch."

"Johnny, is David really dead?"

"Yes, sweetheart. It happened so fast. There was nothing I could do. But right now, you're the one in danger. Leave the house immediately. Throw some clothes in a bag and get out of there as fast as you can. And make sure you're not followed. You know how to do it. David showed us how to 'dry clean' ourselves when we don't want to be followed. Go to Monroe first. Drive in circles through the streets and double back several times. But stay in Monroe. When you're sure you're not being followed, hightail to Albany. If you think you are being followed, rush to the Monroe police station. You'll be safe there."

"Okay," Linda said. "I'll do like you said. I love you, Johnny."

"I love you, too."

As soon as she hung up the phone, Linda slipped on a bathrobe and slippers. Without getting fully dressed, she grabbed an overnight bag and jammed it with clothes. Then, she scribbled a note to her father and left it on the kitchen table.

She exited the house, jumped into her Volkswagen Beetle and headed onto 17A W (Monroe Old Country Road) to Monroe, New York.

Ten minutes after Linda left, a gold Buick pulled into Linda's driveway. A man exited the car and knocked loudly on the front door of Linda's home.

No answer.

He knocked again; this time louder.

Still no answer.

A light went on in the house next door.

The man got back into the gold Buick and drove away.

An hour later, **Mark** banged on the front door of a one-story brick house just outside Albany, New York.

Seconds later, Peter Jacobs opened the front door.

"Mark Marino, I must be dreaming," Jacobs said. He let out a short laugh that sounded more like a soft cough. "You didn't come all the up here at this time of the night to ask for my last installment on your legal fees, did you?"

"No, Jacobs. I came here for a favor," Mark said. "I have a friend in the car who's been shot in the shoulder. He needs immediate medical attention."

"How did you know I'd be home?" Jacobs said.

"Where else could you be?" Mark said. "Unless you get permission, you can't travel more than 100 feet from your home without your court-ordered ankle bracelet alerting the police."

A tall, bespectacled man in his early 50's, Jacobs looked like a meek librarian, which was exactly what he presently was after his run-in with the law that robbed him of his lucrative medical practice.

Too many bets on three-legged horses had forced Jacobs to do things that didn't precisely align with the Hippocratic Oath. After digging a fifty-grand hole for himself, Jacobs decided he could fill in the dirt by selling prescription drugs, specifically morphine, to patients without any specific ailments. His customers sold the drugs to "chemists" who turned it into street heroin, or "horse" as it's referred to in New York City's ghettos.

Fortunately, the only horses Jacobs comes into contact with these days is when he takes his children on the merry-go-round at the New York State Fair.

Mark had taken on Jacobs legal problems without a retainer, and without any payment until Jacobs had completed his three years in jail. After his release, Jacobs paid Mark back in dribs and drags (there are no monetary windfalls working as a librarian), and the present time, he owed only a few hundred dollars to the attorney.

"Bring your friend inside, and let me have a look at him," Jacobs said.

As Mark led Johnny into Jacob's home, Johnny's shoulder felt like someone had inserted the blade of a knife inside it.

"Do you have something for the pain?" Johnny asked Jacob. "My arm and shoulder hurt like hell."

"Do I have something for the pain?" Jacobs said. "As Mark could tell you, giving out painkillers was the reason I lost my license to practice medicine to begin with."

Despite the pain, Johnny could not stifle a laugh. With his hawk-like nose supporting wire-rimmed glasses, Jacobs looked like Sherlock Holmes, sans the double-sided hat.

"But come with me into my library," Jacobs said, "and we'll see what I can come up with."

Jacobs led his two visitors into his library, which was adjacent to the master bedroom. He motioned to his visitors to be quiet, lest they wake his wife, who was presently sawing wood in their bed, and his two children, sleeping in another bedroom opposite the entrance to the library.

On all four sides, the library was filled floor-to-ceiling with books. Jacobs had pilfered almost all of these books from the Albany State Library, a fringe benefit of taking such a low-paying job.

Jacobs went to the far wall, and he reached up to the second shelf from the top. He pulled back on Jules Verne's "Time Machine," and voila! the entire wall shifted sideways, exposing a hidden laboratory that would make a Mad Scientist proud.

"Gentlemen, welcome to my own time machine," Jacobs said.

Jacobs picked up a vial filled with a green-colored liquid. He inserted a long hypodermic needle into the vial, and he injected Johnny's shoulder with the fluid.

"This shit you just gave me, it isn't habit forming, is it Doc?" Johnny said.

"Do not worry, my son," Jacobs said. "In a few moments, your mind will be in the state of euphoria."

"Is that far from the state of New York?" Johnny said. "I don't like going on long trips."

"You'll be on no trip at all," Jacobs said. "There will be no lingering effects of this drug, and you will have no extreme desire to indulge again in the future. That is unless you are unlucky enough to become impregnated with another bullet, which by the way, is still inside your shoulder and needs to come out right away, you know."

"That's why I'm here, Doc," Johnny said.

"Look, Jacobs, we have to stay here for the night," Mark said. "And we're expecting a visitor: a young lady in distress. Considering her brother was murdered tonight, and her boyfriend is about to be operated on by a butcher, you might have to hit her with a few tranquilizers."

"No problem, sir," Jacobs said. "I have plenty more of these goodies on the premises."

Someone knocked lightly on the front door.

"I think our young lady has arrived," Jacobs said. "Shall I answer the door?"

"I think you should check the peephole first," Mark said. "There's a full moon tonight, and we've had enough surprises already."

Chapter Thirty-Seven

Peter Jacobs opened the front door of his home, and before him stood the most beautiful woman he had ever seen.

Linda McKay had shoulder-length jet-black hair and light-green eyes. Her lips were slightly parted, like a little girl ready to cry. A tie-sting around her tiny waist secured a red house dress, and on her feet, a pair of worn slippers curled upward. She forced a smile, but her eyes said otherwise.

"I'm Linda McKay," she told Jacobs.

"Yes, young lady, we've been expecting you," Jacobs said. "Your gentleman friend is in my laboratory. Please, follow me."

He led Linda through his bedroom, into his library, and finally into his laboratory. Johnny rushed towards her, and they embraced.

Suddenly, her mood changed, and her sparkling green eyes became cold granite.

"All right, Johnny. Start explaining how my brother David wound up dead," she said.

After they moved to the library, Johnny calmly explained the events of the previous two nights, and how he was either a victim of circumstances or was being set up for the fall.

When he finished his soliloquy, Linda let out a huge sign, and then she collapsed flat on her back on the library couch. Her body shook like she had Parkinson's, and her eyes were shut tight.

Jacobs slipped into his laboratory. He returned with a hypodermic needle and a vile of off-white liquid. He injected the fluid into Linda's arm, and her shaking stopped immediately.

Jacobs removed his glasses and cleaned them with the bottom part of his shirt.

"I have a spare bedroom that is presently not occupied," he said. "That's where I do my side work, like removing bullets." He turned to Mark. "The young lady can stay here. But I need you to be my assistant in this delicate operation."

Jacobs led the men into a spare bedroom where he ordered Johnny to lie down on the sheet-less king-sized bed. As Jacobs hovered with a Satanic grim etched on his thin lips, Johnny had visions of Dr. Frankenstein administering life to the creature he was creating.

Jacobs injected Johnny with a local anesthetic into his damaged shoulder. Then, with a steady hand, if not a steady mind, Jacobs did a little cutting, and, seconds later, he expertly removed the bullet with a pair of tweezers. He handed the bullet to Mark for inspection. Without looking, Mark dropped it into his pants pocket.

"Hey, don't lose that bullet," Johnny said. "I want to put it on my keychain as a reminder of how much my Uncle Carlo loves me."

Jacobs cleaned, stitched the wound, and bandaged Johnny's shoulder.

Mark's only task during the short medical procedure was to hand Jacobs an eight-ounce glass filled with Dewar's scotch every minute or so. To Johnny's dismay, Jacobs would take a gulp of scotch, wipe his mouth on his sleeve, then continue with the task at hand.

After the bullet was removed, Jacobs injected Johnny with more painkillers, and he said, "Your shoulder will be stiff for about a week. You're lucky the bullet barely touched bone. There's no permanent damage, and there's no reason to see another doctor."

"Unless I want to live," Johnny said.

Jacobs ignored the remark, and he downed the rest of the scotch in the glass. Then, he poured himself another hardy helping of Dewars.

"I'll consume this just before I retire," Jacobs said.

Jacobs removed two pillows and a blanket from the closet, and he flung them onto the bed. Then, he handed Johnny and Mark each a valium. Jacobs popped two valiums into his own mouth and washed it down with the scotch.

"Alright gentlemen, you can sleep here tonight," Jacobs said. "I, for one, am joining my wife in the master bedroom, after I make sure the young lady is resting comfortably."

That said, Jacobs, like a drunken sailor in a dive bar, literally staggered out of the room.

"That guy would be great haunting houses," Johnny said. "You sure he has all his marbles?

"Yeah, he's got all his marbles alright," Mark said. "But they're not in the proper order. Drugs do funny thing's to people's minds. That guy has been a walking drug store since I met him. He was the only inmate in prison selling drugs to the guards, instead of the other way around."

Johnny sat up and said, "So, what's our first move tomorrow?"

"Our first move is to contact David's partner," Mark said. "Do you remember his name?"

"Yes, Hank Peters."

"He's in narcotics, so he shouldn't be too hard to find. One thing's for sure. We have to stay clear of Carlo and his son Vinny. And that means staying out of Little Italy until we get a handle on how to clear your name. Then, we'll worry about those two lowlifes."

"I'm supposed to meet Benny tomorrow night in Brooklyn," Johnny said. "You remember Benny, don't you? He's Mike Bastone's nephew."

"Yeah. I'm not too sure we can trust Mike Bastone," Mark said. "He's in a different crew than Carlo, but they're both made men. And you know how made men stick together."

"Yeah, but Benny's a good friend," Johnny said. "I trust him with my life."

"That's exactly what you'll be doing," Mark said. "What time are you supposed to meet Benny?"

"11 pm."

"Good. That's gives us all day to track down Hank Peters."

When Johnny woke the next morning, the sun was shining brightly through the slits in the bedroom's Venetian blinds. Albany's clean, fresh air was a welcome comfort, so unlike the carbon monoxide pollution which was always present in stuffy and concrete-laden Manhattan. Johnny was accustomed to being awakened by horns honking and people shrieking in the streets. But this morning, all Johnny heard was the cheerful chirping of several sparrows sitting outside his bedroom window.

Next to Johnny, Mark was snoring softly with his back to Johnny, like he didn't have a care in the world. That was Mark's personality – calm and detached; unless he was addressing the jury in the courtroom. Then, he became a raving lunatic, i.e. Charles Darrow on speed. Johnny, on the other hand, was a type 1 personality, high strung with bouts of manic depression with its accompanying high highs and very low lows.

Johnny's elbowed Mark in the side, just enough to get his attention.

"Mark, wake up already," Johnny said. "Let's get moving and get the hell out of here. Those freakin' sparrows are driving me nuts. I'm a New York City kid, not some hayseed dork like Huckleberry Finn."

Mark was still wearing his three-piece suit, which was now quite wrinkled, like a Bowery vagrant who had slept on a cardboard box. Mark reached into his pants pocket, removed a 38 Colt revolver, and placed it on the night table next to the lamp.

"I didn't know you carried a piece," Johnny said.

"Yeah, and it's licensed, too," Mark said. "Not one of those stolen flamethrowers the hoods on Mulberry Street buy up in Harlem."

"That's you, kiddo," Johnny said. "Mister AJ Squared Away. Everything by the book."

"That's how I stay out of trouble," Mark said. "Not like some people I know."

"The last thing I need is a lecture right now," Johnny said. "Let's get this show on the road."

After Johnny and Mark took turns using the bathroom, there was a soft knock on the bedroom door.

"It's me, Linda," she said. "Are you guys decent?"

After being assured the two men were fully dressed, Linda entered the bedroom. She eyed Mark up and down. Then, she finally said, "You look like you slept in your suit."

Mark ignored the remark, and said, "Do you know how we can get in touch with David's partner, Hank Peters? Do you have his home number?"

"No, I don't have his home number," Linda said. "But he's in the Narcotics Division of Midtown South. Let me see If I can get in touch with him at work."

They exited the bedroom and entered the living room, where Jacobs sat on the couch doing the *New York Times* crossword puzzle.

He looked up, spotted his visitors and said, "My wife Helen is in the kitchen making breakfast, Let's go join her in there."

They went into the kitchen, and Johnny spotted Helen Jacobs standing by the kitchen stove. She was, if anything, more odd-looking than her husband. Her hawk-like nose supported black horn-rimmed glasses. And she had pointed ears, which stuck straight up like a rabbit's from under her stringy black hair.

"Sit down at the kitchen table, please," she said. "I'm making scrambled eggs with bacon and toast.

Linda, Johnny, and Mark did as requested, and Jacobs took the fourth seat at the Formica table which looked like it came from a 1950's New York City diner.

Mark turned to Jacobs and said, "Linda needs to use your phone to make a call to the city."

"No problem," Jacobs said. "I'll just add it to the bill that includes room and board, and oh yes, one tiny bullet-removal procedure."

"Put it on my tab," Mark said. "I'll straighten out when my uncle straightens out, and he's a hunchback.

Nonplussed, Jacobs pointed to a rotary-dialed wall phone near the back door.

Linda took out her purse and removed a small back telephone book. She took it with her to the phone and dialed the proper numbers.

A gruff voice answered, saying, "Narcotics Division. Detective Peters speaking."

"Hank, this is Linda, David's sister," she said.

Peters said, "Hello Linda. Is David sick or something? He's not at work yet."

"No, he's not. Something horrible happened last night," she said.

Linda filled in Peters on the sad events of the previous night. Peters listened without saying a word. When she finished her story, she said, "Hank, I need you to speak to someone."

She handed the phone to Mark.

Mark told Peters, "Detective Peters, my name is Mark Marino. I'm Johnny Russo's attorney. He's also my best friend. I don't want to talk over the phone. We're in Albany, but we can be in the city in four hours. Can we meet somewhere?"

"I don't know," Peters said. "What do you want from me?"

"Look, Detective Peters, before David was shot he told us we could trust you," Mark said. "My client is wanted for a murder he didn't commit. David led us to believe that maybe you could help us clear Johnny's name. In fact, that was one of the last things he said before he was shot."

Peters spat out the words, "Why should I help you?"

"Johnny is in love with David's sister, Linda," Mark said. "If you help my client, you'd be helping her, and I know that's what David would have wanted. Please meet with us as soon as possible. Linda will stay here in Albany at the home of a friend. I have reason to believe her life is in danger, too."

Peters said in a more subdued voice, "All right Mr. Lawyer, you win. But I want to tell you this. I knew that David was making a mistake getting involved with that lowlife Russo. I told him so myself. But I'll do what I can do, legally. No more. No less. I'll meet you at the Market Diner downtown off West Street. I can be there at around three pm this afternoon.'

"The Market Diner is fine," Mark said. "But the one downtown is too dangerous for us. It's too close to the neighborhood, and we both have targets on our back. Make it the Market Diner on 12th Avenue and West Street instead."

"All right, three pm sharp," Peters said. And then he hung up the phone without waiting for a reply.

After they both returned to the kitchen table, Linda asked Mark, "Why can't I come, too? And why am I in danger?"

"We're all in danger," Mark said. "Do you remember your brother David saying anything about Johnny's uncle Carlo Russo being involved in selling drugs?"

"No. David never discussed his job with me," Linda said. "But he might have confided in my father. They were always talking about police work and procedures. Does that mean my father could be in danger, too?"

"Anything's possible," Mark said. "Is your father home now?"

"He should be. He worked the overnight shift last night delivering newspapers."

"Call him up and see if he's been notified about David's death."

Linda dialed her home number, and her father answered after five rings in a weary voice.

"Dad, it's me," Linda said. "Did you read the note I left?"

Robert McKay felt too guilty to tell his daughter that another one of his drinking binges had caused him to stagger home at around six am. He had made a beeline to the bedroom and had been sleeping since.

"What note?" he father said.

"Never mind," Linda said. She knew from the sound of his voice that he had been drinking heavily again. "Listen to me, but first sit down. I have some bad news about David..."

But before she could finish, her father heard a knock on the front door.

"One-second, honey," he said. "There's someone at the front door."

"Dad, don't answer the door!"

Still, half in a drunken stupor, her father placed down the receiver. He stumbled over to the front door and opened it.

A man, wearing a woman's stocking over his face, shot him twice in the chest. Robert McKay fell onto his back. The gunman calmed walked over to his prone body and fired two more bullets, aiming for the head. Robert McKay rolled over quickly, and the bullets buried into the floor instead.

Hearing the shots, Linda yelled from the other end of the line, "Dad! Dad!," as the gunman fled from the house.

Chapter Thirty-Eight

New York City Police Detective Hank Peters had seen a lot of dead bodies in his 15 years in the department. He'd seen overdosed bodies; their bodies so thin they looked like someone put them together with sticks and glue. Mob hits; men blasted so many times their bodies had exploded into odd shaped little red chunks lying across the pavements. Car accident victims, their blood and guts smeared into tiny crevices in the highway.

But David McKay didn't look dead.

When the morgue attendant pulled down the white sheet exposing David's face, Peters had expected the worst. Instead, David looked like he was sleeping. His eyes were closed and his lips curved into a gentle smile. Unless someone inspected him closely, there was no visible bullet hole nor the accompanying splatter of blood. The bullet had entered the side of David's head just above the hairline and nestled in his brain. Death was almost instantaneous.

Maybe it was all just a clever joke with David being the antagonist. Maybe he was up to his old tricks again.

Peters pulled the sheet all the way down, exposing David's entire body. The identification tag hung down from his right big toe, like an exhibit marked as evidence in court.

The morgue attendant strutted away like he had more important things to do than to look at another dead body. See one; seen them all. Just another day at the job.

Peters ran his hand along David's anatomy, up his ankle, and he stopped at his peaceful face.

David was ice-cold.

This was no trick; no clever gag to annoy his partner. David was dead alright, and Peters swore he would have no compassion for the killers.

Peters pinched David's chilled cheek and said, "Don't worry buddy, I'll get those bastards for you. You should have let me arrest those guinea cocksuckers when I wanted to. But no, Johnny Russo was dating your sister, and you said he'd become a straight arrow since he got out of the can. Now you're colder than a mackerel, and there's nothing I can do but give you justice, the right way. And that, I swear, is what I am going to do. I'll find out who killed you and then shoot the motherfuckers into the next world; if there is a next world. Just like that. You can take book on it, buddy."

Some men who get arrested sometimes meet misfortune while sitting alone in the police Paddy Wagon. Others get tuned-up by the men-in-blue before they get shoved, battered and bruised, into a police car. Peters hoped he was present when the arrests were made. He'd be the judge, jury, and executioner, and no one in law enforcement would give a damn or even try to stop him. Hell, he'd be saving the taxpayers the expense of a trial, plus the cost of keeping those scumbags fed with a roof over their heads for the rest of their natural fucking lives.

Justice has been done this way since Cain became slightly upset with Abel.

Peters put his lips inches from David's ear and said, "Well, I'll be there when they throw dirt on you. Maybe I'll even throw a fucking rose on your coffin. It don't mean shit. Just another day in Paradise. We'll do our twenty years on the job, and then we get the fuck out. Give them back our shield, and maybe they'll give us a gold watch in return for us risking our lives every fucking day on the force. On the way out the door, they might pat us on the head like a faithful German Shepard. Fuck them all where they breathe, buddy. I'm doing this my way, and fuck the consequences."

The morgue attendant returned and signaled it was time for Peters to leave. Peters pulled the sheet over David's body and exited the morgue. He took the elevator to street level, but he was still fuming.

He said to himself, "Everyone sucks to some extent. Some just suck more than the others. Still, I've got a fucking job to do; a debt to pay. Just like Sam Spade said in the *Maltese Falcon*. When Spade's partner Archer was killed, he had to find the killer even though Spade had been banging Archer's wife for years. In the movie, Spade said, 'When your partner is killed, you're expected to do something about it.' Damn right, I'll do something about it, and quick. And woe to the bastard who tries to stop me."

At St. Anthony's Community Hospital in Warwick, New York, Linda McKay sat alone at her father's bedside in a semi-private room. The other bed was occupied by an old man with tubes sticking out of his body, and an oxygen mask covering his mouth and nose. Linda figured it was just a matter of time, maybe even hours or minutes, before that hospital bed would be filled by somebody else.

The two bullets the doctors had removed from his chest was the least of Robert McKay's problems. When they had opened him up to cut out the bullets, they found his chest was consumed with cancer. They told Linda it was just a matter of time before he passed away, days and maybe even hours, just like the man in the bed next to them.

Robert McKay was conscious but so weak he was barely able to speak. He tried anyway.

"Linda, before I go, there's something I must tell you that I've been hiding for years," he said. "Are you and Johnny Russo serious?"

"Yes, Dad, I love him, and I hope to marry him someday," she said.

Robert McKay just shook his head sadly. "I should have told you this a long time ago. I was going to tell David; let him handle it. But now he's gone, and I have precious little time left in this world."

"Dad, I don't want to hear about your past," Linda said. "What's done is done."

"Linda, this is not only about my past, it's also about your future," he said. "You have to promise me you'll never marry Johnny Russo."

"But dad, I love him," she said.

"Linda, you can't refuse a dying man his last wish. I have nothing against Johnny; you just can't marry him, that's all."

"Dad, so he's Italian from Little Italy, and I know you don't like Italians. It's that old Irish/Italian thing that's been going back a century or more. But Johnny's no hardened criminal. I could never love a man like that. He made a mistake years ago, but he paid for that. Johnny's a good, kind, and loving person, and I love him dearly. That's just the way it is."

"But Linda, you can never marry Johnny in the eyes of God," he said.

Linda did not like the tone and content of what her father had just said.

"Why not?"

He squeezed his daughter's hand and said, "Because he's your brother."

In the last moments of his life, Robert McKay told his daughter a story that had been burning his insides for almost thirty years. It was a story of love and a tale of deceit. But mostly it was about hate.

The man Robert McKay hated was Carlo Russo.

And now Linda McKay would carry that intense hate inside of her, too.

Chapter Thirty-Nine

Johnny Russo deposited the required coins into the pay phone and dialed his Aunt Rita's home phone number. She was the last person he wanted to tell about the events of the past two days, but Aunt Rita had to know.

Rita Italiano had raised Johnny from the time his mother Mary had died after that horrible tragedy three decades earlier. When Mary Russo's weak heart finally stopped beating a few years after her husband Dom was killed by his brother Carlo, Johnny was still wearing knee pants.

Five years ago, when Johnny was grown-up and beyond supervision, Rita had left Little Italy and moved to Uniondale, New York, on Long Island in the Town of Hempstead. She spent her time alone in her one-family brick house, and she very rarely ventured outside, except to run necessary errands.

Try as he may, Johnny could never convince his aunt to come into the city to see him fight. He even offered to have her picked up and returned home in a limo, but she still refused, saying, "Boxing makes me depressed."

Every winter, rather than brave New York's freezing weather and the accompanying snow, she hopped on a plane and headed to

Sarasota, Florida, where she soaked up the sun, at least until the end of April.

Before she flew south, she always gave Johnny a post office box in case he wanted to contact her, which he never did. She never gave Johnny a telephone number, or any other type of contact information; just the post office box. Johnny figured she had a boyfriend down in Sarasota (she was still a good-looking woman), and why not let her have some fun uninterrupted by the troubles up north?

But now Aunt Rita was back from the Sunshine State, and when Johnny called, she answered with the same raspy and spirited voice Johnny had always remembered.

"City morgue. Dr. Cyclops speaking," she said. "You kill 'em; we chill 'em."

"Aunt Rita, it's me, Johnny," he said. "Why do you always answer the phone like that? It gives the creeps."

"Johnny-boy, how have you been," she said. "I haven't heard from you in weeks."

"I've been busy working. But now I'm in a load of trouble, and I need your help."

Johnny told her everything that had transpired in the past few days. He emphasized that he suspected his Uncle Carlo as being the motivating source behind his troubles.

"Where are you now, Johnny?" she said.

"I'm in a phone booth on Route 4 in New Jersey," he said. "Near Paramus. Me and Mark Marino are headed to the uptown Market Diner on 12th Avenue to meet Hank Peters, David McKay's partner in the Narcotics Division of the New York City Police Department. He might be able to bail me out of this hole I'm in."

Aunt Rita and Johnny did not share the same blood, but she felt closer to him than almost anyone else in the world. No one was going to bulldoze her nephew; not while she was still breathing.

"I'll meet you at the Market Diner as soon as I can get my car and my ass in gear," she said. "Don't leave until I get there."

"Aunt Rita, are you crazy?" Johnny said. "The police are after me, and someone is trying to kill me. You'll just be in the way and in deep danger."

"No, you wait there until I get there," she said. "No freaking backtalk. I know what I'm doing."

That said, she slammed down the phone.

Rita went into her bedroom closet, reached onto the top shelf, and removed a hat box. Inside was a blue velvet bag that said in gold lettering: "Crown Royal."

Inside the velvet bag were all her valuables: jewelry, important documents, and old photos from when times were good. She removed an old yellowed envelope. It contained a photo from a wedding a long time ago.

She stared at the group photo. Everyone looked so vibrant; so alive. In the photo were Nancy and Joe, Dom and Mary, and Rita and her husband Johnny Italiano, the Heavyweight Champion of the World. Johnny Russo had been named after his uncle Johnny – a wonderful man, shot to death by an animal named Carlo Russo.

Rita struggled to stop the tears, but they fell down both cheeks anyway.

Rita Italiano never cried in public. At the funerals, she didn't allow a single tear to fall, even when the lowered her husband's body into that black hole in the ground. The years had dimmed the memory, but not the love nor the pain.

All throughout these years, Rita had been faithful to the code of the streets in Little Italy: Never be a rat. Carlo Russo had never been punished for his hateful crimes, but now it was the time to get her cold revenge.

An old torn envelope lay hidden at the bottom of the velvet bag. Rita opened the envelope and read the contents. Satisfied, she placed the envelope into her purse.

Rita donned a light-blue button-down sweater, and then she walked over to her shiny 1958 black Buick, a present from her husband after he had won the title. She turned the key, primed the gas, and headed for Manhattan.

An hour later, she parked her car in the parking lot of the uptown Market Diner.

Inside the Market Diner, a long counter decorated by trays of Danishes and apple turnovers, neatly stacked under glass covers, ran the length of right side the establishment. Opposite the counter, two dozen booths were occupied mostly by burly truck drivers, dressed in red flannel shirts and dirty dungarees.

No tablecloths graced the dark-brown mahogany tables, and dug deep into the top of the tables were words and phrases more suitable for the bathroom walls, and an occasional phone number of someone, who, most likely, did not possess a Social Security Card. People in the rackets don't pay taxes, so who needs a Social Security number anyway?

Aunt Rita spotted Mark and Johnny sitting opposite each other in a booth near the back. She sashayed over, like a model on a runway, and said, "Good evening, gentlemen."

She kissed her nephew's cheek and sat down next to him. She spotted a waitress near a front booth not looking particularly industrious. Rita snapped her fingers and yelled, "Can I get some service here?"

Johnny looked like he had just swallowed a New York City cockroach.

"Aunt Rita, keep it down," he said. "The entire joint is looking at us."

"Sorry, nephew, but I haven't been this full of piss and vinegar in a long time," she said.

The waitress came over, and Rita ordered a double Johnny Black on the rocks.

"And don't pour it like it's medicine," she told the waitress.

"Aunt Rita!" Johnny whispered quite loud.

"It feels good to be angry," she said. "I've been too busy the past years feeling sorry for myself, but now I'm just plain angry. Carlo Russo is finally going to pay for all the misdeeds in his life. And I'm going to be part of the posse that hangs him."

The waitress returned with Rita's drink and placed it on a coaster in front of her.

"Thank you, my dear," Rita told the waitress. "Sorry I was so gruff before. It's been a bad day so far."

"No problem, Ma'am," the waitress said. "People come here all the time to let off steam. That's why we're still in business."

After the waitress left, Rita turned to Johnny and said, "Carlo Russo is no damn good. And another thing, he's not your damn uncle."

Rita removed the old envelope from her purse and handed it to Johnny.

"Read this letter," She said. "I want you both to read it so you'll get the lay of the land. I should have given it to you a long time ago, but things always came up, and I hate to rock the boat. I always felt it was better if you didn't know what had happened in the past. But now you need to know everything."

She took a large swallow of her drink and then she continued: "Johnny, there's a lot of things in that letter that will startle you. But it's all true. I'm here to fill you in on anything that's not clear to you."

Johnny took the wrinkled yellow papers out of the envelope, and he began reading:

To my son John,

I've been a sick woman since the day you were born, and I don't expect to live much longer. You are only five years old now, but later in life, you must know the truth.

Dominick Russo, my husband and a good man, was shot to death on our wedding night. He was killed by his own bother, Carlo, who I fear someday will murder you.

After the pain of my tragic wedding night, I was in the state of shock for days. Your Aunt Rita kept a tight watch on me. She feared I would do harm to myself, and I must admit that I did consider suicide.

But as the days went by, I decided to go back to my old job as the cashier at the Lexington Diner. I wanted to work all day and most of the night, so I wouldn't have time to think.

One of my customers at the Lexington Diner was a truck driver named Robert McKay. He was a thoughtful man who always paid attention to me and the way I looked. But he was married. I didn't care. I had no respect for myself anyway. Our affair was short, and oh so sweet. I never had a man sexually before Robert McKay, and I haven't had one since. I doubt I will ever have one again.

I didn't tell Robert McKay until I was four months pregnant. But what could he do? He was married. His wife was a drunk, he said, but she was still his wife.

I understood.

The only person I could turn to was your Aunt Rita. It was her idea to tell everyone that I was pregnant from Dominick Russo; that we had sex before we were married. A few weeks in the time difference wouldn't make anyone suspicious, she said. Besides, people in our neighborhood have their own problems and always minded their own business.

But for once, Rita was wrong. Carlo Russo was suspicious of everyone. He called me a liar and worse. But I stuck to my story.

They rushed me to the hospital a month early, and you were born prematurely. This made my lie sound even better. But nothing could convince Carlo. He knew his brother better than anyone. He knew Dom would never have sex with me unless we were married.

After you were born, Carlo came to the hospital every day and sat in my room. He never said a word to me. He would just sit and sneer at me. When he left, he'd always spit on the floor and say "Putana!"

One day, Robert McKay came to the hospital to see me and our son. He came out of curiosity and out of compassion. He gave me money. Carlo Russo walked into the room just as Robert McKay was leaving. I knew right away he suspected Robert McKay. He figured why would a stranger be visiting me. I heard later what had happened.

Carlo and one of his goons grabbed Robert McKay as he left the hospital. They beat him and forced him to tell the truth. They made him promise never to see or contact his son again. They said they would kill him and his son if he ever tried. I ever saw Robert McKay again.

When you were six months old, I was pushing you in a carriage on Bayard Street. Carlo spotted us. I tried to turn around and walk the other way, but he blocked our path.

He told me, "One of these days I'm going to kill this little-bastard son of yours. You, I won't touch. You'll kill yourself anyway. It's more fun watching you do yourself, slowly and painfully."

As he walked away, he turned around, pointed at you, and ran his forefinger across his throat.

I'm giving this letter to your Aunt Rita. Carlo won't harm you while she's alive. I don't know why, but he seems to fear her.

After you read this letter, I want you to contact your father, if he's still alive. Don't have any hard feelings towards him. It was just as much my fault as it was his. Please, forgive him.

But most of all, stay away from Carlo Russo. He's not your uncle, and he's not your friend. He's a hated enemy who would take great pleasure in doing you harm. Aunt Rita will help you to do whatever needs to be done.

My son, your mother loves you. I've always led a good life. I never knowingly hurt anyone. I made one mistake, but even some good came from that. I gave birth to you, and I know you are good.

Make me proud of my son. Be a success in life. But as long as Carlo Russo is alive, you are always in danger. Never doubt those words for a moment.

Your Loving Mother,

Mary Italiano Russo.

Aunt Rita watched Johnny closely as he and Mark read the letter. She saw her nephew's face turn white and then a bright red.

She reached across the table and held his hand.

Johnny took a long gulp of his drink. Then, he squeezed his Aunt Rita's hand and smiled.

Johnny looked at his watch, then he said to Mark, "Hank Peters is late. I hope he's not blowing us off."

Aunt Rita finished her drink. Then, she stood and kissed Johnny's cheek.

She said, "It's time I left. The traffic back to Long Island is murder at this time of night. Besides, I think you men might want to talk about something it's better I don't hear about."

Rita nodded at Mark and said, "Take good care of my nephew. I'll be in touch."

She then exited the Market Diner, almost bumping into Hank Peters as she went out the front door.

"Sorry, Ma'am," Peters said.

Rita just smiled at him and continued on her way.

Peters spotted Johnny and Mark at the back table. He barreled over to their table, his face set in the stone of anger.

"I'm Detective Peters," he said.

Seeing Peter's angered face, Johnny dispensed with shaking hands.

"Have a seat, Detective Peters," Mark said. "Would you like something to drink?"

"Yeah, I need a drink," Peters said. "I just came back from the morgue after seeing David. That was a tough sight for me to swallow."

Peters looked at Johnny quizzically. Where had he seen this face before?

The waitress came to the table, and Peters ordered a double Chivas on the rocks.

"With a water chaser," he told her.

It was Mark who spoke first.

"Detective Peters, before we start, I want you to know that my client is innocent in the murder of Diane Hamilton. He's being framed. Nor is he involved with the selling of narcotics."

The waitress returned with Peters' drink and placed it on the table in front of him. He took a long swig of the Scotch, and then he washed it down with the water.

"That's what I figured you'd say," Peters said. "But I have a witness who says Johnny is up to his neck in this mess."

"That's crazy!" Johnny said, in a voice that could be heard from the register up front. "I may have done a little coke now and then. But I never sold the stuff, and I ain't no murderer!"

"Keep your voice down," Mark told Johnny. "Let the man speak."

Peters asked Johnny, "Do you know someone named Gregory Piazza?"

"I don't know him personally, but I read the newspapers," Johnny said. "He's the stool pigeon in the Mafia trial."

"Right," Peters said. "When Piazza first came to us for protection, he only named two people. Paul Miranda and Tony Palumbo. We knew he was lying. After two days of questioning him, and things got pretty rough, he started singing like a canary. Now, he admits that Carlo Russo and his nephew Johnny Italiano were also involved."

"That's a fucking lie!" Johnny said. "I never even met the bastard!"

"But what we needed was for Diane Hamilton to corroborate Piazza's story," Peters said. "And then she turned up dead with your gold boxing glove and chain in her hand. Explain that to me."

Johnny did, relating to Peters the entire events of his night with Diane Hamilton.

"That's all your say-so," Peters said. "You have no one to back up your story, have you?"

Mark figured it was time for him to start acting like Johnny's lawyer.

"Did Piazza make a positive identification of Johnny?" he asked Peters. "Did you show him mugs shots of everyone he mentioned?"

"No, we were about to do that before all this shit hit the fan," Peters said.

"So, Piazza mentioned Johnny's name," Mark said. "But he could have met someone else who passed himself off as Johnny, right?"

"That's possible, but not probable," Peters said. "Who would want to mix up Johnny in all of this?"

"I think I know the answer," Mark said. "What we need to do is do a face-to-face with Piazza and Johnny. I guarantee you he'll say Johnny wasn't the person he met. Where is Piazza now?"

"He's in the Manhattan Correctional Center on Park Row," Peters said.

"So, set up the fucking meeting!" Johnny said. "I'm telling you I don't know this guy from Adam."

Peters took another deep swallow of scotch, followed by a large gulp of water.

"It not that easy," Peters said. "You need a special clearance to see someone in protective custody."

"I'm sure you can get that clearance," Mark said.

"Maybe," Peters said. "I'll make a phone call and find out."

Peters went to the phone booth in the back, right next to the men's room. He put in the required coins, and then he dialed the home phone number of Bill O'Neil, the assistant district attorney in charge of the case. Peters knew that O'Neil had been under the weather and had not been to the office for a few days.

"Bill, this is Hanks Peters," he said. "I'm with Johnny Russo and his lawyer at the uptown Market Diner. They claim Russo never met Piazza and that he didn't kill Diane Hamilton. Russo was with my partner David McKay last night when David was killed in Monroe, New York. Whoever killed David was gunning for Russo, too. What I need to do is confront Piazza with Johnny Russo. Make him made a positive I.D. face to face."

"Forget it," Peters," O'Neil said, in a voice that reeked of the flu. "Arrest Johnny Russo immediately. I don't believe any of this nonsense. Russo's our boy, all right. I have more than enough evidence to indict him for the murder of Diane Hamilton."

"Bill, Russo came here under his own volition," Peters said. "Why would he do that if he were guilty? Piazza said he met with Carlo Russo and his nephew, Johnny Russo. But what if it was someone posing as Russo, and not Russo himself?"

"All right, I'm not feeling that great, but meet me at the Manhattan Correctional Center in one hour," O'Neil said. "If Piazza positively identifies Russo, we'll arrest him on the spot."

"Thanks, Bill."

Peters hung up and went back to the table where Johnny and Mark were waiting with baited breath.

"I just got the okay for Johnny to meet with Piazza downtown," Peters said. "Leave your car here and ride with me."

Chapter Forty

Assistant District Attorney Bill O'Neil paced the lobby inside the Manhattan Correctional Center on Park Row in Downtown Manhattan. During his twenty-five years working in the DA's office, O'Neil had never taken a foolish chance; never put his ass on the line for anyone. "By-the-Book-Bill, they called him. The inside scoop was that O'Neil was so honest, he didn't even cheat on his income taxes.

But Detective Hank Peters was a special kind of cop. He was hard working, with a no-nonsense attitude. And Peters was no fool, who would take the bogus bait and swallow it hook, line, and sinker. If Peters thought that Johnny Russo was being set up, there just might be something to it.

The two men who arrived with Peters in the lobby of the Manhattan Correctional Center looked like typical Mulberry Street hoods. The taller one, whom O'Neil rightfully assumed was Johnny Russo, was just a tad too good-looking for O'Neil's liking. Men like Russo, because of their outstanding looks and street-hood mentality, thought they could charm every woman and outsmart every man.

The shorter man, who O'Neil figured must be Russo's attorney, looked like a miniature fashion plate; a Napoleonic Beau Brummel. He looked arrogant, self-assured, but rough around the edges. O'Neil often faced-off against men like this in court. Their street savvy made them dangerous opponents for the law. And although they were basically good men with fine educations, some form of unbreakable bond impelled then to defend their Italian paisans, some of them the most despicable human beings imaginable, with inhuman vigor.

O'Neil extended his hand to Peters, and Peters took it. He ignored the other two men.

"I got permission to bring Piazza down," O'Neil said. "They'll be two armed marshals with him." He gestured towards Johnny and Mark. "I don't want to hear jack shit from these two. I'm doing this favor for you. Have you frisked these men for weapons?"

"Yes, I have. Before we got into my car," Peters said. "They're clean. So, how are we going to proceed?"

"Ok, this is the drill," O'Neil said. "When Piazza come out of the elevator, I'll shake hands with Russo, so as to identify him to Piazza. When Piazza comes up to us, with the two marshals, one on either side, I want Russo to look directly at Piazza, face to face. Not one word out of him, and no threatening gestures." He stared menacingly into Johnny's eyes, and said, "Get it, Russo? No tricks here. You understand?"

Johnny returned O'Neil's stare with likewise intensity, and said, "I *totally* understand."

Minutes later, the elevator door opened and a small rat-faced man emerged; with one marshal in front of him and the other bringing up the rear. Piazza wore a crumpled three-piece brown suit, and his hair needed a firm hand with a stiff brush.

O'Neil approached Johnny and extended his hand. Johnny took it as Piazza moved to within five feet of them. Piazza and Johnny stared at each other. Johnny was wearing a short smirk across his face. Piazza's head quizzically turned sideways, then he said to O'Neil, "This ain't the guy I know as Johnny Russo."

"Are you sure?" O'Neil said.

"Sure, I'm sure," Piazza said. "The other guy is about the same height, but about 30 pounds lighter. They're about the same age, but that's about it. There's no resemblance whatsoever."

Johnny told O'Neil, "Listen, I have a photo in my wallet I'd like to show to Piazza."

"All right," O'Neil said. "But take it out slowly and no tricks. The marshals here are armed and ready."

Johnny reached into his back pocket and carefully removed his wallet. He flipped through a transparent folder filled with snapshots. He extracted one, and he handed it to O'Neil, who handed it to Piazza.

Piazza looked at the photo for a few seconds, and then he said, "Yeah, that's the guy. No doubt about it."

O'Neil told the marshals, "OK, that's it for now. Take him back upstairs."

Piazza and the two marshals did an about-face and headed back towards the elevator.

Johnny told Peters, "The man in the photo is my cousin is Vinny Russo. I can't prove it, but he killed David McKay, and he tried to kill me, too. I bet he even shot Linda's father. You better get to him before I do. I'll wring his neck."

"Don't be so tough," O'Neil said. "I still have enough evidence to indict you for the murder of Diane Hamilton."

It was Peters who spoke next.

"If you think about it, Bill, we have bullshit evidence against Russo," he said. "It's all circumstantial. I don't think Russo had a damn thing to do with the Hamilton murder."

O'Neil scratched the top of his head, and said, "You may be right. But it's your ballgame, and you better be right. It's both our asses on the line here."

O'Neil shook Peters' hand, and then he strode out of the Manhattan Correctional Center.

Peters, Johnny, and Mark followed Peters out the front door.

As the three men walked briskly down Pearl Street, Johnny told Peters, "There's something else I think you should know."

Johnny told Peters about the contents of the letter his mother had written to him before she died.

Peters immediately realized what puzzled him before about Johnny. It was the sparkle in his eyes and the crooked slant of his smile. Just like David McKay.

"So, that means that you're Linda's and David's half-brother," Peters said.

"Yeah, I haven't fully sorted this out in my head yet," Johnny said. "But please, don't tell Linda about the letter. I need to figure out how to handle this."

"I'm going to let you deal with that one, kid," Petters said. "But I'm going to put Carlo Russo's ass in a sling, and I need you to help me do that. You okay with that?"

"It will be my pleasure, pal," Johnny said. "In fact, nothing would please me more."

After Peters dropped Mark and Johnny off at the uptown Market Diner to pick up Johnny's car, Mark went inside to the pay phone in the back. He dialed Peter Jacobs' number, collect.

Jacobs accepted the charges, and then he said to Mark, "That's going on your tab, too."

"Has Linda McKay called?" Mark said.

"Yes, and I'm afraid that her father has passed away, too," Jacobs said. "I instructed her to return to my humble abode right away. I told her you would make the funeral arrangements for her brother and for her father. I'm sure that was what you wanted me to do, correct?"

"Yes, thank you," Mark said. "But I need for you to handle this delicate matter for me. We are in the middle of one big clusterfuck in New York City. Charge everything to me at my office. I'll contact my secretary immediately and tell her to give you all her cooperation."

"I wasn't expecting this, but I'll do my best," Jacobs said. "The poor girl must be in a tizzy over all this."

"Okay, and tell Linda to stay put with you until we return," Mark said. "We might come back tonight, or tomorrow afternoon at the latest. It's all according to how things go. Tell Linda Johnny is safe, and we're working things out with Detective Peters' help."

"Will do, Mon Capitan," Jacobs said.

Mark exited the Market Diner and slipped into the passenger's seat next to Johnny in the Caddy. Detective Peters sat in the back seat.

"I'm supposed to meet Benny at his uncle's house in Brooklyn at 11 pm," Johnny said. "It's getting late."

"I was just wondering," Peters said. "How did you get the Diane Hamilton ride two nights ago?"

"Benny gave me the ride over the two-way radio," Johnny said. "Do you think he's involved in the frameup?"

"Could be," Peters said. "I'm going with you and Mark to Brooklyn. There may be an ambush waiting for you. If there is, maybe we can nail Carlo and his son Vinny.

"Peters is right," Mark said. "It could have been a frame from the beginning. Maybe Benny's with Carlo. It all adds up."

"Okay, but I doubt it," Johnny said. "That's just not in Benny's makeup. He hates guys like Carlo.

"Let's go, gentlemen," Peters said. "But I'm taking my car. I'll follow you. Maybe I can spot a tail."

At precisely 10:45 pm, Johnny knocked on the door at 1342 73rd Street in the Bensonhurst section of Brooklyn. The wind whistled through the trees, and Johnny felt an eerie tickle down his spine.

No one answered the door.

Johnny knocked a second time.

Still, no answer.

Johnny turned around and glanced at Mark and Peters, sitting in the two separate cars. Like he was in court awaiting the death sentence, Mark sat nervously in Johnny's Caddy; while Peters sat behind the wheel of his unmarked car with his gun pointed out the window and trained on the front door of the house.

Johnny knocked a third time and still no answer.

Johnny stepped lively towards Peters' car, where he told Peters, "Nobody's answering. Maybe we better leave."

"Did you try opening the door?" Peters said.

"No."

"Well, that might be a wise thing to do; don't you think?"

Peters got out of his car and walked over to Johnny's car. He handed Mark his gun, and said, "Keep us covered. You do know how to handle one of these things, don't you?"

"Of course, I do," Mark said. "But why don't we just take off? There's nobody here."

Peters removed a second gun from an ankle holster attached to his right leg.

He told Mark, "No, we're staying. We might find something interesting inside that house. Why? Are you nervous?"

"No, my knees always clang together like cymbals," Mark said.

"Just cover us and don't start shooting unless you have to," Peters said. "You might wing one of us by accident."

Peters and Johnny walked slowly up the steps to the front door of the house. He turned the knob, but the door was locked. Peters glanced carefully in both directions to see if there were any visitors. Seeing none, he reached into his pocket and removed a set of lockpicks. He tried one in the keyhole, and then another. In less than a minute, he heard the favorable "click." He put his right hand on the knob and turned it slowly. The door creaked open.

Peters put the lockpicks back into his pocket, extended his gun with both hands, and started to enter the house. He stopped, reached into the breast pocket of his coat, and took out a flashlight. He shined the light into the house, and both he and Johnny entered.

The door opened into a huge hallway. On the right, a wooden stairway extended up into the darkness. Johnny reached into his pocket and pulled out a 25 caliber automatic.

"I hope you have a license for that rod," Peters said.

"It's Mark's gun, and it's licensed," Johnny said. "He gave it to me while we were driving here; just in case."

"Ok, take a look down here while I go upstairs," Peters said. "If you have a problem, scream your head off, and I'll be down in a flash."

Peters' feet creaked up the stairs, his flashlight leading the way.

Johnny slowly entered an unlit room, and the smell of cigarette smoke smacked him in the face. He slid his hand along the wall, searching for a light switch. He found one, and the room flashed into focus.

Johnny quickly scanned the room, and when his eyes focused on the far right-hand corner of the room, his heart almost stopped.

Benny Bastone, naked below the waist, sat propped up in a brown leather recliner. His eyes bulged, and his mouth stood wide open in a silent bloody scream.

As Johnny inched closer, he realized the horrible death his friend had endured.

A gaping blood hole was where Benny's penis used to be. And, as a message of who-knows-what, the killer had stuffed Benny's bloodied penis into his open mouth.

Johnny yelled for Peters, and seconds later Peters burst into the room, his gun extended.

Peters spotted Benny's disfigured body. He also spotted Johnny kneeling in one corner of the room losing his lunch and dinner.

Chapter Forty-One

As Sinatra did things his way on the radio, Vinny Russo admired himself in the bathroom mirror.

The $50 pink-and-white striped tie perfectly matched Vinny's $100 white silk shirt and his $150 gray silk slacks. He donned a $300 black ultra-suede sports jacket and stuffed a $25 red handkerchief into his top-front jacket pocket.

What good is it to be a gangster unless you dressed like a gangster and spent like a gangster?

He splashed on a little dab of Polo ($50), and Vinny was ready to conquer the world.

Vinny sauntered towards the front door of the Mulberry Street apartment that his father kept as a crash pad across the street from Casa de Carlo. Vinny owned a luxurious house in Bay Ridge Brooklyn and a bungalow in Greenwood Lake, but the spare apartment in Little Italy came in handy when the nightly booze and blow dulled Vinny's senses.

A step from the door, Vinny did an about-face and walked back to the bathroom mirror. He adjusted his tie and patted down an uncooperative strand of hair. He stared into the mirror and smiled.

"It's Showtime!" he yelled to no one in particular.

Vinny saw someone yell that in a movie once. He didn't remember the movie's name, except that it was a musical, and the guy who kept yelling "Show Time!" died of a heart attack at the end of the movie.

Fuck that! It was only a movie.

Vinny frowned, and he exited the bathroom and then the apartment.

Less than a minute later, Vinny entered Casa de Carlo. The bartender Jimmy Pasternak was behind the stick. Vinny ordered a J&B and water, and then he said, "Jimmy, give me the phone."

Jimmy handed Vinny a new cordless model from behind the bar.

Vinny dialed the number of J&A Car Service on Kenmare Street.

Louie the Dispatcher answered, and Vinny said, "Hey, Louie, I'm drinking J&B scotch, and talking to J&A Car Service. How's that for a coincidence?"

"Wonderful," Louie said, blandly. "Now, what can I do for you?"

"I need you to pick up a broad for me and deliver her here to my father's joint on Mulberry Street," Vinny said.

"What's her name, and where's the pickup?"

"It's at the St. Regis Hotel. And her name is Laura Miller."

"St. Regis Hotel? What is she? A high-class hooker?"

"Don't be funny," Vinny said. "The broad's a looker, but she's also the manager of a custom Cadillac showroom uptown: Regal Cadillac. I'm buying a new Caddy with a remote control starter. That is if this broad does the right thing."

"I think what you really need is a limo," Louie said. "All my cars are *stoshabongs*. You know that. Call up Prestige Limo and talk to Benny."

"I don't want a fucking limo, Louie," the Vinny said. "Don't you want the fuckin' business?"

"Sure, kid. Don't get sore," Louie said.

"I know your cars all suck," Vinny said. "That's why I want you to do me a favor and pick her up yourself in your personal Lincoln Continental. All your drivers look like Bowery Bums anyway.

"And I don't?"

"Yeah, you look like a bum, too," Vinny said. "But at least you have a nice car. And don't worry, there's an extra ten-spot in it for you doing me this favor."

"Ten spot! That's worth at least an extra twenty clams."

"Just do it," Vinny said. Then he slammed down the phone.

Vinny sipped his drink and smiled. He knew Benny Bastone was not dispatching any more limos for his uncle; not after what happened to him the previous night.

Vinny thought Butch Salerno and Carlo had gone too far and had taken too much damn pleasure dispatching Benny into the afterworld; if there was an afterworld. Vinny didn't mind whacking someone out. But cutting a guy's dick off and shoving it into his mouth? That was just too damn much. His father and Vinny held Benny down, while Butch did the cutting, with the gleam in his eyes like a mad scientist. Benny was screaming so loud, Vinny swore he felt his own dick being butchered.

At exactly 7:15 pm and 15 minutes late, Laura Miller entered Casa de Carlo, and she was so stunning, the bartender's eyes almost bulged completely out of his head. She spotted Vinny at the bar and sat next to him.

"Sorry, I'm late," she said. "But I was looking for you outside the hotel and not that other fellow, what's his name?"

"Louie."

"Yes, that's right. Louie. He was a perfect gentleman, but a little heavy on the gas pedal."

"Sorry, I tried to hire a limo, but the guy we usually use was not available," Vinny said. "You want to have a drink here or at a table?"

"The table's better," she said

Vinnie snapped his fingers at Hugo, the head waiter, who was standing in the back of the restaurant.

Seconds later, Hugo stood before them. His posture was so erect, Vinny thought he looked like he had a metal rod extending from the top of his head to the base of his spine. Vinny put his arm around Hugo's shoulder and gave him a slight hug. Hugo flinched ever so slightly, and Laura thought that Hugo was clearly uncomfortable in Vinny's presence.

Vinnie told Laura, "This is Hugo, the best damn head waiter in town. And that's because he gives the best damn head in town."

Vinny's smile was a big as an extra-large pizza, heavy on the cheese. But neither Laura nor Hugo saw the humor in his comment.

Vinny waited for a reaction from either of them. But after a few seconds of thick silence, Vinny said, "Hugo, we want the big table in the right-hand corner in the back."

"But sir, it's occupied," Hugo said. "I just seated two couples there ten minutes ago."

"Then unseat them," Vinny said. "Tell them you're sorry, but the table was reserved. They'll understand. If they don't understand, I'll make them an offer they can't refuse."

Hugo sighed. Then, he looked at the ceiling, shook his head, did an about-face, and headed for the large table in the right-hand corner in the back of the restaurant.

"Great head waiter," Vinny told Laura. "But he walks like he's got a broomstick up his ass."

"I think he's very charming," Laura said.

When they were seated at Vinny's favorite table, the feast began.

After they consumed two huge trays of hot and cold antipasto, Vinny wolfed down a double-order of spaghetti and clams; like it was his last meal before heading to the electric chair. Laura dined on a simple veal piccata.

While they waited for their cappuccino and zabaglione, Vinny got down to business.

"I'll take the remote-control Caddy," Vinny said. "But I don't want to wait. What colors do you have in stock, ready to go?"

"We have classic black, midnight blue, or Cadillac red," she said.

"I'll take the Cadillac red," Vinny said. "What the total damages for everything, including tax?"

Laura removed a credit card-sized calculator. She pushed a few buttons, and then she said, "The bill comes to $48,500, tax included. Will you be paying cash, or by check?"

"Which would you prefer?"

"I would prefer a certified bank check. That much cash changing hands might make the IRS interested."

"We wouldn't want to do that, now would we?" Vinny said.

"When can I expect that check?."

"First thing tomorrow morning," he said. "But first you have to do something for me."

Laura forced a slight smile, which looked more like a grimace. Then, she said, "Mr. Russo, I think I can guess what that something might be."

"You're no babe in the woods, sweetheart," Vinny said. He reached his hand under the table and massaged her knee. "We're talking about a lot of money here. Let's put it this way. You and I will go up to my apartment. I'll make you a drink and put on some very romantic music. Then, we'll just play it by ear. No promises. What do you say?"

"That sound fair enough, Mr. Russo," Laura said. "But remember you said, 'No promises.'"

"Yeah, I'll remember," Vinny said. "But you remember you said $48,500. And that's a lot of cabbage in today's money."

The next day, more than a little satisfied with the night before, Vinnie dropped off the cashier's check and picked up his red $48,500 red Cadillac with the remote control starter. Using his father endless money pit, Vinny figured he'd be able to transact for one of these luxury cars once a year, as long as Laura Miller was the manager of Regal Cadillac.

Chapter Forty-Two

The name that constantly came up when Detective Hank Peters was investigating Carlo Russo's involvement in the drug market was a cab driver named Nacho Perez. But there was never any direct evidence to tie Perez to Carlo Russo. After a little trip to the Taxi and Limousine Commission, Peters discovered that Perez worked for Taxi Heaven, on Eight Avenue just below 14th Street; that is when he wasn't doing Carlo's bidding. The word on the street was that Nacho, besides moving Carlo's babania, had no problem doing the heavy lifting, which allegedly included several murders and dozens of beatings.

At the Taxi Heaven garage, Peters confronted the dispatcher, who was standing outside his glass-enclosed office. He stood about five feet tall and five feet wide, and he was smoking a cigar that looked like a burnt piece of rope.

After flashing his police ID, Peters said, "I'm looking for a taxi driver named Nacho Perez. I was told by the Taxi and Limousine Commission that he works here."

"What do you want him for?" the dispatcher said, in a not-so-pleasant voice.

"I'll tell him when I find him," Peters said.

The dispatcher took a long drag of his cigar, and he blew the smoke up into Peters' face.

Peters waved the smoke away and said, "I guess they don't pay you enough here for you to buy decent cigars."

He snatched the cigar from the dispatcher's mouth and stomped it out on the concrete floor. The dispatcher started to say something, but Peters stuck his forefinger under the dispatcher's throat.

"Now, cut out the shit before I stomp *you* out on the floor," Peters said.

The dispatcher froze, and he looked like he was ready to cry.

"Sorry, detective," he said. "This hasn't been one of my better days. I've been swimming in shit since I got out of bed this morning."

Peters lowered his finger and said, "That's okay. I've had a few of those days myself lately. Now, what about Perez?"

"He works here," the dispatcher said. "But I haven't seen him in two days."

"Did he call in sick?"

"Yeah. But that guy's into the white powder pretty good. He's probably on a coke binge. He's done this before. When he runs out of money, he'll be back. Nacho is real tight with the boss. He gets away with murder around here. If it were me, I would have fired him a long time ago."

Peters reached inside his inside jacket pocket. He took out a $5 Macanudo and handed it to the dispatcher.

"Try one of these," Peters said. "You'll live longer and so will your friends. By the way, what's your name?"

"Charlie Nobile."

"Who's your boss Charlie?"

"Butch Salerno. He's from downtown in Little Italy."

A bomb went off in Peter's noggin. Butch Salerno? Carlo's right-hand man? This could get interesting.

"Do you have an address for Perez?" Peters said.

"Sure, let me look it up in my files," Charlie said.

Charlie walked into his office and opened a metal file cabinet. He flipped through several files before he found the right one. He read the file, and then he said to Peters, "Nacho lives at 115 Stanton Street. I think it's just west of Essex Street."

Peters pulled out a roll of bills. He peaked off two twenties and handed them to Charlie.

"Thanks, Charlie," Peters said.

Then, he exited the garage.

Ten minutes later, Peters parked by a fire hydrant in front of 115 Stanton Street, a dilapidated tenement standing amidst mountains of garbage and mounds of dog excrement. Peters stepped inside the building's narrow hallway, and he examined the names on the mailboxes.

There was no listing for Nacho Perez.

Suddenly, two men brushed past Peters. They passed the stairs and headed towards the rear exit to the backyard. Peters turned towards them, and he immediately recognized the tall black man named Snow, one of the top drug dealers on the Lower East Side. Peters had collared Snow a few years earlier, but after some savvy lawyering, Snow copped a plea netting him only three months in the can.

"Hey, I want to talk to you, Snow," Peters said.

Snow spun around, and an angry mask creased his chocolate face. It disappeared fast when Snow recognized the speaker.

"Hey, my man, Detective Peters, what's cooking?" Snow said.

Snow strode back towards the mailboxes, his right hand extended. His companion froze by the stairwell, ready to run.

Peters accepted Snow's extended hand, and he squeezed it in a vice-like grip.

Snow screamed in pain, and his pal immediately sped out the back exit.

"Whatchu doing, man?" Snow yelled in a high-pitched tenor. "You're breaking my hand. I swear! I'm clean! Search me, but let go my fucking hand!"

"You don't really want me to search you, do you?" Peters said. "I know where skells like you hide their stash. Like in that plastic pouch you had last time two inches up your butt. Remember?"

"Look, Peters, I don't want no trouble," Snow said. "Give me a break."

"Ok, I'll give you a break," Peters said. "But I need a favor."

"Whatever you say, man. It's your ballgame."

"I'm looking for Nacho Perez. I was told he lives in this building, but his name is not on any mailbox. Where can I find him?"

Show's face turned pale.

"No, man. I never heard of that dude," Snow said. "You sure you have the right building?"

Deep creases appeared on Peters' forehead. With a turn of the shoulder, he drew back his left arm and drove a straight left into Snow's belly. Snow dropped to his knees, and he started to wretch. But the vomit stuck in his throat.

"Ok, motherfucker," Peters said. "I was going to give you a pass, but now you're fucked. Get up and drop your pants. If I find anything up your butt, you're pinched. With your record, you'll get five years, easy."

Still on his knees, Snow pitched face-forwards until his mug hit the floor inches from Peters' shoes.

"Please don't fuck with my mind," Snow cried. "That dude Nacho will kill me in a split second. He's a dangerous man."

"Well, maybe you'd like to do laundry for Bubba in prison," Peters said. "I know all about you in the can. You rather switch than fight. It's your move. Pick your poison."

Snow spoke with his forehead still touching the ground.

"Look, Nacho just left about a half an hour ago," Snow said. "He's was as high as a kite on blow. When he's like that, all bets are off. He's a fucking animal. I swear, that man loves to kill people."

"Where did he go?" Peters said. "And don't tell me you don't know. That's the wrong answer."

"All right, man," Snow said. "You win."

Snow slowly swung his body backwards until his nose stood even with Peters' belt buckle.

Peters felt sorry for the sad-sack junkie. He was probably better off dead. But Peters had a dead partner, and that was all that mattered to him.

"Start talking, or I start searching," Peters said.

"Nacho hangs out at the Melody Bar on the corner of Houston and Allen," Snow said. "A big Mafia wiseguy owns the place. I don't know his name. That's where Nacho gets his coke. He does odd jobs for the boss-man. Nacho was on his way there to get some more of the white stuff. That's the God's honest truth."

Peters grabbed Snow under both armpits and lifted him to his feet.

"Okay, now get lost," Peters said. "And don't worry about me telling Nacho about what you just told me. Worry about your pal who ran out the back way. He'll rat you out in a split second. I'm leaving this building first. Nobody saw us here except that scumbag who ran out the back door. Wait five minutes before you leave."

That said, Peters exited the tenement.

Chapter Forty-Three

Detective Peters parked his unmarked Plymouth on the corner of Houston and Allen, directly across the street from the Melody Bar. He got out of the car, leaned his back against the hood facing the bar, and waited.

Ten minutes later, a young black hooker approached him. She had impressive breasts, a thin waist, and toothpicks for legs. She wore skin-tight black pants and a purple satin blouse with a neckline low enough to make a cadaver horny. She wore a pretty smile, reinforced by a sparkling set of pearly whites. Her smile reminded Peters of a cold shark cruising for a warm body.

"Wanna go out, mister?" she said.

"No, thank you," Peters said.

"It's only twenty dollars for a blowjob. I could do you right here in your car.

"Sorry, I'm not in the mood."

"You're not a faggot, are you?"

Peter suddenly got an idea.

"Listen, I'm looking for a friend," he said. "You want to make twenty bucks a lot easier."

"Nothing's easier than a blowjob," she said. "But money's money." She put her hands on her hips. "You ain't a cop, are you?"

"No, I'm not a cop," Peters said. "But I think a friend of mine is in that bar across the street."

"What-chu want me to do?"

"I want you to go inside, and see if he's there."

"Why don't you go inside yourself?"

"That's too many questions already."

Peters took a twenty-dollar bill from his wallet and ripped it in half. He gave one half to the girl and pocketed the other half himself.

"The other half is yours when you come back outside."

"I usually get paid in advance."

Peters ignored her remark and said, "Do you know a guy named Nacho Perez?"

After she shook her head, he gave her Nacho's description which he had previously gotten from Nacho's arrest records.

"Walk into the bar and see if he's there," he said. "Use the ladies room so you can check out the entire place. If you see him, don't say a word. Just come outside and tell me."

"You can't use the ladies room in that place unless you buy a drink," she said.

He handed her a dollar bill.

"You can't buy shit for a buck," she said.

Peters handed her another dollar.

The hooker slipped the money inside her bra. Then, she sashayed across Houston Street, her hips rotating in an east to west motion, and she went inside the Melody Bar.

Five minutes later, she sauntered back to Peters' car and said, "The man you are looking for is sitting at a back table taking with another dude, who looks like he came right out of *The Godfather*."

"Thanks," Peters said.

He took out the other half of the twenty and handed it to her.

She smiled, looking like the same cold shark; different warm body.

"Sure you don't want a blowjob?" she said.

"No thanks. Maybe the next time."

"Bye mister," she said. "Maybe I'll see you around."

Peters watched as she wiggled her way across Houston Street.

Suddenly, a white Corvette Stingray cruised to a halt beside her.

After a few seconds of introductions and negotiations, Peters watched as the hooker slithered inside the car. The Stingray sped away, and a cash register clanged in Peters' head.

Everybody's got to make a living.

Peters sat inside the Plymouth, his eyes trained on the entrance of the Melody Bar and waited.

Thirty minutes later, Nacho Perez sauntered out of the bar, accompanied by the man the hooker had described.

It was Carlo Russo.

Carlo flagged down a taxi on Houston. He slipped inside, and the taxi pulled away.

Nacho did an about-face and headed back into the Melody Bar.

Peters did a quick accounting: Nacho Perez, Butch Salerno, and now Carlo Russo. Three peas in a pod. But where exactly did Nacho fit in? Italians don't hire Puerto Ricans, except to wash and wax their cars.

Then, it hit Peters like a kick in the belly.

It was a longshot, but it was worth a try.

Peters walked across the street and into the Melody Bar.

The Melody Bar resembled a 19th-Century Dodge City Saloon. Sawdust covered a wood-planked floor that was stained with beer dropping and much worse. When Peters ambled through the front door, a putrid stench smacked him in the face.

No food was served at the Melody Bar, except for hard-boiled eggs, sold at twenty-five cents a pop which was on display in a large porcelain bowl on the bar.

The clientele was mainly Hispanic and mostly inebriated. The bar extended on the left side of the long, narrow room and faced a string of wooden tables.

Peters stood by the first bar stool by the door. He spotted Nacho at a table in the back near the men's room, speaking animatedly to two other Hispanics. It did not seem like a friendly conversation.

Not trusting the cleanliness of the equipment, Peters ordered a Heineken beer in a bottle with no glass. After taking two sips, he scowled at the hardboiled eggs sitting in the bowl in front of him. Then, he turned and headed for the men's room in the back. As he passed Nacho's table, Nacho menacingly raised his voice at his two companions. Both men shook like tuning forks.

Peters entered the men's room and locked the door behind him. The room was the size of a small closet, with the urinal, toilet bowl, and sink all in view of each other. The sink looked as dirty as the toilet bowl, maybe even worse.

Peters did what he had to do. Then, he removed the .38 Smith and Wesson from his leg holster and verified each chamber. He did the same with the small Ruger LCR-22 carry revolver that he kept under this shirt by the small of his back.

Someone tried to open the bathroom door.

"I'll be right out," Peters said.

He put both guns where they belonged, then he unlocked the bathroom door and exited.

Peters walked directly behind Nacho, who was still berating his companions. He placed his left hand on Nacho's left shoulder and extended his .38 caliber heater in his right hand two inches from the back of Nacho's skull.

"Move a muscle, and I'll blow your brains all over that filthy table," Peters said.

Nacho froze, as the two other men at the table stared at Peters, almost thankfully.

"What-chu crazy, man?" Nacho yelled. He dared not turn around.

Peters grabbed Nacho by the back of his shirt and dragged him to his feet.

Peters spoke loud so that everyone in the joint heard him.

"If anyone tries to be a hero, I'll blow them away," Peters said.

Peters nudged Nacho in the back with the point of his gun.

"Come on, fuckface, we're going for a little walk," Peters said. "One false move and I'll drill you a new asshole.

Peters pushed Macho out the front door, the muzzle of his gun still in contact with Nacho's back.

On the sidewalk, Peters spun Nacho around and threw him against a parked car. At the sight of the gun, a handful of hookers hightailed it down the block.

Nacho stared into Peters' eyes; dumbfounded.

"What's this all about?" Nacho said. "You a copper, or something? No street guy would have the balls to do what you just did to me."

"Yeah, I'm a copper," Peters said. "But I don't always play by the copper rules."

"So, what the fuck do you want me with me?" Nacho said, smiling like he hadn't a care in the world.

"How does murder one sound?" Peters said. "Does the name Diane Hamilton ring a bell?"

That wiped the smile off Nacho's face. Peters knew he had struck pay-dirt, and now it was time for him to spike the football.

Nacho moved his eyes frantically side to side. Peters figured the coke was making him more paranoid than the situation called for. So, to increase Nacho's angst, Peters turned his left hand into a first, and he smashed it half-force into the side of Nacho's face. Nacho gurgled, then he reared his head back and spat a mound of blood into Peters' mug.

Because the AIDS epidemic had just begun in New York City, Peters was not too pleased. Junkies and gay men were falling like flies, and if Nacho wasn't gay, he sure was a junkie.

Peters took out a handkerchief and wiped the blood off his face. And then he smashed the butt on his gun hard on top of Nacho's head. Nacho fell to his knees, in perfect position for Peters to knee him in the face. Nacho's head snapped back and collided with the side of a parked car. Nacho groaned, and he fell sideways onto the pavement.

Peters bent down and cuffed Nacho's hands behind his back. He grabbed Nacho by the back of his shirt collar and dragged him to his feet. Peters hauled Nacho across and street and threw him into the front seat of Peters' unmarked Plymouth.

With his gun aimed at Nacho's head, Peters drove one-handed down Allen Street and headed for the East River, less than a mile away. Two minutes later, Peters parked on South Street under the elevated portion of the East River Drive. He dragged Nacho out of the car and flung him onto the pavement, less than two feet from the water.

"I could blow you away right here, and no one would notice," Peters said. "Dump you in the East River with all the other bodies and abandoned cars. Or, I could just arrest you for the murder of Diane Hamilton. I already have enough evidence to get a conviction. But door number three is your best bet. I want you to give up your bosses. What'll it be?"

Terror clouded Nacho's face.

"Look, man, give me a break, and I'll feed you some heavy fellows," Nacho said. "Big-time Mafia guys. That's what you want, right?"

Peters heard the roar of car engines headed his way. He lifted Nacho to his feet and put his arm around his shoulder like they were best buddies. Peters leaned both of them back against his car to hide the handcuffs. With Police Headquarters just a half a mile away, you never know who could be heading up South Street to the entrance of the East River Drive, less than a mile north from where they were standing.

Two cars sped past them, and after they disappeared north on South Street, Peters transferred his hand from around Nacho's shoulder to around his neck. He squeezed hard, and Nacho made several short choking sounds, which pleased Peters more than he thought it would. Then, he stuck his revolver into Nacho's ribs.

"Man, I didn't kill that broad," Nacho said. "You've got to believe me."

Peters just smiled. He knew it was not against the law for a cop to tell a little white lie, especially if it meant putting bad guys away. Cops lie all the time, and now Peters would use that to his advantage.

"Our sources next to Carlo Russo said he hired you to do it," Peters said. "But he says he just hired you to follow her and that you killed her on your own; because you like killing people."

"That's a lie," Nacho said.

"Look, Carlo's been on our side for a while now," Peters said. "We got him dead in his bed with solid witnesses to his drug dealing. So, he cut a deal with us. Carlo's getting up in age. He doesn't have many years left on this earth, and he doesn't want to spend those years locked up in the can. So, he gave us you, wrapped up in a nice neat package."

"But that's bullshit, and you know it's bullshit," Nacho said. "Carlo's lying through his teeth to save his own ass."

"Maybe he's lying; maybe he's not," Peters said. "Maybe you were acting under his orders, but the truth is, it doesn't make a difference. My partner David McKay was killed, and I'm betting you were in on it. Besides, no one cares what happens to a lowlife drug dealer like you anyway. I could snuff you out now, right here, and nobody would give a fuck. I'd be saving the taxpayers the money for keeping you alive in jail for the rest of your miserable life."

As Peters buried his revolver deeper into Nacho's ribs, tears dripped down both sides of Nacho's face.

"Now, do you feel like talking, or do I just end it right here," Peters said.

Nacho gasped for air; his head moving up and down like a lunatic.

"Okay, I'll talk," Nacho said. "Put that fucking gun away!"

Peters lowered his gun and opened the front passenger door of his car. He opened the glove compartment, took out a small tape recorder, and he snapped it on.

"Okay, start talking," Peters told Nacho. "Say the right things, and maybe I won't put six bullet holes into your worthless body."

The short, thin man parked his blue Chevy in Peter Jacobs' driveway, right behind Linda McKay's Volkswagen. He wore a cheap back suit, not unlike those worn by an undertaker. With a gold-leaf, bound and clasped copy of the King James Bible stuffed under one arm, he knocked on Peter Jacobs' front door.

Linda opened the door and said, "Can I help you?"

"Are you the lady of the house?" he said.

Staring at the bible she said, "No. Neither Mr. or Mrs. Jacobs is at home at the present time. But maybe I can help you."

The man frowned, and said, "Oh, I see. Well, I'm selling the King James Holy Bible at a tremendous discount this week. If you could just give me a minute of your time, maybe I could interest you in buying one."

Linda shook her head and said, "I'm sorry, but I'm not interested. I'm a Catholic, and we don't believe in the St. James Version of the Bible. But if you leave your card, I'll have Mr. Jacobs call you if he's interested."

The man seemed relieved.

"Will they be back soon?" she said. "I could go to the other houses in the neighborhood and then come back later."

Linda looked at her wristwatch and said, "They left about an hour ago. They should be home soon.

The man smiled broadly, and then he said, "Good. Let me leave this Bible with you for them to look at. I'll be back in an hour or so. If they haven't returned by then, I'll take the Bible and leave my card."

He handed her the rather large Bible.

Linda took the Bible and then she said, "Okay, I guess that'll be alright."

"Thank you, Miss," he said, bowing slightly.

Then, he turned around and headed back to his car.

Linda shut the door and flipped the inside lock.

The man backed out of the driveway and drove away.

In his rearview mirror, he saw an ear-splitting explosion, and in seconds, Peter Jacobs' house was reduced to a large mound of smoldering rubble.

Chapter Forty-Four

An orange ball of sun on the Lido Beach horizon melted into the crystal-clear blue waters of the Gulf of Mexico. Summer vacation has just ended for thousands of Florida school children. And except for a sprinkling of middle-aged blue-haired woman working on their suntans and a battalion of seagulls diving for fish, the sixtyish well-muscled man had the entire beach to himself.

Sunny Sarasota, Florida had been Joe Italiano's home since he had barely escaped the dangers of New York City more than three decades earlier.

New Yorkers traditionally flocked to the more popular cities of Miami and Fort Lauderdale on Florida's East Coast. Sarasota, on the other hand, was located on the West Coast of Florida, sixty miles south of Tampa. It is populated by Canadians, Mid-Westerners, and a gaggle of people from Boston and Buffalo. In more than thirty years, Joe had never met a Sarasota resident who was from New York City, and that suited Joe just fine.

Unlike the excesses prevalent on the East Coast of Florida, Sarasota was a cultured and aristocratic town; an unknown treasure that Joe was sure would dramatically change with the expansion of world news primarily caused by the fledgling cable television empire. In Sarasota, tall, lazy palm trees surrounded luxurious high-rise condominiums as far as the eye could see. The beach water was sparkling blue, and it engaged in a perfect marriage with the cool white sand which was as soft as marshmallows.

While Miami had been overrun by people who made their living pumping cocaine up people's noses, Sarasota prospered, unencumbered by such trash. That, too, Joe knew would soon end, but he was determined to enjoy himself to the fullest while the blissful ride lasted.

Joe had always envisioned himself spending his twilight years in Florida. That tragic night more than thirty years ago was now nothing but a bad dream; a nightmare Joe had experienced many times while his children slept in peace and in ignorance.

The relentless Sarasota sun and the lazy peacefulness of his surroundings had been Joe's playmates for the past generation.

There were no more icy nights toiling in the Fulton Fish Market.

No more murder.

No more hate.

No more Mulberry Street.

Joe gingerly lifted himself off his beach chair, and he felt a twinge in his lower back. Old age had crept up sooner than Joe would admit and much sooner than he had expected. He trudged slowly in the sand, each step harder than the last. His journey ended at a tiny straw hut, which was the outdoor bar of the Lido Beach Restaurant and Motel fifty feet further inland. The motel, restaurant, and tiny hut was Joe's main source of income for the past twenty years, but he was allergic to actually standing behind the stick. Besides, he didn't attract the customers like his gorgeous barmaid did.

"Chesty, make me a gin and tonic," Joe said to his barmaid, who was built like Sophia Lauren, and just as pretty.

Chesty smiled, and said, "Okay, poof, you're a gin and tonic."

"Wiseguy," Joe said.

She bent down to where the well-liquor was situated, grabbed the Beefeater, and made Joe his drink. While doing so, her bathing suit dipped ever so slightly, exposing enough skin to make Joe's heart beat a little faster.

She placed the drink in front of Joe, and he said, "Any messages for me?"

"Sorry, boss," she said. "You wife called about ten minutes ago. She said it was very important and to get back to her right away."

"Hand me the phone, sweetheart," Joe said.

After she did, Joe dialed his home phone number. His wife answered on the first ring.

"Hello, baby, what's up? " Joe said.

The tone of her voice sent a chill up Joe's spine.

"Darling, I have bad news from New York City," Nancy said.

"Is Rita sick or something?"

"No, it's Johnny. I can't talk over the phone. Go to a pay phone and call Rita. Please hurry."

"What's the matter?" Joe said. "Is Johnny in trouble with the law again?"

"In a way, yes. But this time it's real bad. It's Carlo."

This was the first time Joe had heard his wife mention that dreaded name in all the years they had been in Sarasota.

Joe went to a pay phone inside the motel and dialed Rita's number.

She told him the bad news, and how Johnny, if he didn't go to jail for murder, would certainly be murdered by Carlo.

Horrid thoughts struggled in Joe's mind, like a swimmer going down for the third time. An hour later, Joe's Chevy Impala was headed towards New York City. If everything went smooth, driving straight through without stopping, except for gas, eats, and the men's room, Joe should be sitting in Rita's Long Island living room in about 24 hours.

Rita was a stand-up broad of the highest order. The grapes of their revenge had fermented for a long time. Now, it was time to savor the wine.

Chapter Forty-Five

Joe Italiano's car cruised to a halt at the toll booth at the end of the Jersey Turnpike. He paid the toll and headed for the Holland Tunnel. As he proceeded on the last leg of his journey, Joe's eyes scanned across the Hudson River.

New York City's skyline looked almost the same as it has thirty years earlier, except for two tall buildings at the south end of Manhattan Island. The Twin Towers of the World Trade Center had replaced the Empire State Building as the city's tallest structures. Joe thought they looked like to seven-foot basketball players posing in a team photo of horse-racing jockeys."

At the Holland Tunnel, the toll booth-collector subtracted two dollars from Joe's ten-dollar bill.

"The last time I was here it cost a quarter," he told the toll booth collector.

"That must have been during the Civil War," the toll booth collector said.

"Yeah, my own Civil War," Joe said.

On the New York side of the Holland Tunnel, Joe followed the signs for "Downtown Manhattan."

He stopped at a phone booth opposite the First Precinct police station and dialed Rita's number.

"I can't believe this is the same city," Joe told her. "It even smells different."

"I thought you were coming straight here," Rita said. "You should've gotten off at Exit 13 of the Turnpike and taken the Verrazano Bridge to the Belt Parkway."

"No, Rita," Joe said. "There's too many bad memories on the Belt Parkway. Besides, I just wanted to see the old neighborhood."

"You'll be sorry," she said. "It's mostly Chinese now. When Nixon took over in 1968, he opened the floodgates of Chinese immigration. Most of the buildings on Mulberry Street are now owned by the Chinese."

"The way the Italians took over the neighborhood from the Irish in the last part of the Nineteenth Century, the Chinese are doing the same to us. It's a natural progression."

"Maybe so," Rita said. "But I don't have to like it."

"Have you heard from Johnny?"

"Yes. He's laying low with his lawyer in an uptown hotel. I haven't told Johnny about you yet."

"Good, I want to work in the dark a little while longer. I'll be over your place in a few hours. Have a good stiff drink ready for me when I get there. I'm sure I'm going to need it."

Joe drove east on Canal Street, and at the corner of Broadway, his heart sank into his stomach. His beloved Dave's Corner was now a Chinese restaurant. Was nothing sacred anymore?

Joe parked his car in a public parking lot on Centre Street near Canal. As he strolled down the block towards Little Italy, a pair of Porsche sunglasses enveloped his face. It's wasn't likely Joe would come across anyone who remembered him, but he wasn't taking any chances.

It was noontime, and the workers at the San Gennaro Feast prepared for the lunchtime traffic. Joe stopped at a sausage stand on Mulberry Street for a bite. He almost choked when the man asked him for three bucks for a tiny piece of sausage stuffed into an even smaller piece of Italian bread.

And the guy didn't even have a gun.

"Are you here every year?" he asked a man who had "Cha Cha's Sausage," in red, white, and green stenciled on a white tea shirt. He was short and stocky, with a moon face and a long droopy moustache.

"Been here 20 years," the man said. "You have a funny accent. You from out of town?"

"Yes, just visiting," Joe said. "When's the feast over?"

"Sunday is the last day. That's when they climb the grease pole. The first one to reach the top wins a prize; like a stuffed animal, or something."

"Are you Cha Cha?" Joe said.

The man declined to answer, and instead, he glared at Joe, not in a friendly manner.

Joe ignored that glare, and he decided to see how much inflation had affected the operation of the feast.

He said, "How much do you pay to the wiseguys for a stand like this?"

The man frowned, and said, "What are you, the F.B.I.?"

"No, just asking," Joe said.

"Well, then ask your questions walking," the man said, pointing his forefinger in a far-away direction. "Around here, we don't like people who ask questions."

Joe decided the neighborhood hadn't changed much. Nobody ever talked to strangers; not Like in Florida where total strangers tell you to "Have a nice day."

Joe took the man's advice, and his three-buck sausage sandwich in hand, he departed the stand.

Taking a big chance, but not really caring, Joe walked down the middle of Mulberry Street, past a zeppola stand, a beer and soda stand, a calzone stand, and a stand where you tried to flip a dime into a tiny circle (sketched around an actual dime) to win a puppy. Joe knew, from the old days, if any rube accidentally did the trick, someone connected with the stand would brush the dime away with a sponge mop. If the rube squawked, the cops, who were being paid off by the stand owners anyway, would tell the man to either be quite and vacate the premises; otherwise they would throw him into the clink for disturbing the peace.

It's amazing what a few bucks distributed into the right hands can do.

Joe stopped at a zeppole stand and bought a dozen zeppole for three bucks, which Joe thought was outrageous for a dozen tiny balls of dough fried in boiling oil, topped with powdered sugar, and stuffed into a small paper bag. During Joe's time in the neighborhood, a dozen zeppole was 50 cents.

Wiseguy inflation at its best.

Joe took the bag of zeppole, and he headed back to the parking lot on Centre Street. As he was hiking back, he couldn't believe he was annoyed instead of being exhilarated by walking through his old neighborhood. Times change, and so do people.

Joe paid the parking lot attendant six bucks to park for less than half-an-hour.

The parking attendant didn't have a gun either.

Joe drove north on Centre Street and stopped by a hydrant. He got out of his car and deposited a quarter into a pay phone that was decorated by a top that looked like a Chinese pagoda.

Bye-bye Little Italy. Hello Chinatown.

Joe dialed Rita's number and told her he was headed to her house in Long Island after he made another phone call. He asked for Hank Peters' number, and Rita gave it to him. He also told her he bought a dozen zeppola for her.

"Great, I haven't had them in years," Rita said. "Were they expensive?"

"You don't want to know," Joe said.

Joe hung up and dialed Peters' number.

"Detective Peters," a surly voice answered.

"Hello, Detective Peters," Joe said. "My name is Joe Italiano. I'm Johnny Russo's uncle. Johnny doesn't even know I'm alive. I'm a ghost from the past; like Casper the Friendly Ghost."

"What can I do for you?" Peters said.

"I'd like to make an appointment to see you. Rita Italiano told me that my nephew said you're a good man.

"Alright," Peters said. "But I want to see Rita, too. Can you arrange that?"

"I most certainly can," Joe said. "How about eight pm tonight, at her home in Long Island?"

Joe gave him Rita's address and phone number.

"I'll see you there at eight," Peters said.

At precisely 8 pm, Detective Peters parked his car in front of Rita's Long Island home.

He knocked on the front door, and Rita answered.

"Detective Peters, I presume," Rita said.

Peters nodded, and Rita asked him to enter.

When he did, Peters spotted a middle-aged man with a full head of mostly black hair heading towards him. Peters figured the man to be in his late 40's or early 50's, and he was astonished to find out that Joe was well into his 60's instead. Joe still had the muscled athletic body of the world-class middleweight he once was.

Joe extended his hand, and said, "Joe Italiano. My pleasure, Detective Peters."

Peters took Joe's hand, and said, "Likewise."

Rita led the two men to the kitchen table, where the two men sat.

"Can I get you something to drink, Detective Peters?" Rita said.

"Sure," Peters said.

"Hard or soft?"

"Hard, if you have it."

"Scotch or bourbon?"

"Scotch is fine. With cubes and a little water."

"It's coming," Rita said.

After she returned with Peters' drink, she sat opposite him.

"Any idea who killed Diane Hamilton?" she said. "It sure wasn't my nephew, Johnny."

"I know who killed her," Peters said. "And, you're right; it wasn't your nephew."

Peters took a sip of his scotch, and then he continued.

"There's something you both should know," Peters said. "My partner David McKay was Johnny's half-brother."

Joe's face turned white, but Rita just smiled.

"I already knew that," Rita said. "I was around at the time." She turned to Joe. "I'm sorry, Joe. I wasn't certain it was the same family, but I knew Mary's lover was named McKay. Sometimes God works in mysterious ways."

Joe turned to Peters and said, "You say you know who killed Diane Hamilton. Can you prove it?"

"There's some evidence, but it's flimsy," Peters said. "Actually, the killer was hired to do the job. I want the person who hired him, but that's not going to be easy. I have the actual killer in custody. But it's his word against the man he said hired him. I need corroboration. So far I've run into to a dead end."

"Who ordered her murder?" Joe said.

"Johnny's uncle, Carlo Russo."

Joe's face turned a deep red.

"Detective Peters, that bastard Carlo thinks he killed me, too," Joe said. "I went on the lam for more than thirty years. But now I'm back to take care of some unfinished business."

Peters stared at Joe with a lopsided grin on his face.

"You're not planning to take the law into your own hands, are you?" Peters said.

"Would you mind if I did, Detective Peters?" Joe said. "Are you that conscientious a police officer. Do you believe in absolute law and order and all those other bullshit beliefs?"

Peters didn't answer.

"Do you believe in revenge, Detective Peters?" Joe said.

Peters smiled and gave Rita his glass.

"Can I have a refill?" he said. "I need another blast, and then I can answer Joe's questions."

Rita did as Peters requested, and then she placed the bottle of scotch on the table in front of him. He grabbed his second drink and downed it with one huge swallow.

"You know, Joe, I've got fifteen years on the force," Peters said. "When you start out on this job, you have all these great ideas about helping the good guys and arresting the bad guys. But it just doesn't work that way. You see, the bad guys have the edge. When they commit a crime, first you have to catch them. Then, you have to prove their guilt so that a jury can convict them.

"If we arrest some poor black man on a drug charge, there's no problem. He can't afford a good lawyer. So, the state gives him a legal aid lawyer, sometimes fresh out of law school. If the lawyer's been around a while, that means he sucks as a lawyer, otherwise, he'd have his own office and his own clients. So, the drug dealer cops a plea and goes right to jail. He did not pass 'Go,' and he did not collect the customary two hundred dollars. Sometimes he's guilty; sometimes he's innocent, and sometimes we don't have enough evidence to convict. But he goes to jail anyway because his lawyer is only interested in clearing his calendar for the next case."

"I take it justice works differently when the person you arrested has the money to obtain a top-notch lawyer," Joe said.

"You bet your ass it does," Peters said. "When you have a shrewd mouthpiece in your corner, he eats up the assistance DA, because if the assistant DA was worth a shit anyway, he'd be in private practice. So, in that case, the rich scum walks, and I'm watching the whole thing in court with my finger up my ass."

He turned to Rita, and said, "Sorry for my French, Ma'am. When I get worked up like this, the dirtiest things come from my mouth."

"Don't worry, Kiddo," Rita said. "I've said worse."

Peters took the bottle of scotch off the table and poured himself another drink, which he again, drowned in one huge gulp.

"I did a complete investigation of Carlo Russo," Peters said. "He's a big-time Mafioso with enough cash to hire the best criminal lawyers in the country. And what do I have? I have a spick junkie who claims he killed Diane Hamilton because Carlo hired him to do it. I'm dead in my bed in court. There's no way I can get a conviction."

Peters had worked himself up into a state of frenzy. He poured himself a fourth scotch, but this time he downed only half.

Rita turned to Joe, and said, "Remind me to stop at the liquor store for some more scotch."

Peters continued: "Carlo Russo killed my partner, and he killed Diane Hamilton, and who knows how many others during his lifetime of crime. He didn't always pull the trigger, but he might as well have. David McKay was the sweetest guy in the world. And even if he wasn't, he was still my partner. And this bastard Carlo Russo is going to pay for it; one way or another. Even if I have to be the judge, jury, and executioner, that bastard is going down! What do I have to lose? A gold watch and a pat on the back after I do my twenty years?"

"Detective Peters, I'm glad to say we all agree with everything you've just said," Joe said. "But what, precisely, is your plan?"

"Joe, I have an idea," Peters said. "During my investigation, I found out something very interesting."

Rita left the table, and she returned with two more glasses and a bucket of ice. She poured the three of them a healthy serving of scotch, draining the rest of the bottle in her own glass.

The three people exchanged ideas, and a plan evolved.

Chapter Forty-Six

Detective Peters' unmarked Plymouth glided to a stop in front of an outdoor parking lot on Monroe Street, in the shadows of the Manhattan Bridge and three blocks from One Police Plaza.

Peters pointed to the red Cadillac parked inside the lot, and said to Joe Italiano, who was sitting next to him, "That's Carlo's Russo's new red Cadillac. It has a remote control starter that Carlo operates from his sixth-floor apartment in Knickerbocker Village across the street. That's so he doesn't get blown to pieces when he starts his car, which has been known to happen to mob guys."

The parking lot was long rather than wide, and the cars were parked around the perimeter in spots marked by white parallel lines on the walls of the surrounding tenements. The unpaved ground was dotted by deep craters, not unlike the surface of the moon. These huge holes were filled with muddy water, caused by the previous night's rain. A twenty-foot long shack that served as the office sat at the left front corner of the lot, and Carlo's Caddy was parked face-in next to the shack.

"How come Carlo's car is parked next to the shack instead of the way the other cars are parked?" Joe said.

Peters smiled and said, "This is a monthly parking lot where everyone has their own parking spot. The owner doesn't take daily parking. Carlo insisted that the owner clear up the spot next to the shack for him so that he doesn't get his feet wet and dirty when it rains. Carlo also put out the word that if anyone dares park in his spot without his permission, he'd give their car four flat tires and break all the windows. And that's if he's in a *good* mood."

"You really *do* do your homework," Joe said.

"I just wanted to give you the lay of the land," Peters said.

Peters drove back to Rita's home in Long Island. When they arrived, Rita had already placed a pot of hot coffee in the middle of the kitchen table.

"After the benders we put on next night, I'm sure none of us wants to look at any more booze," she said.

"Everything was fine until you broke out the bourbon," Joe said. "After we killed the scotch, you should have left well enough alone."

"Yeah, good thing Joe and I are the same size," Peters said. "Otherwise I would've had had to sleep on the couch in my suit."

"Speaking of your suit," Rita said. "I sent it out with your shirt to a pick-up-and-deliver- one-hour cleaners. It should be back soon."

"Pick-up-and-deliver one hour clearers?" Joe said. "That could never happen in Little Italy thirty years ago."

"Welcome to the modern world," Rita said.

As they were sipping their first cup of coffee, they heard a knock on the front door.

Peters stood and pulled out his gun out of his leg holster.

"I'll get it," he whispered. Then, he told Rita and Joe, "Go hide in the bedroom."

They obeyed.

Gun drawn, Peters went to the front door, looked through the peephole, and said, "Who is it?"

"It's me," Johnny said. "Open up."

Gun still drawn, Peters opened the door and in walked Johnny and Mark Marino.

"Where have you two been?" Peters said. "We were starting to worry about you."

"We were holed up in some flea-bag hotel on the Upper West Side," Johnny said. "The bathroom was in the hallway, and the wallpaper was pealing both in our rooms and by the elevator."

"That was the safest place to go," Mark said. "Wiseguys from Little Italy rarely go to the Upper West Side. Too many junkies, too many fags, and too many liberals. It's worse than the Village."

"Yeah, in the Village, men are marrying men and women are marrying women," Peters said. "What a disgrace! What's next? Men marring sheep?"

"Wouldn't surprise me," Johnny said. "Why did you send us out here? And where's my Aunt Rita?"

"Your aunt is in the bedroom with a visitor?" Peters said. "And it's not what you're thinking."

As if on cue, Rita strolled out of the bedroom holding the hands of a well-built middle-aged man with a full head of black curly hair.

She said to her nephew, "Johnny, this is someone I should have introduced to you a long time ago."

"No. Rita. Let me handle this," Joe said. "This is something I have to do, personally."

Joe walked up to Johnny and placed a hand on each of Johnny's broad shoulders.

He looked the younger man directly in his eyes, and said, "I'm your Uncle Joe. In case you haven't heard, I've been dead for more than thirty years."

Johnny stepped back and stared at Joe. He said, "What is this? Some kind of joke?"

"This is no joke," Rita said. "Sit down on the couch, and I'll explain."

Johnny did as he was told, and, as the other two men stood, Rita told Johnny about the great tragedy that had occurred man years ago, before he was born.

When she finished, Johnny scrutinized Joe's face. The family resemblance was unmistakable.

Johnny turned to his aunt and said, "So, that's why you've been going to Florida all these years. I figured you had a man down there or something."

"I did have a man down there," Rita said. "He's one of the bravest men in the world. Your uncle and my brother-in-law Joe Italiano."

Joe turned to Mark and said, "You're Mark Marino, aren't you?"

"Yes sir, I am," Mark said.

Joe took Mark's hand and shook it vibrantly.

"Do me a favor, Mark," Joe said. "Take my nephew back to the Upper West Side hotel, and sit tight. This is something I have to handle myself. There's no reason for the two of you to get involved."

Johnny jumped off the couch and said, "That's bullshit! Why, I can't handle my own problems? I've only been doing it my entire life."

"Sure, you have," Joe said. "But now you have backup. What I have to do is dangerous and more than a little Illegal, to say the least."

Johnny stuck his forefinger into his uncle's chest, and said, "No freaking way! You want to help? Fine. But you ain't counting me out. This is my fight, too."

Joe smiled and hugged his nephew.

He said, "Well, you can't say I didn't try."

It was Mark who spoke next, when he said, "This is some team we have here. A cop. A lawyer. And three close relatives. And we all have one thing in common: we all want Carlo Russo's ass. Why me, you ask? Nobody bothered to ask why I was involving myself in this jackpot."

"You're my friend and my lawyer, that's why," Johnny said.

"There's more to it than that," Mark said.

He sat down on the couch and said, "My older brother, Charlie, worked for Carlo many years ago. Charlie was a good man, but he had a weakness for the ponies. He got into a big hole, and he couldn't pay Carlo what he lost, plus the vig, which came out to be double what my brother had originally lost. He tried to reason with Carlo, but Carlo wouldn't listen.

"One night, my brother went out for a pack of cigarettes, and someone put two bullet holes in the back of his head. The word on the street was that Carlo did it to send a message to the rest of the neighborhood – 'pay me what I demand, or you will die.'

"So, the hell with the law, and let's do what we gotta do – together!"

Everyone agreed.

Two hours later, the phone rang in Casa De Carlo. The bartender answered the phone. A voice said, "Is Vinny Russo there?"

"No, Vinny is on his way here from Greenwood Lake," the bartender said. "He just left and should be here in about an hour. Who's calling?"

"Just a friend. I'll call back later."

"Any message?"

"No, thank you."

Joe Italiano hung up the phone. He turned to Detective Peters and said, "Let's leave now. He's on his way."

"I'm going with you," Johnny Russo said.

"No, you stay put," his uncle said. "They're looking for you, but they don't know me and Detective Peters."

"Yes, you and Mark stay here," Rita said. "Uncle Joe knows what to do."

Johnny reluctantly agreed.

An hour later, Peters parked his unmarked Plymouth on Hester Street, around the corner from Casa De Carlo on Mulberry Street. Peters knew Vinny parked his car in a lot on Baxter Street, and this was the perfect spot to head him off. Peters got out of the car, and Joe slipped behind the wheel as Peters leaned back against the hood of his car.

Five minutes later, Peters spotted Vinny Russo heading east on Hester Street towards them. Before Vinny could turn onto Mulberry Street, Peters grabbed his arm.

"Get your fucking hands off me," Vinny said. Then, he noticed the police detective shield in Peters' other hand. "So, you're a fucking bull. Big deal! What the fuck do you want?"

"You are under arrest for the murder of Diane Hamilton," Peters said. "You have the right to remain silent. Anything you say can and will be used against you in a court of law. You have the right to an attorney. If you cannot afford an attorney, one will be provided for you."

Vinny sneered at Peters, as an angry group of mobsters surrounded them.

"I don't need no free fucking lawyer," Vinny said. Then, he spat on Peters' shoes.

"That's assault right there, asshole," Peters said, pulling out his gun. "You're coming with me."

Peters turned to the crowd of mobsters and said, "Anybody tries to stop me, they *will* get shot."

Peters spun Vinny around and cuffed his hands behind his back. Then, he opened the back door of the Plymouth, flung Vinny into the back seat and got in beside him. He jabbed his gun into Vinny's ribs.

"Let's go!" Peters yelled to Joe.

Tires screeched as Joe's foot pushed the gas pedal to the floor. Seconds later, they were traveling east on Delancey Street headed for the Williamsburg Bridge, one of the three Lower East Side bridges that separate Manhattan from Brooklyn.

Vinny sensed something was wrong, and he said, "What the fuck is going on here? Why are we going to Brooklyn?"

Peters jabbed his gun deeper into Vinny's ribs and said, "Shut the fuck up. If I wanted you dead, you'd be dead already."

Vinny was near tears. He told Peters, "You guys ain't cops. Who the fuck are you? You want money. I'll give you money. What's it going to cost? My father has plenty of cash."

"Just be quiet," Peters said. "Or I'll plug you in the knee."

On the Brooklyn side of the Williamsburg Bridge, Joe took the turnoff onto South Fifth Street, speeding past a long line of people standing by the unemployment office.

They drove in silence through downtown Brooklyn for about five minutes, and then Peters said to Joe, "Make a right at the next corner."

Joe made the right turn, and he came face to face what looked like the remnants of a European war zone during the Second World War. Bricks, garbage and worse filled empty lots where buildings once stood. A solitary tenement tottered in the middle of the block; it's windows broken as well as it spirits.

Peters stuffed a thick woolen sock into Vinny's mouth and bound it with white adhesive tape, which he wrapped several times around Vinny's head. Vinny tried to scream, but it was to no avail.

"Scream all you want, you cocksucker," Peters said. "There's nobody here to hear you. We're in the middle of nowhere."

Peters exited the car first, and he dragged Vinny behind him. Again, Vinny tried to scream, but all he could manage were short gurgling grunts.

Peters pushed Vinny through the entrance of the abandoned tenement, then he pushed, dragged, and kicked Vinny up five flights of stairs. When they finally reached the sixth floor, Peters threw Vinny down on the filthy hallway tiled floor. Then, while keeping Vinny in place with a foot behind the back of his neck, Peters pushed open the door to an abandoned apartment.

The sight of the inside of the apartment made Peters wretch. Human feces dotted the floor, and squadrons of cockroaches scatted in all directions. Used hypodermic needles were scattered everywhere with used cellophane packets sitting next to them.

In a room that must have been the living room, a torn couch sat with rusty springs bleeding from the upholstery. As tears streamed down both sides of Vinny's face, Peters tied Vinny with a length of rope to a chair sitting next to the couch. As Peters incapacitated Vinny, frantic roaches ran down Vinny's legs and across his chest.

Peters almost felt sorry for him.

"I'll be back for you later," Peters told Vinny. "Don't go anywhere."

Vinny's eyes begged Peters to cut him loose. But Peters just turned and exited the apartment. He bounded down the steps two at a time.

When he exited the building, he ran to the car and motioned for Joe to slide over to the passenger's seat.

"I'll drive," Peters said. "You haven't been around here for more than thirty years. Things have changed since then."

"I'll say," Joe said. "This was a nice neighborhood in the 1950's. What animals did this?"

"The animals you just saw on the unemployment line did this," Peters said. "They don't want to work a decent job. They just want to get high at all costs. And it's Carlo Russo and his son Vinny who's selling them the junk."

"I can't believe Carlo's into dope," Joe said. "Dope dealing has been forbidden by the bosses like forever. The bosses feel that is you sell dope and get pinched, with all the big time you're facing, you're likely to become a rat. Who needs that kind of aggravation? Plus, Carlo must be making a mint with the gambling and the shylocking. Why get involved with drugs?"

"Because Carlo is a money-hungry bastard," Peters said. "He won't be happy until he has all the money in the world."

"In a little while, all Carlo's money won't mean shit," Joe said.

"In a little while, Carlo Russo won't mean shit either," Peters said.

Peters directed the car over the Williamsburg Bridge and back into Manhattan.

Chapter Forty-Seven

Thirty minutes later, Detective Hank Peters, Joe Italiano, Johnny Russo, Mark Marino, and Rita Italiano sat in a tiny one-bedroom apartment Joe Italiano had just rented on Ludlow Street, a stone's throw away from Little Italy.

The apartment was located in an old tenement in a quickly deteriorating neighborhood, which Mulberry Street wiseguys avoided like the law. From the looks of things, it had been vacant for some time, and the people who had lived there left and they neglected to take the furniture with them. It was a win-win for Joe. A month-to-month lease on a furnished apartment for $300 a month, with only a one month's security deposit.

The good news was that Joe didn't even expect to spend two nights in this dump let alone two months. He just rented the apartment as a base of operations that was close to Little Italy, so he could make his maneuvers on the sly and then disappear quickly before he rode off into the New York City sunset, for good.

Suddenly, Peters started issuing orders like he was General Pershing at the Argonne Forest.

"All right, we've got to move quickly," Peters said. He wiped a drop of sweat from his brow. "Joe, call Casa DeCarlo. I'm sure Carlo's there by now. He does his biggest business during the San Gennaro Feast, and he doesn't want the bartenders making themselves partners."

"I bought the recording device you asked for," Mark told Peters. "Do you want me to wire-up Johnny now?"

"No, we won't need to do that for a couple of hours," Peters told mark. "Rita could do that later. Right now, I want you to go back out to Brooklyn to where Vinny is."

Peters opened up a medium-sized cardboard box. It contained a push-button corded telephone. He handed it to Mark.

"There's a telephone jack in the apartment where we have Vinny holed up," Peters said. "I used the place for surveillance a while back, and I left the jack in and the service on. When you get there, plug it in, and wait for a call. Now, get your ass in gear."

Mark was gone in a flash.

Joe dialed the phone number of Case de Carlo. Jimmy the bartender answered.

"Is Carlo Russo there?" Joe said.

"One moment, please," the bartender said. Then, he yelled towards the back of the restaurant, "Carlo, you're wanted on the phone!"

Carlo grabbed the phone and said, "Carlo Russo speaking."

"Carlo, this is an old friend," Joe said. "I need some money, and I need it fast. I have your son Vinny tied up, so to speak. I know he's your only son, and I know you wouldn't want anything happening to him. Right, Carlo?"

Carlo walked to the far end of the bar where no one could overhear the conversation.

"Is this some kind of joke?" Carlo said. "Well, I don't find it funny at all."

"It's no joke, Carlo. If you think I'm a comedian, how about I send you Vinny's right ear? I'm sure you'll get a big kick out of that."

"All right, asshole. Don't do something you'll regret later. How much do you want? Maybe something can be arranged."

"Fine hundred thousand dollars. Cash."

"*Are you fucking crazy!* Not even my son is worth that kind of money!"

"Come on, Carlo," Joe said. "Who you fooling? Half a mill is a drop in the bucket to you. With all the money you've robbed and stolen in the past 40 years, you should have no trouble coming up with that kind of cash."

"How do I know my son is still alive?"

"Good question. I'm glad you're paying attention. I'm going to give you a phone number. Call this number at exactly seven pm, on the button. You'll speak to your son."

Joe gave Carlo the phone number.

Then, Carlo said, "When do you want the money?"

"Tonight at midnight."

"Now I know you're fucking crazy. The banks are closed now. I can't come up with that kind of cash tonight."

"Bullshit!" Joe said. "You have a trap somewhere near you with millions in cash. That's how you operate. You never want to be too far from your money at any time."

"I need more time," Carlo said.

"You have until midnight tonight. If I don't have the money by then, Vinny will turn into a pumpkin. A dead pumpkin."

"It just can't be done!"

"I'm sure Vinny will be glad to hear that."

Carlo paused, and then he said, "I'll see what I can do."

"You do that. Now remember, call that number at exactly seven pm. And make sure Butch Salerno is with you. That's all for now. Ciao."

After Joe hung up the phone, he wore a wicked smile on this face. He winked at Rita, who was smiling broadly.

"It feels great having that son-of-a-bitch by the balls," Joe said.

"I'll feel a lot better when we cut them off," Rita said.

Carlo Russo paced slowly in his apartment above Case De Carlo; first to one end of the living room, then back to the other end.

He thought:

How dare someone shakedown Carlo Russo. I'm a man of respect. I do the shaking down; not the other way around. If my son Vinny wasn't so occupied trying to bang every broad in town, this never would have happened. A HALF A MILLION BUCKS! The kid just ain't worth that much cash! But what'll I'll lose in respect if I don't keep my only son alive will cost me so much more than money. If I let Vinny die, I'll be a dead duck myself. People are just waiting for me to fuck up so that they can take over my rackets.

Carlo stopped pacing. He picked up the phone and dialed Butch Salerno's number.

"Butch, this is important," Carlo said. "Meet me at my apartment in an hour. Bring your car and bring two loaded guns. With extra ammunition."

"What's up, boss?" Butch said.

"Never mind. I'll fill you in later. This could be a long night."

Carlo exited the tenement building, and he pushed his way through the dense crowd of the San Gennaro Feast. Hungry patrons lined up three deep at all the food stands, and Mulberry Street was now approaching pedestrian gridlock. Carlo pushed his way through the mob like an African warrior wielding a machete in the jungle.

As he walked, Carlo took a deep breath, and his lungs filled up with the pungent aroma of sausage and peppers roasting over hot coals and the sweet smell of zeppole boiling in hot oil. He made a mental note to demand more money from the owners of the more prosperous food stands.

They wouldn't dare say no. Carlo was the only game in town. It was Carlo Russo who ruled the rackets on Mulberry Street, and make no mistake, the San Gennaro Feast was indeed a racket. Carlo threw a few measly bucks at Most Precious Blood Church, who supposedly ran the feast, but everyone on Mulberry Street knew that was a joke. It was Carlo who was in charge of the feast's finances, and everyone knew they had to pay him in order to stay and earn. And it was Carlo who would tell them how much to pay, and they better like it, or else. The East River was not that far away from Mulberry Street.

Carlo finally reached the corner of Mulberry and Hester. His heart beat like a jackhammer, and his shirt was drenched in sweat. He approached his car, which as parked by a hydrant. A parking ticket adorned the windshield under the windshield wiper. Carlo ripped off the ticket, shredded it into little pieces and flung them onto the pavement.

"It must be a fucking meter maid," Carlo thought.

The Fifth Precinct cops knew better than to give Carlo a parking ticket.

Because of the overspill of traffic in the neighborhood due to the feast, a five-minute ride to his Knickerbocker Village apartment took nearly 30 minutes. Carlo cursed in Sicilian throughout the entire ride.

Carlo parked in his customary spot next to the parking lot's shack, and he crossed the street to Knickerbocker's entrance. He rode the elevator to his sixth-floor two-bedroom apartment facing the parking lot.

As he put the key into the front door lock, Carlo wondered if maybe his enemies were already inside. He turned the key ever so slowly. Then, with a sudden thrust, he shoved the door open and rushed inside, his six-inch push-button stiletto leading the way.

He saw no one, but Carlo was no fool. He had lived this long in the underworld by being meticulously careful at all times.

His knife extended, Carlo searched the entire apartment; in the closets, behind the draperies, and even under the beds.

Satisfied his apartment was clean, Carlo poured himself three inches of Crown Royal, neat. Mentally and physically exhausted, he plopped down on the couch and drank his drink.

Butch Salerno arrived minutes later.

"What's the matter, boss?" Butch said. "You look like you've seen a ghost."

Carlo looked at Butch with tired eyes.

"Butch, they got my kid, Vinny," Carlo said. "They want a half a mill for me to get him back in one piece. I want you to make the exchange. If you can do it without giving up the cash, half is yours."

Carlo knew that he would whack Butch rather than give him $250,000, and Butch knew it, too. So, Carlo figured, as a nice gesture and to stay alive, Butch, if he didn't have to give up the cash to get Vinny back, would refuse Carlo's magnanimous gesture.

Carlo told Butch to stay put, while Carlo went into the bedroom and closed the door behind him. He went into the closet and dragged out a huge chest which had covered the safe he had installed inside the closet floor. The safe was only ten inches deep, otherwise, it would have fallen through the ceiling of the floor below. But it was five-feet-square and was big enough to accommodate a few million in hundred-dollar bills, give or take a few thou. Carlo had scattered millions more in safety deposit boxes thought the United States and parts of Sicily; just in case.

Carlo wanted a few million bucks close to him at all times. Almost every day, Carlo counted his cash, just for the thrill of feeling the crisp bills running through his fingers. At his age, counting cash was even more pleasurable than having sex with a warm female body. Money was power, and sex was for kids like Vinny.

Carlo counted out half a mill, which caused a sharp pain inside Carlo's chest.

What the hell, Carlo could always make more money. And the visual of Carlo allowing his only son to be killed, when Vinny could be saved with Carlo's money, was too stark for Carlo to even contemplate. Sure, Vinny was basically worthless and a drain on Carlo's soul. But the kid had to be saved for Carlo to remain the big man on Mulberry Street.

At seven pm, Carlo dialed the phone number the caller had given him earlier.

Mark Marino answered the phone inside the dilapidated Brooklyn apartment. Mark wore a multicolored woolen ski mask over his head, exposing only his eyes and mouth, and he held a handkerchief over his mouth to muffle the sound of his voice.

Vinny sat a few feet away, still tied to the chair, and his mouth still taped shut.

"Okay, talk to your son," Mark said into the phone.

Mark unraveled the tape that was covering Vinny's mouth, and not too gently at that. Clusters of Vinny's hair stuck to the tape. Vinny tried to scream, but the sock in his mouth got in the way.

Vinny spit out the sock and said, "Motherfucker! That hurt!"

Mark shrugged his shoulders, and as he held the phone near Vinny's mouth, he pointed his gun at Vinny's head.

"Say the wrong thing, and I'll blow out your brains," Mark said.

"Yeah, pop it's me," Vinny said into the phone. "They grabbed me coming to work. There was nothing I could do. Just do what they say. They only want money."

"They'll get the money, but it's coming out of your hide," Carlo said. "From now on life's going to be a lot different for you. No more fucking around. You're going to have to earn your keep here. No more free rides."

Mark snatched the phone from Vinny's mouth and put it to his own.

"Someone will be up to see you in a little while," Mark told Carlo. "Do exactly as that person says, and your son lives. Fuck around, and Vinny gets two in the head."

Mark slammed down the receiver and pulled the phone jack out of the wall. Then, he shoved the sock back into Vinny's mouth and re-taped his mouth shut.

Mark sat on the wooden chair he had brought with him. He pulled out a paperback from his jacket pocket and commenced reading the first chapter of *The Godfather*.

While reading, he wondered, "Does life imitate art, or is it the other way around?"

A few minutes after he hung up the phone, Carlo heard a knock on the front door of his apartment. With Butch breathing down his neck, Carlo peered through the peephole. Then, he opened the door.

Johnny Russo entered followed by Joe Italiano. Butch and Carlo examined Joe, but nothing registered. As far as they were concerned, it was the first time they had ever seen him.

Carlo said to Johnny, "So, you're involved in this kidnapping scheme. What makes you think I'm going to forget this blatant disrespect?"

"Who gives a fuck what you forget or don't forget, *Uncle Carlo*," Johnny said. "You're not my uncle, but I guess you knew that since the minute I was born."

Butch stood facing Joe, trying to figure out where he had seen this man before.

Joe's smile was as wide as Butch's shoulders.

"Do I look familiar, gentlemen," Joe said. "You haven't seen my handsome face for a long time, now have you?"

Joe's face didn't ring a bell, but his voice ignited a cold chill down Carlo's spine. Carlo's face turned white, then a bright red. His eyes burned with intense hate.

"*No, it can't be you*," Carlo said. "You're dead! I killed you myself!"

"You shot me alright," Joe said. "But I'm still alive." He extended his hand. "Here, feel my hand. It's a little cold, maybe. But blood circulates slowly at our age."

Joe winked at Carlo, and said, "I've been on a little vacation. But now I'm back to collect my just due. I don't want to kill you, Carlo. Although I should. All I want is my nephew's name cleared and a huge chunk of your precious cash. It's that simple."

Carlo decided to what he did best. He lied.

"They have no evidence on Johnny for that broad's murder," Carlo said, his eyes darting from side to side. "I just wanted him to take the rap for a little while until I could pull some strings."

"Is that why you tried to kill me in Greenwood Lake?" Johnny said.

"I didn't want you, Johnny Boy," Carlo said. "I wanted that cop, David McKay. You just happened to be with him. He had evidence on me that could have sent me away for a very long time. I had to take him out to save my own ass."

"But why hang Diane Hamilton's murder on me?" Johnny said. "You know I had nothing to do with that."

Carlo's voice went up an octave, and he spoke like he was pleading for his life.

"That was another coincidence," Carlo said. "I hired this spick cab driver to kill her. Diane always took cabs, so we figured it was easy. But the broad was smart. She knew we were on to her. So, she hired a limo, and you just happened to be the driver. The spick followed the limo until she got out. Then, he picked her up and did what he had to do."

At "Commander Center" in the Ludlow Street apartment, Rita smiled, as the device secured under her nephew's shirt transmitted Carlo's voice into a tape recorder.

"This sounds like bullshit to me," Joe said. "Let's get on with the business at hand."

Then, he said to Carlo, "You have the money, of course?"

"Yeah, I got the cash," Carlo said. "But how are we going to do this? I'm just not to give you my money and let you walk out of here, just like that. How do I know you're not going to kill my son anyway?"

"It's very simple, Carlo," Joe said. "First of all, we'll just sit here and stared at each other for the next couple of hours. We're not ready for the exchange just yet. When it's time, the phone will ring three times. Then, it will stop. Then, ring three times again. That's our signal to continue with the program."

A circular dining room table surrounded by four chairs sat by the window facing the parking lot. Joe glanced through the window, and he spotted Carlo's car parked in the parking lot by the shack. Then, he took a seat and the table and motioned for the other three men to join him.

"Hey Carlo, where's your hospitality?" Joe said. "Don't you have any refreshments for a long-lost pal like me?"

Carlo bent down and pulled open the bottom door of a wooden cabinet. He extracted a bottle of Dewars and a bottle of Crown Royal, and he placed them both on the dining room table. Then, he went into the kitchen and returned with two glasses and a bucket of ice. He set the two glasses in front of Johnny and Joe.

"Help yourself," Carlo said.

"What's the matter?" Joe said. "You and Butch ain't drinking?"

Carlo answered Joe with total silence.

Joe poured Johnny and himself a hefty helping of scotch.

"What's the matter, boys?" Joe said to Carlo and Butch. "Don't be like that. We're all one big happy family, right Carlo?"

Carlo stared straight into Joe's eyes. The venom was obvious, just like it had been a generation ago.

Joe raised he glass towards Johnny, and said, "Well, how about a toast?"

Joe's smile looked youthful, almost angelic. But his eyes signaled Satan's revenge.

"Here to the past," Joe said.

He and Johnny touched glasses.

"Ah salute," Johnny said.

The scotch burned down Joe's throat as did the hatred in his heart.

Joe pointed his glass at Carlo.

"Here's to my brother Johnny and my sister Mary," Joe said. "Here's to my brother-in-law, Dominick. All good people. May they rest in peace."

Joe poured himself and Johnny another scotch. Then he said, "But most of all, Carlo, here's to the fires in hell where you will burn for all eternity."

For the next half hour, no one said a word, and you could cut the hatred hanging in the room with a meat cleaver.

Finally, Joe said to Carlo, "When we get out signal, here's what we do. You stay here with me. Butch goes with Johnny. There's a phone where we have Vinny. When Butch gets there, he calls back here. Then, you give me the money, and Butch gets Vinny."

Joe showed Carlo's his bright white teeth.

"Now, of course, I want to frisk you and Butch to make sure you don't try to play any games," Joe said. "After you get your son, and we get your money, I will disappear for another 30 years, and this time I'm taking my nephew with me."

"That's fine by me," Carlo said.

Joe reached into his inside jacket pocket and pulled out a .38 caliber revolver. Butch made a move for his, but Carlo stopped Butch with a wave of his hand.

"Sorry, Butch, but I want to have the only gun," Joe said.

Then, Joe said to Johnny, "Frisk Butch."

Johnny located a .38 caliber revolver in Butch's shoulder holster and .22 caliber automatic under a strap around Butch's right leg. He handed them to Joe.

Johnny frisked Carlo, and he found only one concealed gun, a .38 automatic, which he also handed to Joe

Joe gave his gun to Johnny, and said, "Cover them."

While Johnny did as he was told, Joe removed the bullets from Butch's .38 and the clip from his .22 automatic. Then, he removed the bullets from Carlo's 38.

Joe exited the apartment and went into the hallway. He walked to the incinerator where he dropped the bullets and the three guns down the chute.

Back in the apartment, Joe asked for his gun back, and Johnny gave it to him. Joe placed the gun in the holster under his left armpit. Then, he said to Carlo, "I don't have time to search the entire apartment for more guns, which I'm sure you have. So, I'm not letting you and Butch out of my sight. So, let's all have a drink. That will cheer you two fellows up a bit."

Carlo and Butch still refused, so Joe poured him and Johnny another scotch.

The minutes past like fat snails.

Butch fell asleep at the kitchen table, his head laying on his folded arms. He snored loud enough to shake the silverware.

Joe and Carlo played an unfriendly game of gin rummy; while Johnny sat back and observed the intense card battle between the two old enemies.

Joe won hand after hand, and he delighted in watching Carlo's rage increase until it seems like his red forehead was about to explode.

At 11 pm, the phone rang three times. Then, it stopped. Then, it rang three times again.

"Okay, guys. That's our cue," Joe said. "Johnny, you drive Butch to where Vinny is. Butch, when you get there, call here. Then, Butch gets Vinny, and I get Carlo's cash."

Joe pointed his finger at Carlo, and said, "And there's one more thing I forgot to tell you. Once Butch calls here, and you give me the cash, I need to make a phone call to give the okay for the switch. If you try anything funny, and I don't make that phone call, both Butch and Vinny get plugged. For good."

Butch and Johnny exited the apartment. A stolen car, with keys left in the ignition, both supplied by Detective Hank Peters, sat by a hydrant in front of Knickerbocker Village. Johnny jumped behind the wheel, and Butch sat next to him. In minutes, they were heading over the Manhattan Bridge into Brooklyn.

In Carlo's apartment, Joe and Carlo still sat at the kitchen table; face to face, both their mugs filled with unbridled hate.

It was Joe who spoke first, when he said, "Deal the cards, Carlo. I enjoy beating your brains in playing gin."

Chapter Forty-Eight

Johnny parked the stolen car in front of the abandoned tenement in the Williamsburg section of Brooklyn. He got out of the car, paced to the passenger side, and opened the door for Butch.

"Vinny's in an apartment on the last floor," Johnny said.

The street was deserted, and the ancient question-mark-shaped lampposts stationed along the street shed no light. It seemed like human civilization had already acknowledged that this street no longer existed.

Just six blocks away, a gaggle of cars scurried along the elevated Brooklyn-Queens Expressway. It could have been four million miles away for all that it mattered.

Butch got out of the car, and Johnny told him, "Look up at the window on the last floor."

Butch craned his neck towards the gray star-less sky. He spotted a solitary figure wearing a ski mask waving down at them from the window.

Johnny motioned for Mark to come down.

"When he gets down here, you go up to the open apartment on the last floor," Johnny told Butch. "There's a phone up there. Call Carlo and tell him to give Joe the money. Then our business is over."

Butch stared at Johnny with a face only the devil could duplicate and said, "That's what you think, kid."

Johnny couldn't stop the cold chill from trickling down his spine. Even in his old age, Butch Salerno was one scary motherfucker.

Johnny reached into the glove compartment of the stolen car and removed a cordless telephone.

"This is an extension to the phone upstairs," Johnny told Butch. "I can hear everything you're saying upstairs. So, there better be no tricks. When you finished talking with Carlo, pull the phone out of the wall and throw it out the window. After you do that, we'll leave. You and Vinny can find your own way back to the city."

"You gotta be fucking kidding me!" Butch said. "There's no cabs anywhere near here."

Johnny pointed up the block and said, "There's a subway just three blocks away."

"I don't take subways," Butch said.

"Then fucking walk," Johnny said.

Seconds later, Mark skipped out of the abandoned tenement, a gun in his right hand. He was still wearing the ski mask. Mark nudged Butch in the back with the gun and said, "Get moving."

Johnny told Butch, "Remember, no tricks on the phone."

Butch nodded, and then he entered the abandoned tenement.

"That Butch is one scary motherfucker," Johnny said. "I know him all my life, but I never realized what a mean cocksucker he is until I stood on the other side of the fence."

"You were always on the other side of the fence," Mark said. "You just never realized it."

It took Butch what seemed like a lifetime to negotiate the six flights of stairs. All the way up, Butch fantasized how he was going to kill Johnny Russo and his midget mouthpiece Mark Marino, who thought he had fooled Butch by wearing a ski mask. Carlo had contacts all over the country. It was just a matter of time before

Carlo found those two, along with Joe Italiano, who Butch thought had been dead for the past three decades. Now that Carlo knew Joe was still alive, there was no place Joe could hide.

When Butch finished climbing the stairs, he was puffing like a steam locomotive. He saw an apartment door open, and he entered the apartment. He spotted Vinny tied to a chair with tape covering his mouth. Butch had no knife to cut Vinny's bonds. So, he put his elbow through a window and used a broken piece of glass, which neatly did the trick. Then, he ripped the tape off Vinny's mouth.

Vinny spit out the sock and said, "Motherfucker! That fucking hurt!"

"Your pain is going to get much worse, kid," Butch said. "Your father is steaming mad."

"Fuck him, too," Vinny said "I didn't do nothing. I'm the victim here."

"Tell it to your old man," Butch said. "But first, I got to call him and tell him to give the cash to Joe Italiano. Five hundred thousand big ones. They're waiting in your father's apartment."

"Who the fuck is Joe Italiano?" Vinny said.

"He's a ghost from the past. I'll explain later. But first, we have to finish this fiasco."

"Fuck the phone call," Vinny said. "I'm free now. What are they gonna do?"

"Well, for openers, Joe has a gun on your father. Another thing is, how the fuck are we going to get out of here alive? Johnny and Mark have guns downstairs. We have nothing but our pricks in our hands. "

"We could hide in the building. Then, when they come looking for us, we could ambush them."

"You couldn't ambush yourself," Butch said. "Stop trying to be a hero. The only thing your old man is losing is money. He's not exactly overjoyed about that, but he can always make more money. When we get back to Little Italy, we'll do what we have to do. Right now, they have all the trump cards. But, tomorrow is another day."

Butch grabbed the phone and dialed Carlo's number. When Carlo answered, Butch said, "Yeah, Carlo. I've got Vinny. Give Joe the cash. We'll be alright."

"Alright, Butch," Carlo said, staring darts at Joe Italiano. "This will all be over in a few minutes. This fuck, Joe Italiano thinks he can disappear just like that. But no, I'll hunt him and his nephew Johnny down like dirty dogs. There's nowhere on earth they can hide from me."

That said, Carlo hung up the phone.

Back in Brooklyn, Butch pulled the phone from the wall and stared down at the two men waiting below.

"Catch, Johnny," Butch said. "I'll be seeing you soon."

Butch threw the phone out of the window. It crashed to the pavement below and broke into little pieces.

Mark took off his ski mask and looked up and Butch and Vinny, a big smile spread across his face. He flung the mask away, pointed a forefinger to his face, and then he flung his middle finger upward in an Italian salute.

Butch and Vinny both smiled and nodded their heads.

Vinny yelled down to Johnny and Mark, "Keep smiling, you two fucks. This ain't over."

"Just say your prayers, gentlemen," Mark said.

Johnny and Mark got into the stolen car with Johnny behind the wheel. He started the engine and drove to the corner where he stopped the car. Both he and Mark turned back towards the abandoned building.

The first explosion blew the top floor off the building. The second explosion, five seconds later, blew the bottom floor out from under what remained. Two loud blasts, blocks away from civilization, transformed the abandoned building into a massive pile of smoking debris.

Abandoned buildings collapse in New York City all the time; giving evidence to the city's fatal decay. Nobody investigates the collapses, and quite frankly, nobody cares.

Johnny took delight in the fact that Butch Salerno and Vinny Russo would never receive the respect of a mob funeral. No long black limousines. No flowers surrounding their luxurious coffins. No tears from their families. No cries for revenge.

Nothing, but a huge mound of bricks on an abandoned block in the middle of nowhere.

Eventually, maybe years later, a bulldozer would come to clean up the mess. But, as for Butch and Vinny, rats and wild dogs would devour their flesh and blood, leaving nothing but bones that could never be identified, if anyone gave a fuck in the first place. The city would just chalk up the bones as being the remains of two squatters whose luck had just plain run out.

A swell ending for a couple of swell guys.

Johnny made three right turns, and he stopped in front of Butch and Vinny's tomb. He got out of the car, opened the trunk and removed a crucifix. He placed the crucifix on top of the mound of debris and said a silent prayer.

"That's the least I can do," Johnny told Mark, who was now standing next to him. "May they rest in peace."

"Not those two," Mark said. "Right now, they're in a hot place with no cold water and no air conditioning."

"Maybe," Johnny said. "But let God be the judge. That's above our pay grade."

"That's always been your problem," Mark said. "You give the worst of the worst the benefit of the doubt."

"Like I said," Johnny said. "Let God be the judge."

In the distance, a church bell tolled midnight.

"Let's get the hell out of here," Mark said.

They got back into the car, and Johnny floored the gas as he headed back to Manhattan.

Chapter Forty-Nine

Joe stood up from the kitchen table in Carlo's Knickerbocker Village apartment.

"Okay, Carlo. Give me the dough, and I'll be on my way," Joe said.

Carlo motioned with his forefinger past the living room towards the far wall and said, "It's in the bedroom in a suitcase."

Joe pulled out his gun, and he directed Carlo to walk in front of him.

Inside the bedroom, Carlo slid a suitcase out from under the bed and snapped it open. Hundred-dollar bills sparkled from the glow of the 100-watt bulb that dangled from the ceiling on a chain.

Joe rubbed his hands together like a miser and said, "I bet there's plenty more where this came from."

Carlo stiffened, and said, "Hey, the deal was for half a mil. You're not reneging on that, are you?"

Joe smiled and patted Carlo's back.

"No, Carlo. A deal is a deal," Joe said. "That's enough money to last me and my nephew Johnny for two lifetimes. We're not greedy bastards like you."

"Want to count it?"

"No. It looks about right. Maybe you stiffed us a bit, but what's a few thousand bucks, more or less, amongst friends?"

Carlo closed the suitcase and handed it to Joe.

"I just have one more phone call to make, and I'll be on my way," Joe said.

Joe picked up and dialed the bedroom phone while pointing his gun at Carlo's heart. Rita answered.

"I'm all finished here," Joe said.

"That fine," Rita said. "But stall Carlo for another ten minutes."

"Negative," Joe said.

"Look, Joe. Everything is almost set," Rita said. "Detective Peters needs another ten minutes to get things right."

"Okay, will do," Joe said.

Joe hung up the phone and motioned with his gun for Carlo to go back into the kitchen.

"Sit down, and deal the cards," Joe said.

Looking quite puzzled, Carlo sat down at the kitchen table. He gathered up the playing cards and arranged them in a neat rectangular deck; never taking his eyes off Joe's gun.

"What's this bullshit about playing cards again?" Carlo said. "You got your money, now get the fuck out!"

Joe pointed his gun at Carlo and said, "I've got the gun. I make the rules. I want to beat your ass in gin one more time."

"Alright, you win," Carlo said. "But I'm winning the next game, and it's the last game, win or lose. You say different, and you're going to have to use that gun."

Joe put his gun on the table in front of him, and said, "What gun? I don't have a gun. Now deal the fucking cards."

Joe knew there was no way Carlo could overpower him. Of course, Joe's body had deteriorated with age, but he was still in great shape. Carlo's body was soft and flabby from too much rich food and too many blow jobs. Joe wished Carlo would make a move, just so he could beat him with his fists.

Joe saw Carlo glance at the gun and then divert his eyes.

"If you want the gun, just try and take it," Joe said.

Carlo just glared at him.

Joe needed to kill more time, and he had an idea.

"You know what? I just changed the rules," Joe said. "One hand of gin. Winner take all. I'll put up the half mil you just gave me, and you get another half mil from the bedroom where you have your stash hidden. But first, get the rest of the money up."

"Fuck you!" Carlo said. Spit flew from his mouth and landed on Joe's chest.

Joe snatched his gun and flipped over the table. Then, he grabbed Carlo's arm and twisted it behind his back. He pushed Carlo in the direction of the bedroom.

"I'll make you show me where the rest of your stash is," Joe said.

He shoved Carlo into the bedroom and hurled him against the wall.

Joe grabbed the mattress and flung it off the bed. He did the same with the box spring, but there was no sign of the hidden money Joe knew was there.

"Well, it ain't under there," Joe said. "Open the closet."

Carlo stood frozen with his back against the wall; a crucifix hung directly over his head.

Joe smacked Carlo, hard, across the face.

"*I SAID OPEN THE FUCKING CLOSET!*" Joe said.

Carlo stumbled towards the closet door. He turned towards Joe; his eyes begging for mercy. Carlo bent forward, laid his forehead against the closet door and cried.

Joe kicked Carlo, hard, in the seat of the pants.

"*AGAIN! I SAID OPEN THE CLOSET DOOR!*" Joe said.

Carlo snapped to attention, and he opened the closet door.

"Pull that chest out of the closet," Joe said.

When Carlo didn't move fast enough, Joe smashed the gun on top of Carlo's skull. Streams of blood seeped down the sides of Carlo's face, over his nose, and onto his lips.

Joe dragged the chest out of the closet. He bent down and inspected the floor. He spotted the telltale lines around the perimeter. Joe bent down slowly, put his hands on the floor, and slid them one way, and then the opposite way. The panel glided open, and thousands, maybe tens of thousands of hundred-dollar bill stared Joe in the face

Joe grabbed a fistful of bills and threw them at Carlos face, who was now on all fours, frantically crawling around the bedroom, like a cockroach when the lights go on.

Joe grabbed Carlo by the collar. He dragged him to his feet and back to the closet.

"Count out a half a million, and put the rest back," Joe said.

After Carlo did what he was told, they went back to the kitchen. Joe righted the fallen table, and both men took a seat facing each other. The second half a million stood on the table in front of them.

Without warning, Carlo shrieked and banged his head on the table, once, twice, three times, causing a lump, the size of a walnut, to sprout on Carlo's forehead. Joe spotted drops of snot falling from Carlo's nose.

Joe took a handkerchief out of his pants pocket and tossed it onto Carlo's head.

"Wipe your nose, you scurvy bastard," Joe said.

Sounding like a London foghorn, Carlo blew his nose, hard. Then, he lay his head on the table and bawled like a little girl whose ponytail had been tugged by the class bully.

Carlo looked pitiful; a beaten man. Conquered by his own greed.

Joe shuffled the cards. He laid them face down in a stack and glanced at his wristwatch.

"I don't have time for a game of gin," Joe said. "High card wins the million. You get to keep the rest in your bedroom, which, from the looks of things, must be a few million more. You have my word, if you win, I'll leave without a dime of your money."

Carlo's head rose from the table, and Joe imagined he saw the face of the Devil superimposed over Carlo's.

"Your word!" Carlo said. "Your *word* don't mean shit. A few minutes ago, you were happy with a half a million. Now, you want double. And then you'll want to take the rest of the money in the closet."

"If I wanted all the money, you'd be dead already, and I'd be gone with all of your cash," Joe said. "Now, I'm giving you a chance to break even. You'd be a fool not to take it."

Carlo grabbed the deck of cards and spread them face-down on the table.

"You pick first," Carlo said.

"Sure, I'll pick first," Joe said. "You see, Carlo, I don't need your money. I have plenty of my own. Win or lose, I'm sitting pretty. But losing a million dollars will destroy you. Even if you have ten million more in the closet."

Joe selected a card from the middle of the deck and placed it face up.

It was the eight of hearts.

Joe pointed his index finger at Carlo and said, "Now, it's your turn."

Carlo looked hungrily at the cards laid out in front of him. He reached for a card at the top of the deck. Then, he changed his mind and fingered the bottom of the deck.

"Make up your mind, Carlo," Joe said. "It doesn't make a difference. Once a loser, always a loser."

Carlo finally selected a card from the deck, and he turned it over.

It was the seven of spades.

Joe scooped up the second half a million and married it to the other half a million in the suitcase.

Joe stood up and said, "Well Carlo, I'm leaving. Sorry I can't stay for some espresso."

Carlo rose slowly to his feet. Smoldering hate burned inside him.

"I'll find you, you prick," Carlo said. "If it takes the rest of my life, I'll find you and your cocksucking nephew."

Joe tried to force a smile and said, "I need a little head start. You have a choice. Either I tie you in that chair, or I sock you one on the chin. Take your pick."

Carlo stood up and straightened his shoulders. He stuck his chest out and his chin back.

"Go ahead, hit me," Carlo said.

"My pleasure," Joe said.

Joe fired a short right hand, snapped from the shoulder, which exploded onto Carlo's jaw. He was out cold before he hit the floor.

Joe went through Carlo's pockets. He located Carlo's apartment keys and slipped them into his pocket. Joe picked up his suitcase and exited the apartment.

Just to be safe, Joe took the stairs instead of the elevator to the lobby. He exited Knickerbocker Village and walked one block east to a parked car sitting under the Manhattan Bridge. He got into the back seat.

Hank Peters sat behind the wheel, and Rita sat in the passenger's seat. From their vantage point, they could see both the entrance to Knickerbocker Village and Carlo's car parked next to the shack in the parking lot across the street.

"Carlo will be out for a few minutes," Joe said. "I tried not to slug him too hard."

He put his hand on Rita's shoulder and said, "And you lady, should be home knitting sweaters."

"Not on your life," Rita said. "I wouldn't miss this for all the money in the world."

Five minutes later, Johnny drove the stolen car next to Detective Peters' unmarked car under the Manhattan Bridge. Mark sat next to Johnny.

Johnny rolled down the window and said to Peters, "You've got the money?"

"We got it," Peters said.

"Where's Carlo?"

"The creep's still in his apartment. Joe gave him a love tap on the chin and put his lights out for a while. He should be down any minute now."

It was Mark who spoke next. He said to Peters, "Our end is finished. They won't be needing any flowers."

Joe Italiano told his nephew, "We have everything under control here, Johnny. I want you, Mark, and Rita to go back to the Ludlow Street apartment and wait for us. Me and Detective Peters can handle the rest."

No one moved or uttered a single word.

Finally, Rita said, "No fucking way! Excuse my French. But there's no fucking way I'm leaving now."

Johnny parked his car directly behind Peters' car, and everyone watched and waited in silence.

Carlo Russo lay flat on his back in the kitchen of his Knickerbocker Village apartment. Suddenly, his eyes shot open, and he felt a trickle of blood rolling out the side of his mouth. He slowly got to his feet, rubbed his chin, and staggered to the bathroom.

Carlo ran the faucet, and he threw cold water onto his face. He put his nose an inch from the mirror, and he spotted just a slight puffiness on his upper lip.

Carlo wondered how long he had been out. He figured it was too late to chase Joe Italiano. He'd have to move fast to get all the airports covered. But Carlo figured Joe was too smart to take any kind of public transportation. That meant Joe had a car and was driving to wherever his final destination was.

Carlo smiled. He had plenty of time to locate Joe and Johnny. Let them stew in their own fear, knowing that Carlo would never quit until they both were dead.

Carlo went into the kitchen, pulled open the oven door, and removed a 45 magnum revolver. This time there would be no mistakes. Carlo just didn't want to kill Joe; he wanted to carve Joe into little pieces, then drop them in the ocean where they would become bait.

Carlo grabbed his fedora and headed for the front door.

Suddenly, stark terror engulfed Carlo. He rushed into the bedroom and flung open the closet door.

The rest of his fortune on the closet floor smiled at him. It bugged Carlo, but, damn it, Joe Italiano was a man of his word.

Relieved, Carlo closed the sliding panel and put the chest back into the closet. Carlo's right hand barely touched the front doorknob when he remembered. He opened the kitchen utensil drawer and took out the remote control car starter. Carlo stuck his head out the kitchen window and pressed the starter button. He could hear his car hum to life.

Carlo smiled and exited the apartment.

While the two cars waited under the Manhattan Bridge, lightning flashed, followed by the roar of thunder and an immediate downpour of rain. Luckily, the overhead bridge stopped the rain from pelting down on the two cars.

Detective Peters turned to Joe in the back seat, and he saw Joe's hand shaking as he unsuccessfully tried to marry a match to a Marlboro. Peters saved the day with a flip of his Bic, and Joe blew the smoke out the open window.

"I haven't been this nervous since the day I was married," Joe said.

"Quiet guys," Rita said. "Carlo is leaving Knickerbocker."

The occupants of the two cars watched as Carlo, his fedora-covered head bent into the slanting rain, trudged across Monroe Street towards his car parked next to the parking lot shack.

Carlo opened the driver's door to his car and sat behind the wheel. He removed a note which was taped to the rearview mirror. The note said:

Dear Carlo, there was no way to wire your car because of the remote control starter. But the shack right next to your car will explode in your face in about two seconds. Bye, bye, you piece of shit!

Carlo sat transfixed in his seat. For a split second, he couldn't move. Then, his heart beating like a tom-tom, Carlo tried to push open the driver's door.

Detective Peters fingered a button on the back box he was holding. And as soon as Carlo made his move, Rita leaned across Peters' lap and pressed down hard on the button.

"Die, you motherfucker," she screamed.

Carlo jumped from the car right into the explosion. His head flew off his shoulders, and pieces of the rest of his body, along with parts of his red caddy, littered the parking lot and Monroe Street behind him, as far as fifty feet away.

"Holy shit!" Johnny whispered to Mark.

Johnny pulled his car alongside Peters' car and said, "Let's get the hell out of here before the cops come."

Peters face absolutely glowed when he smiled and said, "You forget, kid, I am the cops."

Johnny got out of the car and stared at the wreckage less than a block away. Mark did the same.

Peters rubbed his hands together like a greedy miser. "Boy, when I fix a blast, I sure fix a blast, now don't I?"

Joe handed Peters Carlo's house keys.

"Hurry up," Joe told Peters. "There's millions of dollars under a sliding door in the bedroom closet. I have a million here in the suitcase. The four of you can split it up. And the four of you can divvy up whatever's in the apartment, too. I don't want a dime of Carlo's money. I don't need it, and if I did, I still wouldn't take his blood money."

"Make that a three-way split," Rita said. "I wouldn't take a dime of that bastard's money either."

"You're a real stand-up broad," Joe said.

He leaned over the front seat and kissed her on the cheek.

"Did you say millions of dollars?" Mark said.

"That's right, millions of dollars," Joe said. "You three men deserve it."

"Fuck that," Johnny said. "I don't want a penny of Carlo's money either. If I did, I'd never sleep at night."

Rita smiled and turned to Joe.

She said, "So, the cop and the lawyer get to keep all Carlo's money. Why am I not surprised? Neither profession ever turns down a nickel."

"Damn right," Peters said.

He got out of the car and said to Mark, "I hope you're not insane, too."

"Not in the least," Mark said. "Let's make this quick."

"Rita and Joe, get in Johnny's car and scram," Peters said. "We'll catch up with you later on Ludlow Street."

Joe and Rita got into the back seat of Johnny's car, and Johnny got behind the wheel.

Joe took one last look at what remained of Carlo and his car.

He said to no one in particular, "Well, I'll be a son-of-a-bitch."

"And I'll be that son-of-a-bitch's sister-in-law," Rita said.

In seconds, Johnny's car was on Pike Street heading north.

After the others had left, Peters said to Mark, "We're taking the stairs up and down, not the elevator."

Peters opened the truck and removed two huge satchels. He gave them both to Mark and then he said. "When we get to Carlo's apartment, you go inside and clean out the closet. I'll cover you from the hallway outside the apartment door in case someone gets nosy."

As sirens blared in the distance, and residents facing Monroe Street threw open their windows, the two men hurried down Monroe Street and into Knickerbocker Village.

Chapter Fifty

The Ludlow Street Apartment looked like the site of a New Years' Eve celebration. Only the noise-makers were missing.

The unholy four of Joe, Rita, Johnny, and Detective Peters sat around the kitchen table drinking champagne from recently purchased crystal glasses. Peters had a case of the bubbly on ice, and from the look of things, no bottle would remain untouched.

Only Mark, a new multi-millionaire, seemed not to be enjoying the fun. He sat alone on the couch, a straight scotch in his hand and a pained expression on his face.

Johnny walked over to the couch and put his hand on Mark's shoulder. He said, "What's the matter, counselor? You just came into a few million in cash. The least you can do is smile."

Mark put his glass up in a toast and said, "Here's to the future. May we always be friends."

He downed his scotch in one gulp.

Johnny went back and said to his uncle, "Uncle Joe, do you have a job for me down in Sarasota? Me and Linda have no one up here anymore, and Sarasota sounds mighty good. "

"Sure, Johnny," Joe said. "I've done very well for myself the last 30-odd years in Sarasota. Made some very wise investments. Own a few diversified businesses. But now it's time for me to take it easy. I'll make you part-owner, and you can manage my restaurant on Lido Beach, which is making a mint. Have you discussed these things with Linda? You know you do have a little problem, like her being your half-sister."

"Considering all the shit we've been through lately, I haven't spoken to her in a few days," Johnny said. "I don't even know what I'm going to say, or where even to begin."

The room stood silent as Mark glanced at his wristwatch.

Johnny turned to Mark and said. "Hey, paisan, stop looking at your watch like your car is parked at a meter. Have another drink."

Johnny poured Mark another scotch, and he handed him the drink.

Again, Mark downed it in one huge gulp.

Peters took off his holster and placed it on top of the television set.

"Well, one thing's for sure," he said. "I'm turning in my badge as soon as possible. I've got this back injury I've been hiding. I used to love this cops-and-robbers game, but since David's gone, I've lost my taste for it. I'll play up my back injury, which is for real and get off on full disability. Thanks to Carlo Russo, it's not that I need the money. But my pension is blood money. I've earned it, and I'm keeping it."

"What do you plan on doing?" Joe said.

"I was thinking about opening my own business for years," Peters said. "Not a bar or a restaurant. Too many hassles. All I know how to do is being a cop. So, I figured a detective agency is right up my alley."

"Funny you should mention that," Joe said. "I already own a detective agency in Sarasota. It's one of my wise investments. I have half a dozen ex-cops working for me. The most dangerous thing they have to do is take photos of cheating husbands. I could make you a partner."

"Thanks, Joe, it's something to think about," Peters said.

"And if you like the setup, you could take over the entire business," Joe said. "I'm in my mid-60's now. I need a break."

Rita slowly twirled a crystal champagne glass in front of her eyes. The light from the overhead fixture reflected bright colors onto her face.

"You know, Joe, now that Johnny's on the move, I think is time for me to move south permanently," Rita said. "What do you think? Can you put me up for good?"

"Why not?" Joe said. "But I thought you said it was too hot in the summer in Florida."

"I can take the heat better than I can take Johnny no longer being close by me," Rita said.

Suddenly, there was a knock on the front door. Since they weren't expecting company, Peters grabbed for his gun in the holster on top of the television set.

"Relax, Detective," Mark said. "I know who it is."

Mark got up from the couch and opened the front door of the apartment. Peter Jacobs entered. Jacobs looked haggard; like he hadn't slept in days.

Mark introduced Jacobs to Rita and Joe.

"How's Linda doing?" Johnny asked Jacobs. "We've been so busy, I haven't had time to talk to her."

Jacobs' eyes bulged almost completely out of his head. He looked at Mark for help. Mark handed him a glass of champagne instead.

Jacobs pushed the glass away and said, "I'll have something a little stronger if you don't mind."

He pointed to the bottle of Dewars sitting on the table.

While Peters poured Jacobs the scotch, Jacobs said, "Please make it a strong one. With all the murders lately, I'm shaking like a leaf."

Johnny sensed something was wrong, and he said to Mark, "What the hell is going on here?"

Jacobs said to Mark, "You mean he doesn't know?"

"*KNOW WHAT!*" Johnny screamed.

Mark placed his hand on Johnny's shoulder and said, "I'm sorry, but with what's all been going on, I just couldn't bring myself to tell you. The truth is that Linda's dead. They blew up Jacobs home two days ago, and Linda was the only one home. The house basically disintegrated. Jacobs took care of all the funeral arrangements. There was no need for a casket."

Johnny sat on the couch, and he began to sob; so hard, his entire body shook. His aunt Rita sat down next to him, and she placed his head in her lap. As he cried, she gently stroked his black, curly hair.

Joe glanced at his wristwatch. It was almost 4 am. As the head of the family, he decided to take charge; as always.

"My cars parked around the corner," he said. "Johnny, you're coming with me right now. I can make it to Sarasota in about 20 hours. Even less, if you help me with the driving."

"Count me in, too," Rita said. "If we're smart, the three of us have to get out of New York City right away. Carlo was a made-guy; which means every Mafioso in the country will be looking for us if they find out who was responsible for Carlo's death."

"Don't be too sure of that," Mark said. "That was old-school Mafia bullshit. Nowadays, it's every man for himself. When some mob guy gets whacked, the others put on a show of false sorrow. When the reality is that the dead man's territory gets split up, and everyone, except the dead guy, prospers."

Johnny excused himself and went into the bathroom. He locked the door behind him. He doused his face with cold water, and then he stared into the mirror.

His eyes were bloodshot, his cheeks were sagging, and his complexion was a sickly off-white. Johnny figured he looked ten years older than he did just a few short days ago.

Considering both Linda and David were now dead, Johnny could either bite the barrel, or man-up and get on with his life. While assessing the possibilities, Johnny fingered the pistol inside his jacket pocket.

Things had always been rough for Johnny Russo since the day he was born. But through hard work and perseverance, Johnny had survived the hardships and sometimes even prospered.

But this type of hardship was too unbearable for words. A simple bullet into his brain would solve his problems, permanently.

Johnny recalled a movie he once saw, *All That Jazz*, starring Roy Schnieder, in which Schnieder's character, a tap dancer, would, before he went on stage, stare into a mirror, just like Johnny was now doing, smile and say, "It's Showtime!"

Johnny removed the gun from his jacket pocket.

He placed the gun to his temple, smiled, and said, "IT'S SHOWTIME!"

Then, he said out loud, "CLICK! CLICK! CLICK!"

Johnny opened the small bathroom window. He pitched the gun through the window, and it fell onto the deserted backyard below.

Johnny knew that only a coward would commit suicide. And Johnny Russo was no coward.

Ready for whatever the world would throw at him next, Johnny went back into the living room.

"Okay, let's get this show on the road," Johnny said.

Hugs and handshakes filled the room, and then they all exited the apartment.

Outside, in front of the building, Peters got into this unmarked car and drove off into the darkness. Joe, Rita, and Johnny got into Joe's car and began their journey down south.

That left Mark and Jacobs alone and in need of a cab. As they headed north towards Houston Street, where cabs always passed, even in the middle of the night, Mark handed Jacobs a satchel containing $200,000 of Carlo's cash.

"Your homeowner's insurance will pay for your house and the furniture," Mark said. "This is a little extra for your troubles."

Jacobs opened the satchel, glanced at the money, and then closed the satchel.

"My, my," Jacobs said. "I do think you fellows made a killing tonight."

"More than you'll ever know, Peter Jacobs," Mark said. "More than you'll ever know."

The End

www.ingramcontent.com/pod-product-compliance
Lightning Source LLC
Chambersburg PA
CBHW070525220526
45467CB00003B/849